Threats in Context

Threats in Context: Identify, Analyze, Anticipate begins with the premise that a risk assessment is relevant primarily to—and hinges upon—the correct evaluation of the threat. According to the author, all the other stages of the risk evaluation are, in fact, dependent on getting the understanding and measurement of the threat right.

Despite this truism, many risk assessment methods (i.e., the process of determining the threat) tend to rush through a vague typology, offer minimal classifications, utilize an often-outdated list of potential malevolent actions—all of which are based on precedent occurrences. There should be a way to improve on this: a way to provide security practitioners and analysts better tools to deal with the task of analyzing threats and risk and to prepare for such contingencies appropriately.

The book begins with a retrospective on the threats from the 1960s through to the present. The list is long and includes hijackings and airport attacks, piracy, drug smuggling, attacks on trains, pipelines, citywide multi-site attacks, road attacks, workplace shootings, lone wolf attacks, drone attacks, bombings, improvised explosive device (IED) attacks, sniper attacks, random stabbings, and more.

Terrorism, workplace violence, and active shooter scenarios all present asymmetric problems and unique challenges that require new ways of thinking, operationally, of risk to properly prevent, mitigate, and respond to such threats. The author demonstrates how to develop an appropriate methodology to define both current and emerging threats, providing a five-step process to self-evaluate—to determine an organization's, a location's, or a facility's threats and to plan risk mitigation strategies to accurately identify, minimize, and neutralize such threats.

Coverage progressively builds from correctly identifying the root threats—both global and local—to a subsequent understanding of the corollary relationship between threat, vulnerability, and risk, with the threat serving as the fundamental cornerstone of the risk evaluation. As such, *Threats in Context* will serve as a pivotal resource to security professionals from all backgrounds serving in a variety of fields and industries.

Threats in Context
Identify, Analyze, Anticipate

Jean Perois

CRC Press
Taylor & Francis Group
Boca Raton London New York

CRC Press is an imprint of the
Taylor & Francis Group, an **informa** business

First edition published 2023
by CRC Press
6000 Broken Sound Parkway NW, Suite 300, Boca Raton, FL 33487-2742

and by CRC Press
4 Park Square, Milton Park, Abingdon, Oxon, OX14 4RN

CRC Press is an imprint of Taylor & Francis Group, LLC

Library of Congress Cataloging-in-Publication Data
Names: Perois, Jean, author.
Title: Threats in context : identify, analyze, anticipate / Jean Perois.
Identifiers: LCCN 2022036815 (print) | LCCN 2022036816 (ebook) |
ISBN 9780367548971 (hardback) | ISBN 9781032420271 (paperback) |
ISBN 9781003091080 (ebook)
Subjects: LCSH: Risk assessment. | Risk management. | Threats.
Classification: LCC HD61 P47 2023 (print) |
LCC HD61 (ebook) | DDC 658.15/5–dc23/eng/20221107
LC record available at https://lccn.loc.gov/2022036815
LC ebook record available at https://lccn.loc.gov/2022036816

ISBN: 9780367548971 (hbk)
ISBN: 9781032420271 (pbk)
ISBN: 9781003091080 (ebk)

DOI: 10.4324/9781003091080

Typeset in Palatino
by Newgen Publishing UK

CONTENTS

ABOUT THE AUTHOR

Jean Perois, a security practitioner with several decades of experience in the Middle East, is now teaching at undergraduate and postgraduate level in several colleges and at the Military academy of St-Cyr Coëtquidan.

He is still a security analyst for a French consultancy firm for which he covers the Middle-Eastern region.

Jean Perois holds a PhD in politics and International Relations from the University of Leicester (UK), is a Certified Protection Professional (CPP), and is a Chartered Security Professional (CSyP).

He now lives in France.

ACKNOWLEDGMENTS

I would like to thank particularly:

- Angelo M'Ba, my former undergraduate student at the Catholic University in Rennes, who acted as an extraordinary research assistant in this book. His work in Chapter 1 has been invaluable. Thank you, Angelo, for this dedication, and best wishes for your further studies.
- My editor, Mark Listewnik, for his patience and friendly support and all the people who worked on my manuscript at CRC Press.
- My wife Caroline, my home editor, and my support in all my endeavors. Without her indefectible support and editorial skills, this book would not exist.

Introduction

This book has been in the making for a long time. Not the writing of it, but the reflection about what constitutes a threat and the reality of it. As a security practitioner operating in the Middle East, I have experienced all the threats changes since 9/11 and experienced and used most of the methods of risk evaluation on the market. I have used some extensively – often because they were mandatory like the API 780 – and enjoyed using others – like the Biringer et al.'s method of risk assessment – when I had the choice. I always had the feeling that in a risk assessment, the issue of the threat was the most underdeveloped, and rested on simple – I am tempted to say simplistic – definitions of threats, be they agents or modi operandi. For almost seven years, I thought about security forecasting and tried to organize my approach while writing a PhD dissertation in a British university.

Sometimes, the line between academia and the world of industrial or corporate security was almost imperceptible, but thinking about my profession from a theoretical standpoint while I was confronted daily to the pragmatic approach of the method I used, I became convinced that threat analysis and security forecast should be joined and thus improved by adopting a more generic, academic approach to the subject. Nowadays, think tanks, the Central Intelligence Agency (CIA), most intelligence services produce such security forecast, available to a wide audience. Life does not always confirm these predictions, but the exercise is essential, and security practitioners should follow suit. The topic of my PhD research was simply to see how the wise use of theories of international relations could provide a solid base from which the security analyst could improve its prognostication of threats.

Uncovering the future fascinates humans and have done so for immemorial times. Examples are numerous of oracles predicting the issue of a battle by deciphering the viscera of sacrificed birds, goats and sometimes humans. But a bit like with alchemy, a disappointing science, one does not transform lead in gold and the future will remain for all of us unreadable and will condemn us to renewed surprises.

And yet, I believe that this attempt to read the crystal ball is a valuable exercise. Most of the time, forecasting is simply a linear projection of the recent events slightly altered with each new attack appearing in the security landscape. As mentioned above, I have a big part of my professional life thinking about the best way to anticipate "undesired security events". Strong from this experience and years of reflection, I have tried to devise a method, studied most existing ones, and if I eventually got my PhD, I still had not been able to replace the crystal ball of my grandmother (My grandmother was a professional fortune teller and had a quite respectable clientele, so I guess that wanting to delve into the future runs into the family).

At the same time, what are we expected to do when we are tasked to draft a threat assessment in our security risk assessment, if it is not a forecast?? There must, therefore, be a bit of a fortune teller in each security practitioner.

To write a book on the evolution of security threats is unnerving. The feeling that whatever you write will be mocked in ten years' time is unpleasant.

Before getting into the substance of this book, let me put something straight. As a security practitioner, your job is not to write an essay or a theory on the future of the security situation in your region. You have been selected to protect a facility, a factory, an office, any entity, and geostrategic thoughts are not expected of you. Keeping a target-centric perspective remains essential. But it is impossible to focus on your task without observing the surroundings and the security environment, or without measuring and assessing the political forces at work in the region, the role of your facility in the industrial and/or political landscape, its social impact and the way it is perceived at a global level, since it will decline itself down to the level of the city or village where your facility is installed.

In simple words, you have to analyze the big picture, make simple connections, imagine the ramifications that transform the global threat into a target-threat and build your security master plan around this analysis.

2

While I was working on completing this book, an incredible event occurred that definitely qualified as a disruptive event: Russia invaded Ukraine. The swift reaction of the European union to this act of aggression made me realize two things. The first one was that this event had surprised all observers, except perhaps the American intelligence services who had warned that Putin was preparing his army for an attack. We, Europeans, did not believe it could happen!

We were wrong. But the sanctions taken immediately by the European were my second occasion of amazement. The Nordstream project, the goal of which is to deliver Russian gas to Germany, came to an immediate standstill. And most industrial cooperation projects with Russian involvement were brutally stopped in their tracks. This made me realize the importance, for security managers, to have an evacuation plan at the ready, should such adventure occur again. The upper management would probably not forgive their CSO if he or she was to tell them, "I am sorry, I have no plan, this event totally surprised me!" I guess that from this brutal event, a new pressing priority made itself evident. As soon as we deploy people, we must envision a withdrawal, limited or even total, and we must work on that as soon as the decision to deploy people in volatile security environments is taken. In my experience as a security manager, evacuation plan came once the whole security system was in place, and all policies and procedures were running. There seemed never any urgency in building this plan. And I worked in places that some would consider as unstable. Even in Saudi Arabia in 2004–5 when the situation worsened to the point where shootouts between Islamists and the Saudi police and national guard became almost a daily occurrence, I was asked for an evacuation plan after six months of presence in the country. The fast attack of the Russians on a sovereign country might change this attitude. One can expect that customers will want evacuation plans, detailed, incremental even when the situation appears calm. Like 9/11, but of course to a lesser extent, this attack on Ukraine might change the security paradigm for times to come. Not only Vladimir Putin resuscitated a moribund North Atlantic Treaty Organization (NATO), but it relaunched a security industry that was resting on its laurels.

Another interesting consequence of the Russian attack was less spectacular but particularly worrying. The US satellite system KA-SAT was the victim of a cyberattack. One of the consequences was that it paralyzed almost 6,000 German wind turbines. One week after the attack, the wind turbines were still not repaired by lack of electronic components.

3

Cyberattacks are often less spectacular – there are no destruction, no blood, no noise, no cadavers. But they can be extremely effective. A few weeks before the Russian attack, several European major ports had been victim of cyberattacks. Hamburg (Germany), Rotterdam (Netherlands) and Antwerp (Belgium) had been hit with the consequences of oil distribution that had been affected in the north of Europe. Some experts suggested that Russia was behind the attacks. A trial run before the real stuff?

Although I never had much taste for it, I think that if I were a young security cadre, I would try to train myself in cybersecurity, the ideal situation being to become both a CPP[1] and a CISSP.[2] I am too old for that, and my interest is now in analysis, but this profile will probably be expected from the new generation of security experts. Be that as it may, what we thought was a thing of the past has reappeared as the ultimate disruptive event, courtesy of Vladimir Putin.

For those who operate in volatile or fragile security environments, it will not change much. Those protecting oil and gas facilities in the Middle East, particularly for western owners, already take these disruptive events into account. It is rather the suddenness of it and its unpleasant closeness to areas that had been at peace for over seven decades that created the shock. A salutary shock, hopefully. I have never really believed that war would never come back to Europe. I have been confirmed in this feeling and do not need to get any credit from it.

Some do compare these events in Ukraine to the shock of 9/11. I do not think it can be compared, but what is comparable is that this attack shattered the dream of perpetual peace that Europeans had come to believe, as 9/11, in more instantaneous time, damaged Fukuyama's dream of the end of history.

This brutal event confirmed somehow the priority that must be given to disruptive events over disruptive techniques. In both cases, keep yourself informed and stay aware of any developments, political and technical, and never become complacent; it is so easy to feel isolated in a far-off place, with no peers to talk to. This is a very lonesome situation that I have known, and I know how difficult it can be to maintain enthusiasm in certain circumstances.

And remember this famous sentence by the French philosopher Maurice Blondel (1861–1949) that applies particularly well to our profession: The future should not be predicted, but prepared.

This book is the result of decades of experience as a security risk assessor in countries that take security seriously. I am convinced that you will find, in both the theoretical aspects and the shared experience, food for thought and recipes for improvement.

NOTES

1 A Certified Protection Professional, a certification by ASIS International.
2 Certified Information Systems Security Professional, a certification managed by the International Information Systems Security Certification Consortium (ISC²).

1

An Abridged History of Threats from the Late 60s to Today

A Retrospective

This chapter will be a very abridged summary[1] of the most important and spectacular attacks against the West from the plane hijackings of the 70s to the specific evolution of maritime piracy techniques, as well as attacks on land assets (linear assets such as pipelines and trains, iconic buildings and closer to us indiscriminate individuals). This chapter will highlight the problem of new threats and how copycat approach allows security agencies to find an appropriate response and bring the specific modus operandi (MO) to an end.

1.1 SELECTING ATTACKS: ON WHICH CRITERIA?

When I drafted the proposal for this book, I had in mind for this chapter to draw a list of the most spectacular attacks of the last 40 years, and try to establish along a time line the trends of terror attacks, privileged modi operandi, duration of supremacy, creation and evolution of the countermeasure responses and eventually abandonment while a new modus operandi made its way to the headlines and inspired copycats. Or a terrorist curve that would try to explain why some MOs were effective only for a limited period, then challenged and defeated by the progress of government agencies, leading to its abandonment until a new scenario, original deadly and properly executed managed to thwart existing security, that will look for an appropriate response, defeating this new threat, until a new one appears, and this in almost endless circles.

I thought it would be an easy task only half conscious of the magnitude of the task, and I quickly realized that it would be far more time consuming and complicated than I had anticipated. I had for me that I had lived through these times, and had quite vivid memories of some of the most infamous attacks – at least on the European continent – and that I remembered well how adult people – namely, my parents, my grandparents and their friends – reacted to these events, which were quite new to this generation who had been actors or children of the war. I was often too young to read the analyses of the pundits of the days (journalists, politicians, academics), and somehow, my family members' reactions were the barometer of my own response. Terrorist attacks have an emotional potential that far surpasses the immediate analyses of the why and how, particularly in the early days of the 1970s when it took the western world by surprise.

When I braced myself up and started working on this chapter, I became conscious that the task might be overwhelming and that I would not be able to lead it to its end. I put that chapter on hold and worked on the less complicated portions of the book. Something else bothered me. It has become so easy to collect information today on the internet, and terrorists attacks have become so numerous and commented and analyzed that the task seemed suddenly far less interesting to me because not essential to the topic. Then I remembered that one of the assessors of the book project wrote that he had loved the chapter plan and that he really looked forward to reading some chapters, this one being one of them. I decided that would it be only for this man and the trust he placed in me that I owed it to him to write it. The question was, when would I find time to collect all these data, classify them, organize them by types, dates, countries and the like? And which criteria should be used to justify the presence of an attack? The number of deaths? It could be one, but it would not reflect the emotional impact "the effect" this event had on the western world psyche. The Achille Lauro drama ended up with only one casualty, and yet it held the world in suspense until its conclusion. The nature and numbers of victims? In that case, only terrorist attacks committed in Muslim countries would be listed, attacks in Muslim countries often resulting in hundreds of casualties. The impact of the attacks? But the impact where? For whom? Who are we to decide that attacks on some communities are more or less important than attacks on other communities. This reminds me of an anecdote of my days in South Africa. One day, president Thabo Mbeki, Nelson Mandela's successor, made a declaration that said in essence, that he was fed up with the whites complaining permanently about insecurity, because the black victims of insecurity were far more numerous among the black population. He basically treated us (I say "us," as I am white) like spoiled kids while he had to deal with the real security issues. The white community was outraged. But I have to say that President Mbeki, a man I deeply admire, was right on this point. The problem was that he purposely refused to take into account the emotional and traumatic aspect of insecurity for the white community unaware an unconcerned by the security difficulties faced by the black community. I could be criticized identically here on that idea that I have listed mainly actions against westerns targets, that were traumatic events to Western audiences while the innumerable attacks against other communities were mostly ignored. These days, one could say that my approach is the attitude of a white male, privileged (undoubtedly), old (I can accept that although I do not really like it) and rich (If only…). I accept the reproach, without shame. I have decided to select events that marked the young man I was, and the old man I am now. It is a very reflexive approach, but I have always believed in reflexivity. In fact, I do not want to waste time trying to reach objectivity or impartiality, since it is not of this world. I write for an audience who might share, or might not, many of my cultural and social idiosyncrasies, and I am sure that readers get my point.

Then, while I was really thinking about dropping that chapter, as often in life, luck struck. One of my most brilliant undergraduate students at the Catholic University of Rennes, Angelo M'ba, asked me – after one of the final exams of the year, whether I would have some work for him as a research assistant during summer, if possible in the security field? This was the sign I expected. I discussed my problems with this chapter and told him he would have to list, classify and organize terrorist attacks since the 1970s in order to allow me to write the analysis and trends of these events. He was not frightened by the task and became my research assistant on a voluntary basis. I thank him again here as this chapter could never have been written without his help and dedication. Thank you, Angelo!

9

As you will notice, quite a substantial number of attacks are listed below. Many of them we are familiar with. Others I discovered. All had, in a way, a bearing on the world we live in and somehow modified our relationship to security. I often say that it is all about perception and that events marked with emotions are the ones who stay with us forever. One example? The first event I remember: I was coming back from primary school in the afternoon. It was a short walk from the school to our Lilliputian villa – we called it "the bungalow" – and when I arrived home, ready for a traditional bread butter and chocolate bar back-from-school snack, I found my mother in tears, her ears stuck to the radio – a big rounded brown and yellow block we had in the lounge. Tears were running along her face; she was almost disheveled and she was hanging to every word the speaker was uttering. I had never seen my mother in that state of disarray. I still had my entire family and I was not accustomed to the idea of death that permeates us slowly with the loss of grandparents, uncles, or family friends while we grow up in an emotional cocoon. As a matter of fact, I had never seen my mother cry at all, or cannot remember it since I have no real recollection of any such event before that day – or they are stored in a place I cannot access anymore. She was 28 years old then and she looked as if an unfathomable catastrophe had just struck her, or our family, or the country – although this did not occur to me at that time. I threw my satchel on the floor and came close to her, bewildered! I am sure some of you have already guessed.

It was the 22nd November of 1963, and President John Kennedy had been shot in Dallas, and was fighting for his life. In hindsight, one can only marvel at the fact that a young woman in the outskirts of Paris, with little education, a job that is now obsolete – she was a standard operator in a big pharmaceutical company – but with vivid memories of the Germans leaving France and the Americans replacing them and an unremarkable intelligence, could feel such an emotion for the assassination of a US president somewhere in the state of Texas on the other side of the Atlantic Ocean. But these were different times. The Americans were still in France, De Gaulle had not yet decided to expel them (this would happen in march 1967). The world was still very much a postwar world and leaders and the population were still marked by the war and would be to the end of their lives. You probably wonder why I am telling this story? Simply to illustrate the fact that emotionally charged events stay with you forever, and occupy a special place in your brain and your heart. This is my first political memory, not because it was important, but because of the emotional impact it had on my mother and how she transmitted her distress to me, unwillingly but like a formidable and irresistible wave.

Closer to us, everyone remembers where they were when the Twin Towers were attacked on September 11, 2001. The reason is identical. The emotional impact of the news puts it in a specific place where it will stay forever and those who lived through it will be marked for ever. Another one, although not a security incident, was an event that marked humanity like no other event, the day when the Americans landed on the moon: July 21, 1969. The whole population of the street where my grandparents were living, in the department of Savoy, in the French Alps, abandoned their TVs and went to the street, to look at the moon that I remember bright and almost full. It was a very clear night and the temperature was pleasant; I was 12. Watching the moon, all these blue collars and pensioners, dressed in their blue uniform (workers dressed like this in those days and widows dressed in black outfit and covered their hair), looked at the moon and tried to integrate that men were walking there while they had just recovered from the war that had destroyed their lives one short generation ago. How was it possible? How had the Americans achieved such an incredible feat? The emotion was palpable, and that night we were not all Americans – this idea is a modern idea that nobody would have understood then – we were in awe in front of the intelligence and extraordinary dynamism of the American people for whom nothing seemed impossible.

This chapter is not about the history of political movements who used terrorism as a means of action. Why groups of people politically motivated decided to use terrorism as a preferred mode of action is certainly interesting but would not be of interest for the security practitioner to whom I am speaking now. This book intends to be a book for the modern security practitioners and who is neither interested in the histories of the sect of the Hashishin, (who gave us the word assassin)[2] nor the thug tribe of India (who gave us the word thug, of course) nor of the adventures of the anarchists of the turn of the 20th century in France. Although they certainly are very interesting topics for scholars, historians and academics, our security practitioner has certainly more important cats to whip and did not buy this book to hear about such adventures.

Yet it might of interest to him or her to have a broad idea of what terrorism means in the modern world, and by modern, I mean from the time where men started to wear ties…

When did it begin (planting bombs, not wearing ties)? Terrorist actions having almost always been with us, (Guy Fawkes and the gunpowder plot, 1605), we need to choose arbitrarily a date that our readers can relate to. I suggest we start our study at the very beginning of the 20th century, with the rise of nationalism and the beginning of the end of multicultural empires (mainly The Austro-Hungarian and the Ottoman empire). Terrorist theorists are usually stemming from mid-19th-century Europe. Following in the steps of Marx and Bakunin, Karl Heinzen was the first to conceptualize the use of violence by individuals to bring political changes in what he considered as the immoral social situation of his time, in a pamphlet titled *Mord und Freiheit* in 1853. We owe him the concept of Freedom Fighter (*Freiheitskampfer*). Heinzen advocated violence, assassination and even mass murder as a means to reach one's political goals! A man with a vision...

But their failure to really modify the political/monarchical system in Europe pushed these exalted activists toward more violence and a more extreme tactics. Unable to overthrow the existing regimes and even to gain a wide support within the peasantry and the masses, they opted for different tactics. Targeted assassination became their favored modus operandi. It had the advantage of being more palatable to the public, since it targeted only crowned heads or representative of an abhorred system. The list is long of such successful attacks. The Czar Alexander II of Russia, killed in 1881 by the groups *Narodnaya Volya*, is probably the most emblematic example. These murders rested on basic principles that assured a certain success until the outbreak of the First World War. Attacking symbols of oppression could be seen as acts of courage. People assassinated were the flag bearers of oppression, and political assassination spared the life of the population. Modernity also reinforced the capabilities of our terrorists. The invention of dynamite by Alfred Nobel in 1867 offered more spectacular opportunities – and less hazardous outcomes for the perpetrators. Simultaneously, the development of communications technologies and the growth of education permitted an amplified echo to their deeds. Newspapers becoming an integral part of daily life of populations meant that any terrorist event could be known and commented in no time in distant parts of the world. The development of the railways added to this information spreading of news and ideas. Another factor was the migration of European masses around the world that helped the dissemination of such ideas (and actions) creating a possible inspiration for groups of downtrodden minorities, not to mention the domestic migration of large chunks of the peasantry to the great urban centers of Europe and the United States allowing a diffusion of revolutionary ideas.

The assassination of Czar Alexander led to a spate of terrorists (they were called anarchists in those days) throughout Europe and the

Americas. Russian rebels were the leaders of this trend; they played the role of terrorist camps in Afghanistan, training all sorts of anarchists in the techniques of assassination and bombings. French, Germans, Italians and Spanish returned from these training camps to carry out their deeds, often triggering a chain of retribution between themselves and the local authorities, amplified by the press and encouraging vocations. The solutions found by the authorities of the day are not that different from the ones chosen by our current western governments. Immigration controls and extradition treaties were put in place, and executed to put an end to the wave of assassinations. In 1904, a Secret Protocol for the International War on Anarchism also known as the St. Petersburg Protocol, championed by Germany and Russia, arranged national policies for the rendition of anarchists to their origin countries and the exchange of surveilled information on anarchists. The following year, an administrative convention was signed for the exchange of information regarding individuals professing ideas hostile to their governments. One of the last but most consequential event of this anarchist period was when on this fateful day of 28 June 1914, Gavrilo Princip, a Serb nationalist, ended brutally the life of the archduke Franz-Ferdinand of Austria and the archduchess Sophie – igniting by the spiraling game of alliances, a kind of pre-Eisenhower domino effect, that led to the first industrial conflict, resulting in the loss of approximately 20 million lives around the globe, mainly Europeans.

I see some of my students raising their hands. "Wasn't this a political assassination, sir, rather than a terrorist act?" Very good question, indeed. And not a very easy one to answer. We all know that one's terrorist is another's freedom fighter and the same goes for acts of terror. I guess that when the target is an operative politician, we would call it today a political assassination – precisely because it spares the lives of innocent passersby, while our modern terrorists-murderers do not hold in high esteem the lives of those who do not espouse their causes. When the target is chosen randomly in order to instil fear in populations, put pressure on authorities to change a course of action, by blind attacks on innocent people, we are talking terrorism. Yet one cannot imagine that the act of Princip had not been planned in Belgrade or Sarajevo by a group of motivated people – anarchists-nationalists – who expected this murder to trigger a violent reaction from the Austro-Hungarian monarchy, which it did. I am also convinced that the Austro-Hungarian crown saw these Serbians as a bunch of rag-tag terrorists, while these nationalists saw themselves as perfectly legitimate irredentists! Amazingly, we end up with a political assassination (the act itself) that can qualify then as a terrorist act since it was planned, prepared and performed clandestinely by a group of people who intended to bring down a government and tried to gain independence from the Empire. Difficult to be impartial in this instance. The difference between a terrorist and a freedom fighter being really whether the latter can reach successfully their objective (Menahem Begin for Israel, Nelson Mandela for South Africa are examples). What makes a terrorist is that he does not succeed...yet.

One can see that the debate on who qualifies as a terrorist and on which criteria is an open file and will remain so for many years to come.

Be that as it may, coming back to the Sarajevo assassination, one must admit that for a single terrorist act, ill prepared and not so well executed, the outcome was a resounding success, probably far beyond their masterminds' expectations. Between the wars, terrorism was not really on fashion; the rise of nationalism and popular movements such as Italian Fascism and German Nazism, the 1929 financial crisis, the great Stalinist purges in Russia and the Spanish Civil war were events of sufficient magnitude and interest to attract those who could otherwise have opted for a terrorist career. The Second World War was even more devastating than the first. About 50 million people died, but the main victim of this war was Europe and its overwhelming beneficiary the United States of America who, with 1% of human losses, established themselves as the sole and undisputed power in the world. Within the next 15 years, France and Britain, the two major colonial powers of the previous century, were going to lose almost all of their overseas possessions, to find – at least for France – some solace in the initially successful construction of the European Union with an atrophied, but still potentially dangerous West Germany (Bonn replacing Weimar and Berlin). Russia did not fare much better than a mauled Europe. Russia had taken the blunt of the German fury, and its population and its infrastructure had paid an enormous price. Let us be honest, Russia, or the Soviets, were never a threat for the United States. In spite of what scholars and politicians may have said for decades, there was never any possibility of a hot war between the two powers. The reason is simple: Russia never was, not even a fraction of a second, a superpower. They were a huge expanse of land, directed by a minority elite, having invested their poor resources in an extraordinary military apparatus. But that does not make a country a great power. During the Cold War, the Soviet economy was an economical dwarf. Even today, with the discovery of hydrocarbons, Russia ranks at the 11th place of the world gross domestic product (GDP), behind South Korea's![3] They may have been flattered by being called a superpower since that gave them a status – Stalin must really have enjoyed this recognition. But they simply were a military power, conscious of the precarity of their situation, threatened of annihilation by the only power left at the end of the war, the United States of America, untouched and unscathed (500,000 casualties compared to the 20 million deaths of the soviet armies during the conflict) who had to invest all their resources into military equipment, eventually preventing this massive but sparsely populated country to develop and progress. Russia was, and still is, in spite of its hydrocarbon recent riches, and military capability, an economic dwarf. Having borne the brunt of the war, it started the postwar period in a precarious situation, ruined, devastated, almost as exhausted as their German archrival. But while Germany was going to benefit from the Marshall plan, that Stalin was offered and refused, Russia had to fend for itself, while assuming at the same time the leadership of most of the have-not newly and soon-to-be decolonized countries (I am tempted to say quasi-countries) of the world.

Russia, like China, was always too poor to be a real menace to the western world. Russia's efforts to maintain military parity with the United States coupled with a useless and costly campaign in Afghanistan logically ended in Russia throwing in the towel in 1989. And no, the mujahidin were not crucial to this victory. The reason was elsewhere in Europe, and was simple. The communist dream had exhausted itself and the population had had enough of it.

Even the creation of the state of Israel – who was to become the focal point (Rationale? Pretext? Excuse?) of so many terrorist actions to come – was first dealt with success by Israel through military means (1948, 1956 and 1967).

1.2 WHY ARE THESE EVENTS IMPORTANT?

One might think that I cannot resist the temptation to list spectacular events in order to make my book dramatic reading. This is not the case. Having an idea of what happened in our modern era in terms of terrorism provides an idea about the security environment. To paraphrase Gilles Kepel, the famous expert on Islamism, I would say that it provides a *terrorism of atmosphere*,[4] that gives ideas to potential terrorists and while, at the same time, signposting the evolution of the counter terrorism techniques that rely to these MOs. When a technique works, it generates copycats' actions almost immediately. Security forces need a bit of time to learn to counter these attacks. During this period, attacks multiply with success. When the countermeasures have been developed and success- fully tested – plane hijacking is a good illustration of this – by security forces, terrorists start to experience fiascos. After a few failures, terrorists realize that ratio cost-benefit, or return on investment becomes negative, costly and counterproductive politically and start looking for new MOs, opportunities and scenarios.

Yes, I admit that the most glamorous attacks only concern a minority of us (unless you work for airports, major companies, oil and gas indus- tries, nuclear facilities, some government entities, which is after all, quite a number of us...). Most of our daily security routine does not consider the entire destruction of our building and casualties counting by the hundreds. Yet we need examples, we need references, because these references are part of the *terrorism of atmosphere* and major events will guide less resourceful terrorists. By knowing them, we are more disposed to understand the mentality and approach of our adversaries.

1.3 WHY CHOOSE 1970 AS A STARTING DATE?

As Brian Michael Jenkins of the Rand corporation posited in an article published in the *Hill* on July 30, 2015, "Terrorists in the 1970s perfected their repertoire. They employed 6 basic tactics, some of which had been practiced for centuries: assassination, bombings, kidnapping, airline hijacking, barricaded hostage situations and armed assault".[5]

After the expeditive victory in June 1967, the myth of Israel invinci- bility was firmly established, and Arab leaders started to believe that only terrorism as an alternative way of waging war to Israel would provide a better ratio of cost-benefit than head-on hopeless and often humiliating confrontations. Although Arab armies thought that it would be impos- sible to achieve, the 1973 confrontation turned, at least initially, to their advantage. To the total surprise of the Israel – and the US – governments, eventually, the massive support of their indefectible American ally deprived the Arab coalition from a deserved military victory. This humil- iating and frustrating situation would be the trigger for a new type of struggle that would be the terrorism of the 1970s spearheaded by the PLO, the FPLP and several pro-Palestinians organizations. Many Arabs thought that since America was ready to support Israel at any cost, expelling Jews from Palestine by force would never occur and that other means of actions should be envisioned, and new tactics developed. From that moment, a kind of golden age of modern terrorism began and was to last for the following three decades.

In a recent article published in the *Télégramme*, my local newspaper in Brittany, Marc Trevidic, former anti-terrorism examining judge, makes some very interesting remarks about the evolution of terrorism in recent years. He is a man of experience. From 2000 to 2015, he was an examining magistrate at the *Tribunal de Grande Instance de Paris*, specializing in fighting terrorism. He represented clients in the 1980 Paris synagogue bombing,[6] 2002 Karachi bus bombing[7] and the Assassination of the monks of Tibhirine,[8] among other cases.

The interesting point he makes is that, until recently, terrorist organizations were very "organized", and worked for a cause. In spite of the terrible acts they committed, most of these organization (Al-Qaeda, Abou Nidal, the IRA or the ETA)[9] were focused on an objective, and terror had been chosen as the strategy to reach that goal. It seems that Daesh (aka ISIL – the Islamic State of Iraq and the Levant) changed this dynamic. Daesh called for murder in an irrational way. The West became the designated enemy. There was no possible compromise or negotiation. Daesh inaugurated a new kind of fight to death that we had not seen for a long time. Hatred replaced politics. The destruction of antic cities, the gruesome decapitations of innocent people by teenagers, the gore display of unimaginable tortures on social networks, dwarfed the political objectives of their competitors (like Al-Qaeda who was acting in a more classical way). Hatred seems to be the main source of motivation; violence became the tool and terror the expected outcome and it found in western frustrated migrant populations a fertile breeding ground. More importantly, there was suddenly no need for a political conscience, a conceptual intelligence, a kind of grasp of the complexities of the struggle, a knowledge of Marxism-Leninism or Maoist theories, a historical basis that created a link between supposed grievances and contemporaneous sufferings. Terrorism opened its arm to the least gifted, the least educated, the most violent, the most primitive. The new generation of terrorists are neither intellectuals acting reluctantly as criminals, nor soldiers serving a cause. They are, most of them, social failures, frustrated individuals, many of them petty criminals with multiple mentions on their criminal records, maladjusted individuals whose main drive is social revenge (brandishing racism as the excuse) and who find this new form of brutal anarchy the only way to compensate for their feeling of personal failure and malaise. A comparison between the intellectual backgrounds of the 9/11 terrorists – and even those historical leaders of the 1970s – and the abysmal level of this new brand of terrorists in Europe is striking. Is this new type of threat agents having an impact on the way security analysts should evaluate the threat? The level of education of the terrorists of the last quarter of the 20th century and even that of some of the 9/11 criminals is disproportionate to that of the recent recruits of terrorist movement in this first quarter of the 21st century. It cannot have no impact on the threat assessment. Rationality and political objectives are not anymore the only backgrounds to the possible threats that we, security practitioners, will have to understand and prepare against. I do not want to use the word quality here; my purpose is not apologetic, but there seemed to be, in the terrorist movement of the 1970s, an intellectual touch, a conceptualization of the terrorist act as the only way to obtain political gains against an overwhelmingly powerful enemy – an approach in the tradition of the anarchists of the pre-1914 era. This seems to be entirely absent from the motivations of our recent stabbers and cutthroats. The fate of the Palestinian people appears more as a pretext than the "cause" it used to be. Many of the neo-terrorists who pretend to act in the name of the oppressed Palestine would be in great difficulty lo locate Palestine on a map.

Since hatred, frustration and resentment seem to have replaced politics and power struggles in the minds or our adversaries, we need to reassess our traditional analysis of the threat.

I believe that the trilogy, *terrorist, criminal and disgruntled employee* commonly used to define the threat in most risk assessments methods needs to be revaluated. Creating a barrier between the nature of threats does not resist a serious analysis of recent incidents. The same person can be a terrorist, a criminal and a disgruntled employee, in different phases, with different degrees of commitment. Helping criminals or terrorists in response to a professional unsatisfaction and to redress a personal grievance is to make oneself an accessory and a terrorist. The disgruntled employee needs to be considered in their relation with terrorism; the motivations for this type express themselves now in much wider range, stemming from the new racialist, decolonial and transversal struggles that seem to be the flavor of the day, making its identification by security practitioners more complicated than it used to be. Although we must still work the nature and type of the threat, we will need to refine our interpretation of their possible motivations. What used to be simple, sometimes simplistic, will need to be reassessed, the profiles of employees taking now first place in our analysis. The new set of motivations based on frustrations rather than political motivation will impact our analysis and probably emphasize a threat becoming more internal than external in nature.

Instead of disgruntled employees who want to redress and injustice, we may face frustrated employees who may want to harm other fellow workers and colleagues simply because they feel unsatisfied and hateful toward almost everyone. What the company you are supposed to protect symbolically represents appears suddenly much less important than the capability of an employee to commit a terrorist act simply out of frustration and anger. Consequently, the chances are that the threat will drift from the external toward the internal.

Let us take a recent example that shocked the French judiciary establishment. On Thursday October 3, 2019, during lunchtime, an employee of the Paris *Prefecture de Police*, Mickael Harpon, a French citizen from the *Antilles Françaises*[10] – la Martinique – stabbed and killed four of his colleagues, wounding a fifth one, before a young officer shot him dead. The man had been employed at the Prefecture de Police for four years and was well noted. He apparently auto-radicalized, and decided to kill unbelievers all by himself and without any complaint being raised about his change of behavior that had been noticed by all and sundry. Converting to Islam in 2008, married to a Muslim woman in 2014, M.H appeared to have been seduced by a rigorist vision of Islam and its appeal to violence as part of a kind of personal jihad. The night preceding the killing, and after a night of religious hysteria, where he was heard by the neighbors yelling many times Allahu Akbar, he sent religious message to his wife, and after the bloodbath decided to die as a martyr by confronting an armed policeman with his blood-spattered knife. What is interesting for us practitioners is that his religious drift had been noticed by his colleagues as early as 2015 – that is, four years before the attack by some comments, his refusal to condemn the Charlie Hebdo attacks, changes in behavior particularly towards women, observed by his colleagues. Two of them – keep in mind that he was working as a maintenance IT specialist at the Intelligence Directorate of the Prefecture de Police (PP) de Paris, a secret defense habilitation position, and had therefore access to the identity and history of all undercover police officers of the country working on Islamist networks – although conscious of the abnormal behavior of the man, decided not to report him to their hierarchy. Two months later, while the signs of radicalization were becoming more visible, they still decided not to report the behavioral change. The man had been employed at the

PP since 2003. No mention of his drift toward terrorism was noted in his personal file.

There are of course many lessons to learn from this example, and I am sure that this attack created a powerful and salutary shock in this administration. But there were signs that pointed toward a change in psychology and the possibility of danger. And yet, nobody had the courage to bring this situation to the hierarchy. The inquest confirmed the terrorist character of the attack underlining the hybrid profile of the killer, operating at the edge between terrorism and psychiatry. A profile more and more frequent that does not facilitate our job, since the psychiatric component is always detected after the action...

For the security practitioner, this drama tends to illustrate that the internal threat is probably becoming more important than the external and colluding threat. And that the solution to this new paradigm should follow two axes. 1) security awareness must become part of the normal security arsenal and rendered mandatory in companies And 2) the possibility of reporting abnormal or changing behaviors must be facilitated and anonymity guaranteed. People must have the possibility to report any suspicious behavior without designating themselves for retribution. I will discuss this more in detail and provide simple solutions when the nature and types of threats are discussed (Chapter 2).

In the following pages, I will list a number of terrorist actions that have occurred since the 1970s and list them under four categories: terror in the air, terror at sea, terror in cities – and in linear networks – train, pipelines and the recent trends in terror attacks. Two words of warning:

1. The idea being to find examples relevant to this discussion, most of the data were collected on Wikipedia. I know the reluctance of some to use Wikipedia, but this is not an academic article, and the information gathered through wiki are, in my opinion, truthful enough to illustrate my purpose.
2. One must be aware that there have been more than 200,000 officially registered terrorist attacks since 1970[11] and that what will follow is a small (and inevitably biased) sampling of so many attacks.
3. The attacks I have selected are essentially attacks against western objectives, because these are the ones, we – my audience of western security practitioners and I – want to hear about. One must be conscious though that the rest of the world is also hit by terrorism, and probably more so than the west.

1.4 TERROR IN THE AIR

Terrorist acts related to airplanes and airports have a dramatic touch to them that make them unique. The idea of falling from the sky still alive and getting pulverized on touching the ground terrifies any human being and there is nothing more dreadful than imagining yourself falling from the sky and meeting the earth at close to 200 kilometers per hour. Be that as it may, there is an inherent perfume of danger with the airplane that obviously speaks to all of us, and this includes terrorists. Terror in the air started very early in the history of aviation. The excellent book by Price and Forrest titled Practical Aviation security[12] lists the early attempts at hijacking as early as 1930 in the United States. I do not know if the phenomenon occurred as early in Europe, but I remember perfectly the heydays of political hijacking in the early 1970s, how they started, why, and how and why they passed.

1.4.1 Air Attacks

The golden age of air hijacking was the five-year period 1968–1972. During this five-year period, the world experienced 326 hijack attempts, or one every 5.6 days. The incidents were frequent and often just an inconvenience […]. Most incidents occurred in the United States: There were two distinct types: hijackings for transportation elsewhere and hijackings for extortion with the threat of harm. Between 1968 and 1972, there were 90 recorded transport attempts to Cuba.[13]

I perfectly remember this period as an incessant breaking news – although this term was not employed in the 1970s, of ceaseless politically motivated hijackings, most of them related with the situation in the Middle East, an indirect consequence of the humiliating rout of the Arab armies in 1967.

Here are a few of the most marking attacks of this troubled period.

1.4.2 7 March 1970: Eastern Air Lines Shuttle Flight 1320

Eastern Air Lines Shuttle Flight 1320, carrying passengers from Newark to Boston, was hijacked around 7:30 p.m. on March 17, 1970, by John J. Divivo who was armed. Captain Robert Wilbur Jr., 35, a former US Air Force pilot who had only been promoted to captain six months earlier, was shot in his arm by the hijacker. Despite his wounds, he flew his aircraft safely to a landing while talking to the tower, telling them his copilot was shot and needed an ambulance. His copilot, First Officer James Hartley, 30, was shot without warning by Divivo and collapsed. Despite being mortally wounded, Hartley recovered sufficiently to rip the gun from Divivo's hand, and shot the would-be hijacker three times before lapsing into unconsciousness, and eventually death. Although wounded and slumped between the seats, Divivo arose and began clawing at Captain Wilbur, attempting to force a crash. Wilbur hit Divivo over the head with the gun he had retrieved from the center console. The pilot was able to land the plane safely at Logan International Airport, and the hijacker was arrested immediately. On October 31, 1970, Divivo hanged himself while awaiting trial.

1.4.3 17 December 1973: Rome Airport Attacks and Hijacking

The 1973 Rome airport attacks and hijacking were a set of Palestinian terrorist attacks originating at Leonardo da Vinci–Fiumicino International Airport in Fiumicino, Lazio, Italy, and resulting in the deaths of 34 people (and 20 people injured). The attacks began with an airport terminal invasion and hostage-taking, followed by the firebombing of Pan American World Airways Flight 110.

1.4.4 8 September 1974: TWA Flight 841 (Hijacking and Bombing)

A Boeing operating as TWA Flight 841 from Tel Aviv to New York City via Athens and Rome crashed into the Ionian Sea, killing all aboard (88 victims). It has been determined that the plane had been destroyed by a bomb hidden in the cargo hold. The detonation of the bomb destroyed the systems responsible for operating the plane's control surfaces, causing the plane to pitch up until it stalled and dove into the sea.

1.4.5 January 1975: Paris-Orly Airport Attacks (Airport Attack)

On 13 and 19 January 1975, two El Al aircrafts at Paris-Orly Airport, France, were subject to attempted grenade-launchers attacks by Popular Front for the Liberation of Palestine (PFLP) terrorists led by the famous terrorist Carlos (aka Carlos The Jackal). While the intended attacks failed, there was collateral damage and the second attack resulted in gunfighting and a 17-hour hostage situation. These incidents did result in 23 people getting injured but no death was reported.

1.4.6 2 June 1985: Air India Flight 182 (Hijacking)

Air India Flight 182 was an Air India flight operating on the Montreal–London–Delhi route. On 23 June 1985, it was operated using Boeing 747-237B registered VT-EFO. It disintegrated in midair en route from Montreal to London, at an altitude of 31,000 feet (9,400 m) over the Atlantic Ocean, as a result of the explosion from a bomb planted by Canadian Sikh militants known commonly as Khalistanis.

The remnants of the airliner fell into the ocean, killing all aboard: 329 people, including 268 Canadian citizens, 27 British citizens and 24 Indian citizens. The bombing of Air India Flight 182 is the largest mass killing in Canadian history, the deadliest aviation incident in the history of Air India and was the deadliest act of aviation terrorism until the 9/11 attacks.

1.4.7 19 June 1985: Frankfurt Airport Bombing (Airport Attack)

On 19 June 1985, a bombing at the Frankfurt Airport, West Germany, killed three and wounded 74 people. A second bomb was found and defused not far from the first explosion. About 30 groups claimed responsibility, among them an unprecedented group calling itself Arab Revolutionary Organization, having done so because of West German intelligence recruiting Arabs to assassinate members of Arab revolutionary movements in Lebanon.

1.4.8 21 December 1988: Lockerbie Bombing/PAN AM 103

This incident was probably the most media covered terrorist act until surpassed by 9/11 and one of the most complicated – and politically loaded act of terrorism. Its ramifications and the progress of the international inquiry were discussed daily in the medias and it fascinated the world because, this time, the responsibility of a sovereign state was involved (The Libyan Islamic Republic of Muamar Gadhafi) instead of groups supported by states.

The facts: The Pan Am Flight 103 was a regularly scheduled transatlantic flight from Frankfurt to Detroit via a stopover in London and New York City. The aircraft operating the transatlantic leg of the route was destroyed by a bomb, killing all 243 passengers and 16 crew, in what became known as the Lockerbie bombing.

Until 9/11, it was one of the world's most lethal acts of air terrorism and one of the largest and most complex acts of international terrorism ever investigated by the FBI. Solving the case required unprecedented international cooperation—and hours upon hours of painstaking work. With the midair explosion 30,000 feet up, debris rained down over 845 square miles across Scotland. FBI agents and international investigators combed the countryside on hands and knees looking for clues in virtually every blade of grass, eventually turning up thousands of pieces of evidence. They also traversed the globe, interviewing more than 10,000 individuals in dozens of countries. Participating in the investigation were an array of international police organizations from countries such as Germany, Austria, Switzerland and, of course, Great Britain (including Scotland). This evidence led to two Libyan intelligence operatives. In November 1991, the United States and Scotland simultaneously indicted the pair for planting the bomb. On January 31, 2001, after years of working to extradite the men and bring the case to trial, Abdel Basset Ali Al-Megrahi was found guilty of the crime. The codefendant was found not guilty and released. Eventually, on May 1, 2003, the Libyan government formally accepted responsibility for the bombing and agreed to pay nearly $3 billion to the victims' families.[14]

1.4.9 11 September 2001 Attacks

These are the most dramatic terrorist events of the twenty first century. All has been written about these events, all and more than that. These attacks triggered a trillion of conspiracy theories the purpose of which was to lighten the guilt of the culprits and try to incriminate the US government, some of them going as far as pointing at the CIA regarding the responsibility of these attacks. No need to discuss these preposterous and indecent theories.

1.4.10 A Short Reminder

The September 11 attacks were a series of four coordinated terrorist attacks by the terrorist group Al-Qaeda against the United States on the morning of Tuesday, September 11, 2001. The attacks resulted in a record in several fields. A total of 2,977 people lost their life in these attacks, over 25,000 people were injured, many with substantial long-term health consequences, in addition to at least $10 billion in infrastructure and property damage. It is the deadliest terrorist attack in human history and the single deadliest incident for firefighters and law enforcement officers in the history of the United States, with 340 and 72 killed, respectively. As I mentioned at the beginning of this paragraph, these attacks triggered an avalanche of conspiracy theories, some more credible than others – this is why conspiracy theories exist – because they offer credible alternatives – a consequence of the burgeoning social network mentality where everything can be said, and almost everything is believed. What I find more worrying is that these conspiracy theories are still very popular in many Arab and Muslim countries nowadays.

1.4.11 The Conspiracy Theories

The most prominent conspiracy theory is that the collapse of the Twin Towers and the World Trade Center were the result of controlled demolitions rather than structural failure due to impact and fire. Another prominent belief is that the Pentagon was hit by a missile launched by elements from inside the US government or that a commercial airliner was allowed to do so via an effective stand-down of the American military. Possible motives claimed by conspiracy theorists for such actions include justifying the invasions of Afghanistan and Iraq (even though the US government concluded that Iraq was not involved in the attacks and had probably planned the invasion of Afghanistan for a very long time) to advance their geostrategic interests, such as plans to construct a natural gas pipeline through Afghanistan. Other conspiracy theories revolve around authorities having advance knowledge of the attacks and deliberately ignoring or assisting the attackers.[15]

Whatever the theories, 9/11 was probably a trauma of the magnitude of the Pearl Harbor attack in 1941 and rallied the US population as a single man behind their government. The flag effect functioned beautifully in that situation and it is quite understandable.

1. 30 December 2006: Madrid-Barajas Airport bombing (airport attack)
   On December 30, 2006, a bomb planted in a van exploded in the Terminal 4 parking area at the Madrid–Barajas Airport in Spain, killing two and injuring 52. On 9 January 2007, the Basque nationalist and separatist organization ETA[16] claimed responsibility for the attack. The attack, one of the most powerful carried out by ETA, damaged the airport terminal and destroyed the entire parking structure.

2. 31 October 2015: Metrojet flight 9268 (midair plane bombing)
   Metrojet Flight 9268 was an international chartered passenger flight, operated by Russian airline Kogalymavia (branded as Metrojet). An Airbus A321-231 operating the flight was destroyed by a bomb above the northern Sinai Peninsula following its departure from Sharm El Sheikh International Airport, Egypt en route to Pulkovo Airport, Saint Petersburg, Russia. All 224 passengers and crew on board were killed. The cause of the crash was most likely an onboard explosive device as concluded by Russian investigators. For these experts, the cause of the crash was an improvised explosive device containing up to one kg of TNT.[17]

   The analysis of the black box confirmed the hypothesis of a bomb exploding midair. The attack was claimed by the ISIL.

3. 22 March 2016: Brussels bombing (airport attacks)
   On the morning of 22 March 2016, three coordinated suicide bombings occurred in Brussels, two at Brussels Airport in Zaventem, and one at Maalbeek metro station in central Brussels. Thirty-two civilians and three terrorists were killed, and more than 300 people were injured. Another bomb was found during a search of the airport. The ISIL claimed responsibility for the attacks.

1.5 TERROR AT SEA

Terror at sea has also known its heydays through the 1970s and the 1980s, and I perfectly remember how the Achille Lauro seajacking left the world spellbound for days. It was not yet the time of CNN breaking news and continuous 24/7 news channel, but we watched the evening news with anxiety and incomprehension.

But like with air terror, seajacking lost its appeal and another threat started to appear in the late 90s, something we thought were a thing of the past: piracy. Not the flamboyant one personified by Errol Flynn, not even the one personified by Captain Jack Sparrow, no, something more brutal and far less glamorous.

In the 1990s, several hotspots of piracy appeared on the maps of the oceans. Again, the purpose here is not to make a list of these incidents, and a very good summary can be found in Michael McNicholas' book *Maritime security.*[18]

Here are a few of the major attacks perpetrated at sea in the modern era:

1. 7 October 1985: The Achille Lauro hijacking
   The *Achille Lauro* hijacking happened on October 7, 1985, when the Italian MS *Achille Lauro* was hijacked by four men representing the Palestine Liberation Front off the coast of Egypt, as she was sailing from Alexandria to Ashdod, Israel. A 69-year-old Jewish American man in a wheelchair, Leon Klinghoffer, was murdered by the hijackers and thrown overboard. I am not sure that the Palestinian cause benefitted from this abject execution.
2. 27 February 2004: SuperFerry 14 attack (naval bombing)
   'SuperFerry 14', the deadliest terrorist attack in The Philippines, killed a total of 116 people. The blast occurred on 27 February 2004 in Manila Bay, claiming the title of the world's deadliest terrorist attack at sea until today. At 11 pm on 27 February 2004, the 10,192-ton ferry departed from Manila for Cagayan de Oro City, carrying 899 passengers and crew onboard. An hour after departure, just off either El Fraile or Corregidor Island, an explosion onboard started a fire that engulfed the ship. The attack was conducted by Abu Sayyaf, a Jihadist militant and pirate terrorist organization.

   Investigators believe the Superferry was targeted because its owners, WG&A, refused a request for $1m in protection money from Abu Sayyaf in 2003.

   The Abu Sayyaf group claimed responsibility soon after the incident, but the government initially dismissed the claim as a "propaganda ploy". In March, however, a group of Abu Sayyaf members were arrested over the incident – including one man who allegedly confessed to planting the bomb. This incident highlighted the porous border between terrorism and organized crime. Apparently, blackmailing ended up in mass murder, and this incident may have decided other shipping companies to pay the price for tranquility.

1.5.1 Maritime Security: A Large Panel of Threats

Maritime security comprises many activities, and is a complex world for the security practitioners. The main threats encountered in maritime security are:

- Illegal military (or paramilitary) activity
- Terrorism
- Trafficking
- Piracy

27

1.5.1.1 Illegal Paramilitary or Illegal Military Activity

These are all the events that make the headlines and the breaking news when official and semiofficial naval units face each other in areas of tension in the world seas. Such events occur at a regular frequency in the Persian Gulf when incidents between the Iranian speedboats and western navies occur, reflecting the tensions between Iran and its southern neighbors (the Gulf Cooperation Council [GCC] sheikhdoms) supported by the United States. In Eastern Mediterranean, the navy of the neo-sultan Erdogan taunt the international law of the sea, violate the Greek territorial waters, and threaten Greek and French ships with no significant retaliation whatsoever from NATO and the European Union.[19] This is what happens in the China sea when American, Chinese and Japanese navies try to intimidate each other to impose their sovereignty on this gigantic and coveted mass of water sprinkled with strategically located islands. Let us be honest, this is not really the domain of the security manager. Although, as a security professional, you might be involved at the periphery of that space, particularly if you work for the shipping industry and you have to protect merchant ships and tankers or in the oil and gas industry where there is a continuity of action from the state to the company. Most of your job will about deterrence, prevention, and effective security plans, never to reply to a physical attack. Anything above that is of the domain of the navy or the coast guards, military or paramilitary paction. This is why I shall not spend too much time on that topic.

1.5.1.2 Terrorism

Terrorism at sea is a complex issue. It is sometimes intertwined with criminal activities, and what is displayed in the headlines as a terrorist attack is often a mix of criminal operation (piracy, kidnap and ransom, etc.) coupled with a political intent or part of a criminal association between criminals and activists. Dryad Global (DG) defines terrorism as "The unofficial or unauthorized use of violence and intimidation in the pursuit of political aims". I prefer this simple definition to some official convoluted definitions that want to mean that states – and by this, it is meant western states – cannot be terrorists – although with the advent of rogue and failed states – a convenient means to distinguish us from them – these subtleties in definition are not necessary anymore. Western decision makers can sleep soundly.

DG considers maritime terrorism on a grand scale, citing the examples of standoff attacks – such as the terrorist attacks in Aden and Mogadishu, as well as simply firing on vessels at sea, a technique much favored by the defunct Tamil tiger's terrorist group.[20]

The second type of aggression that they mention is the direct attack (blast attack) either through a charge detonated from a distance, or through a suicide operator.

Illustrating the second category, the attack on the USS Cole, on October 12, 2000, where suicide operators exploded a small boat alongside the USS Cole – a Navy Destroyer – as it was refueling in the Yemeni port of Aden is still in everyone's memory. The blast ripped a 40-foot-wide hole near the waterline of the Cole, killing 17 American sailors and injuring 37 others.

1.5.1.3 Trafficking

Trafficking is again rarely in the hands of the security professionals, but they often act at the periphery of these traffics. The coast guards, the navy and often a cooperation between the police, the intelligence and coast guards are working together to work on the many and varied traffics that exist in the maritime industry. For the security manager, a strict application of the ISPS requirements along with a healthy relationship with local authorities is the best possible approach to the countering these various threats.

There are mainly three axes of traffic currently present on most continents. First, the traffic of people, worth – according to DG – $150 billion a year, coming second to drug as the most profitable illegal business on the planet. The trafficking has been highlighted these last years with the transport in appalling conditions – but a very steep price – of migrants crossing the Mediterranean to reach the shores of Europe where they expect to find a better life. This year, 900 migrants died doing the crossing.

Weapons is the second most common illegal act of trafficking at sea and is of course present in the vicinity of areas of conflict. Libya is, at the moment, at the core of incessant smuggling operation to support one or the other contender to power in Tripoli. Here the chances that you, as a security practitioner, become involved in operations of this magnitude, is a possibility, but a rather small one. But again, you can be at the periphery of this traffic, depending on your location and the composition of your workforce.

Drugs is the most consistent of traffic, since being illegal in most countries as well as in great demand, there is no chance of improvement regarding drug trafficking at sea.

1.5.1.4 Piracy

Piracy does not concern many security managers unless they protect a facility with a maritime facade or they work as a security manager in a company involved in shipping and transport. Obviously, a port security manager or a manager of companies working in a port environment (shipping companies, cargo transport companies, terminals, oil and gas companies, pipeline security, etc.) would be concerned by piracy as a threat. In most cases, the ISPS will be the reference guide, but maritime threats are not easy to counter, because security managers have normally very few means at their disposal. Coast guards, and navies are traditionally the response to maritime threats. Nevertheless, security managers may be tasked with protecting facilities, pipelines or ships. There, prevention will be the best chance of success and the place where security managers can add value. A strong security program will help and provide deterrence, help detection and help delay capabilities.

1.5.2 What Is the Future of Attacks at Sea?

Attacks at sea to hijack ships or keep people hostages for resale seem today rather out of fashion. They had their moment of glory, but companies have equipped their vessels with adequate equipment and response teams, and a better cooperation between merchant navies and intervention forces has changed the situation and attacks seem less frequent (or perhaps they are less advertised?) mainly as a criminal activity, but its goals have now been concentrated on criminal activities and immediate profits. DG tells us that the aim of piracy is to extract the maximum monetary value possible by:

- *Hit and run* – Theft of ships' cash and/or stores
- *Kidnap for ransom* – removal of persons to extort release money
- *Hijack for ransom* – detention of the target to extort release money
- *Stealing ship and cargo* – targeting of vessels (often during ship-ship operations) to remove cargo.

These criminal acts are favored by a number of objective factors:

To start with, there are some legal and jurisdictional opportunities in certain areas of the world where sea sovereignty is not properly established and where local navies and coast guard units have neither the will nor the means to police the sea routes.

30

Favorable geography comes as a second factor. Areas of kidnapping share a number of critical geographic elements, vast areas, sea routes, and little police force at sea, reflecting often conflicts and disorders in the country owning the maritime domain. In countries politically or economically fragile, there is usually very little money left to equip coast guards and find quality ships able to rival those of the smugglers. This weakness of law enforcement is a direct result of political instability and economic incapacity and perhaps it might also benefit some people in governments that may have some interest in financing piracy. This is what falls under the label of permissive political environments, when members close to the power inner circle derive huge profits from illegal maritime activities, under the indifferent eye of part of the responsible administration. We can talk about either a kind of cultural acceptability or, more bluntly, sheer corruption of the elites. By cultural acceptability, we mean that in some areas of south Asia and Africa, there has always been a tradition of piracy that is accepted as a fact of life. It is a natural redistribution of riches and has been part of some populations living for as far as history has been recorded. Although paying lip service to international regulations, and signing all binding international agreements, the leaders of the countries concerned by this cultural trait will tend to consider its consequences as a fact of life that maintains a balance within the population groups and that they consider as a parallel acceptable economy.

And yet, when I see the cruise liners, with several thousands of people on board and the destruction capability of such ships – imagine one of these cruisers crashing in Venice – I am surprised that no incident occurred these last years. Such an attack would be far less complicated to organize than the attacks on the Twin Towers and/or the Pentagon. Unless of course, security on these big liners is really top-class. I admit that I have absolutely no knowledge about the situation.

1.6 TERROR IN CITIES – LAND ATTACKS

Terrors in cities are often those that impact our imagination the most. Because most of us live in towns, what happens in a train station, a school or a shopping mall has therefore more power on our imagination because this is where we could have been, us or those who are dear to us.

In this section, I will cite a few events that marked my generation starting with the traumatic Munich massacre during the 1972 Olympic games.

1.7 THE MUNICH MASSACRE ON 6 SEPTEMBER 1972

The Munich massacre was an attack during the 1972 Summer Olympics in Munich, West Germany, by eight members of the Palestinian terrorist group Black September, who took nine members of the Israeli Olympic team hostages, after killing two of them.

The hostage-takers demanded the release of 234 Palestinians and non-Arabs jailed in Israel, along with two West German insurgents held by the West German penitentiary system, Andreas Baader and Ulrike Meinhof, the founders of the West German Red Army Faction. The hostage-takers threw the body of Weinberg out of the front door of the residence to demonstrate their resolve. Israel's response was immediate and absolute: There would be no negotiation. Israel's official policy at the time was to refuse to negotiate with terrorists under any circumstances, as according to the Israeli government such negotiations would give an incentive to future attacks.

On 8 September, Israeli planes bombed ten Palestine Liberation Organization (PLO) bases in Syria and Lebanon in response to the massacre, killing an estimated 200 people. A campaign of retaliation was launched by the Israeli government of Golda Meir that can be resumed in the book written by one of the members of the commando who took the lives of several Palestinians considered as the masterminds behind the massacre. The book Ephraim's revenge by Jonas George published in 1984 offers a romanticized account of the deeds of the commando, making it one of the most captivating books I ever read.

1.8 THE BOLOGNA CENTRAL STATION ATTACK

On 2 August 1980 in Bologna – Italy – 85 people were killed and nearly 200 more wounded during a terrorist bombing episode at the city's Central Station. According to some reports, the *Nuclei Armati Rivoluzionari*, a neofascist terrorist organization, executed the attack. Other theories were also proposed. The Bologna Massacre is regarded as Western Europe's fourth deadliest terror attack after the Nice attack, Paris attacks and Madrid train bombings.

1.9 18 APRIL 1983: US EMBASSY BOMBING, BEIRUT (SUICIDE ATTACK)

On 18 April 1983, the US embassy was destroyed by a suicide bomber in Beirut, Lebanon, that killed 32 Lebanese, 17 Americans and 14 visitors and passersby. It was the deadliest attack on a US diplomatic mission up to that time, and was considered the beginning of Islamist attacks on US targets. In all, 63 people were killed (including the suicide bomber) and 120 others were injured.

1.10 26 FEBRUARY 1993: 1993 WORLD TRADE CENTER BOMBING (BOMBING)

The 1993 World Trade Center bombing was a terrorist attack on the World Trade Center, carried out on February 26, 1993, when a truck bomb detonated below the North Tower of the World Trade Center in New York City. It intended to send the North Tower crashing into the South Tower, bringing both towers down and killing tens of thousands of people. It failed to do so, but killed six people, including a pregnant woman, and injured over 1,000.

1.10.1 19 April 1995: Oklahoma City Bombing (Bombing)

The Oklahoma City bombing was a domestic terrorist truck bombing of the Alfred P. Murrah Federal Building in Oklahoma City, Oklahoma, United States, on Wednesday, 19 April 1995. Perpetrated by anti-government extremists Timothy McVeigh and Terry Nichols, the bombing happened at 9:02 am and killed at least 168 people, injured more than 680 others, and destroyed more than one third of the building, which had to be demolished. The blast destroyed or damaged 324 other buildings within a 16-block radius, shattered glass in 258 nearby buildings, and destroyed or burned 86 cars, causing an estimated $652 million worth of damage.

1.10.2 11 March 2004: Madrid Train Bombs (Bombing – Attacks on Station)

The 2004 Madrid train bombings (also known in Spain as 11M) were nearly simultaneous, coordinated bombings against the Cercanías commuter train system of Madrid, Spain, on the morning of 11 March 2004—three days before Spain's general elections. The explosions killed 193 people and injured around 2,000.

1.10.3 1 September 2004: Beslan School Siege (Armed Attack)

On 1 September 2004, armed Chechen rebels took approximately 1,200 children and adults hostage at a school in Beslan, North Ossetia, Russia, at approximately 9:00 a.m. local time. The siege ended on 3 September 2004, with more than 330 killed, including 186 children, and more than 700 people wounded.

Chechen warlord Shamil Basayev claimed responsibility for the attack. It is considered to be the deadliest school shooting in history.

1.10.4 7 July 2005: London Transport Bombings (Bombing)

The 7 July 2005 London bombings, often referred to as 7/7, were a series of four coordinated Islamist suicide attacks in London, England, that targeted commuters travelling on the city's public transport system during the morning rush hour. 52 people lost their lives while 700 people were injured. The four suicide bombers died, obviously.

1.10.5 22 July 2011: Breivik Shootings or the 2011 Norway Attacks (Armed Attack)

The 2011 Norway attacks, referred to in Norway as 22 July or as 22/7, were two sequential domestic terrorist attacks by Anders Behring Breivik against the government, the civilian population and a Workers' Youth League (AUF) summer camp, in which 77 people were killed.

The first attack was a car bomb explosion in Oslo within Regjeringskvartalet, the executive government quarter of Norway, at 15:25 p.m. The bomb was placed inside a van next to the tower block housing the office of the then Prime Minister Jens Stoltenberg. The explosion killed eight people and injured at least 209 people, 12 severely.

The second attack occurred less than two hours later at a summer camp on the island of Utøya in Tyrifjorden, Viken. The camp was organized by the AUF, the youth division of the ruling Norwegian Labor Party (AP). Breivik, dressed in a homemade police uniform and showing false identification, took a ferry to the island and opened fire at the participants, killing 69 and injuring at least 110, 55 seriously.

The attack was the deadliest in Norway since the Second World War. A survey found that one in four Norwegians knew someone affected.

1.10.6 7 January 2015: Charlie Hebdo Shootings (Armed Attack)

On 7 January 2015, at about 11:30 a.m. CET local time, two French Muslim brothers, Saïd and Chérif Kouachi, forced their way into the offices of the French satirical weekly newspaper Charlie Hebdo in Paris. Armed with rifles and other weapons, they killed 12 people and injured 11 others. The gunmen identified themselves as belonging to the Islamic terrorist group Al-Qaeda in the Arabian Peninsula, which took responsibility for the attack.

Several related attacks followed in the Île-de-France region on 7–9 January 2015, including the Hypercacher kosher supermarket siege where a terrorist held 19 hostages, of whom he murdered four Jewish people (next event).

1.10.7 9 January 2015: Hyper Cacher Kosher Deli Siege

The Hypercacher kosher supermarket siege was an attack and hostage crisis that occurred in Porte de Vincennes (20th arrondissement of Paris) in the wake of the Charlie Hebdo shooting two days earlier, and concurrently with the Dammartin-en-Goële hostage crisis in which the two Charlie Hebdo gunmen were cornered and killed.

Amedy Coulibaly had pledged allegiance to the Islamic State of Iraq and the Levant, and was a close friend of Saïd and Chérif Kouachi (whom he had met in jail in 2005), the gunmen in the Charlie Hebdo attack. Armed with a submachine gun, an assault rifle and two Tokarev pistols, he entered and attacked the people in the kosher food supermarket. Coulibaly murdered four Jewish hostages, and held 15 other hostages during a siege in which he demanded that the Kouachi brothers not be harmed. The police ended the siege by storming the store and killing Coulibaly.

1.10.8 13 November 2015: Paris Attacks (Suicide Bombing)

The November 2015 Paris attacks were a series of coordinated terrorist attacks that took place on Friday 13 November 2015 in Paris, France, and the city's northern suburb, Saint-Denis. Three suicide bombers struck outside the Stade de France in Saint-Denis, during an international football match, after failing to gain entry to the stadium. Another group of attackers then fired on crowded cafés and restaurants in Paris, with one of them also blowing himself up. A third group carried out another mass shooting and took hostages at a rock concert attended by 1,500 people in the Bataclan theater.

The attackers killed 130 people, including 90 at the Bataclan theater. Another 416 people were injured, almost 100 critically. Seven of the attackers were also killed. The attacks were the deadliest in France since the Second World War, and the deadliest in the European Union since the Madrid train bombings of 2004.

1.10.9 14 July 2016: Nice Attack (Vehicle-Ramming – Public Space)

On the evening of July 14, 2016, a 19-ton cargo truck was deliberately driven into crowds of people celebrating Bastille Day on the *Promenade des Anglais* in Nice, France, resulting in the deaths of 86 people and the injury of 458 others. The driver was Mohamed Lahouaiej-Bouhlel, a Tunisian citizen living in France. The attack ended following an exchange of gunfire, during which Lahouaiej-Bouhlel was shot dead by the police.

1.10.10 24 August 2020: Syria Pipeline Attack

On Monday, 24 August 2020, 5:51 a.m., an explosion caused by a "terrorist attack" against a major gas pipeline in Syria caused a temporary countrywide blackout. Reporting on Monday, the official Syrian Arab News Agency (SANA) cited Minister of Petroleum and Mineral Resources Ali Ghanem as saying that the entire country was left without power overnight after the blast at the Arab Gas Pipeline that feeds the country's southern power stations.

The pipeline explosion was the latest in a string of alleged attacks against the government's energy infrastructure.

It is always interesting to see that these are the great inventions of the late 19th early 20th century that seem to attract our bad apples. On the land front, railways – and by railways I means trains, metros but also stations, seem to have an irresistible appeal to terrorists. The metro attack in Japan is an interesting example, when Japanese terrorists decided to poison the couloirs du metro and succeeded in creating a terrible panic.

1.10.10.1 The End of the Hollywood Type World Attacks

The last few years saw developments that underlines a loss of capabilities and imagination from our adversaries. The attack of iconic targets having lost momentum, there has been a shift from logistically demanding attacks to a sort of marauding terror action, hostile vehicle assaults, seeing alleged lone wolves attacking all and sundry while shouting Allahu Akbar with gusto. The number of these attacks (rams and blades) have reached a sickening regularity and have probably made some florists and candle sellers quite rich. The Brits seem to have been the most proactive in this domain's response, prepositioning police teams close to London's iconic/critical areas that proved their effectiveness during the last two attacks in London. The French have not yet reached that level of commitment and preparation. Although they have specific units trained to deal with several kind of terror attacks (hostage taking seems to be a French specialty), they are far too dispersed to be able to face the multiplicity of these attacks. France is facing daily attacks from North and sub-Saharan Africans who consider everything that represents the French Republic a systemic enemy, although they were born in the country, are often third- or fourth-generation French citizens, and have been fed, instructed and looked after since their birth. Police, firefighters and even doctors are regularly ambushed in suburbs where what the French press calls "Les jeunes" (the young ones), protecting their lucrative drug business, reign supreme. This situation will either totally degenerate or a bit of discipline will need to be restored.

But I do not see any of our politicians being able to reverse the trend. Sad, really because it creates a culture of insecurity that makes the job of security manager in the private sector more complicated. The potential threat agents are becoming more elusive and difficult to protect from without discriminating. These attacks, all claimed by Daesh or the Islamic state have probably never been ordered by the vacillating movement. It is probably the only way to these dispirited and full of hatred people to claim an allegiance to something Muslim and anti-West. Although these attacks are classified by the parquet as terrorist attacks, is this really what they are? Young and idle, frustrated and not very bright young people might find solace in attacking native people in the streets with a knife shouting Allahu Akbar; does that make this a terrorist attack? Or a simple criminal act? It is not an easy question. My generation was faced with terrorists who were part of terror networks, receiving orders from their chiefs in the mountains of Pakistan, or in backstreets of Lebanon, selecting, training and deploying/dispatching people to commit their acts, securing huge funds to launch massive operations that necessitated a substantial number of trained actors and required discipline and absolute dedication. These actors sworn allegiance to a leader or an emir and were ready to sacrifice their lives for him and the cause.

The last generation of marauding attackers and truck ramming drivers do not need orders, or money, and not much courage, rather desperation. Although most of them end up dead, shot by the police, their return on investment, from a jihadist's perspective, is impressive. Because, if this is the case, the problem will be difficult to solve. In France, specialized service follows these networks and classify their members as Fiches S. But their number is growing much faster than the police elements who track them, and their demographic stamina will make the work more and more complicated. There are not many ways of countering this threat. Thousands of people of big cities suburbs might shift from alcohol, drugs and motorbike rodeos to martyrdom, with a very shallow knowledge of religion and for reasons difficult to apprehend. It has been said that all these recidivist offenders have been recruited in jail by other politically and religiously motivated activists. Maybe they find a way to take revenge on the country who gave shelter to their parents or grandparents who were ill-treated by their hosts? Who knows? But this is definitely not our problem.

Our problem is to understand how some people can suddenly turn nasty and decide to betray the company that employs them. At the moment, there is an overlapping area between criminal violence and terrorist violence because both populations are represented by the same ethnic and religious group.

Why am I making this point? Because it is very difficult for a security practitioner working in an organization where these populations are highly represented to know when one is leaving the first group to enter the second. Both are worlds of violence, but for the security practitioner, terrorism always ranks higher than petty crime and violence. Of course, if you are in retail security, your daily job is about fighting thieves, but the idea of an individual entering the shop on a sale day and killing in an ocean of blood all the females in the lobby should be your fist concern (the *Hypercacher* syndrome). Low probability. High consequence should always take precedence over high-probability low-consequence events.

Second question: Why is it important to differentiate the nature of the adversary? Because of the possible consequences of their action. A theft of IT accessories may be irritating, but the deaths of innocent people is an issue of another entirely different magnitude.

1.11 RECENT ATTACK TRENDS

Although we still denote a large number of bombing attacks, contemporary times have seen the emergence of new trends in terrorist actions. These last years have seen the expression *lone wolf* enter the world of breaking news in an exponential way.

1.11.1 Lone-Wolf Attacks

A lone wolf has been defined as:

> A lone actor, lone-actor terrorist, or lone wolf is someone who prepares and commits violent acts alone, outside of any command structure and without material assistance from any group. They may be influenced or motivated by the ideology and beliefs of an external group and may act in support of such a group.
>
> *Wikipedia*

This sounds very nice but does not resist the reality of the facts. It has been proved, again and again, that alleged lone wolves had all benefited from logistical support from friends and/or family to prepare their attacks. The link between the Kouachi brothers of Charlie Hebdo and Amedy Coulibaly of the Kasher supermarket have been established without doubt. As soon as a lone wolf is arrested or shot by the police, a string of arrestations follows: brothers, sisters, parents who knew about the actions and helped, voluntarily. As a conclusion, the concept of lone wolf does not resist a good investigation.

For those interested, the list of lone wolf attacks is long and will easily be accessible on the net.

1.12 NEW TECHNIQUES

Sometimes, it is technical things that bring a bit of fresh air in modi operandi. The use of drones, although they have been in existence for quite some time, suddenly became the flavor of the day a few years ago, and their use seems less frequent these days and more and more the monopoly of military and paramilitary groups.

1.12.1 Drone Attacks

Between 1994 and 2018, more than 14 planned or attempted terrorist attacks took place using aerial drones. Some of these were:

- in 1994, Aum Shinrikyo attempted to use a remote-controlled helicopter to spray sarin gas, but tests failed as the helicopter crashed;
- in 2013, a planned attack by Al-Qaeda in Pakistan using multiple drones was stopped by local law enforcement;
- in 2014, the Islamic State began using commercial off-the-shelf and homemade aerial drones at scale during military operations in Iraq and Syria;
- in August 2018, two GPS-guided drones, laden with explosives, were used in a failed attempt to assassinate Venezuelan President Maduro; and,
- in January 2018, a swarm of 13 homemade aerial drones attacked two Russian military bases in Syria.

Drones were for a while an extraordinary means of surveillance and attack. The Houthi rebels of Yemen seem to have exploited very well this new technique, particularly in their attacks on the Saudi-Yemeni border. But its efficiency was very relative and its attractiveness waned.

1.12.1.1 2 July 2019: Attack on a Saudi Arabian Airport

That was the second attack in two months on an airport in southwestern Saudi Arabia. It wounded nine people, according to a Saudi-led coalition statement. Yemen's Iranian-backed Houthi rebels claimed responsibility for a drone attack Tuesday on Abha International Airport, according to the Houthi-run Al-Masirah news agency. The Saudi-led coalition fighting the rebels confirmed the drone attack and said it believed Tehran was involved in the operation.

The BBC highlighted some recent threats made by the Islamic State and its future use of drones and they can be found at https://inews.co.uk/news/uk/drone-terror-attack-jihadists-britain-matter-time-security-sources-warn-89904

1.12.2 Cyberterrorism

Cyberterrorism is obviously a threat to be taken seriously. In many organizations, IT security is the domain of the IT manager, and my experience with these people is that they do not see the point of working with people like us, whom they seem to consider as an inferior security species. I might have been unlucky in my career, but my relationship with IT managers has always been more complicated than with HR managers (who often end up doing our job, in smaller organizations). The IT threat is complex. Because the authors do not expose themselves physically and are quite good at covering their tracks, they fear nothing. But there again, we must be cautious with the myth of the lone wolf hacker. It has appeared during these last years that state-sponsored hacking was much more prominent than the American hacker in his garage, you know the one we see in Netflix series, and most of the serious hacking is organized from Russia, in China, Iran, Turkey and probably our democracies as well. State hacking is part of the arsenal of states and it does make sense that this investment pays.

I was working in Saudi Arabia when the Saudi Aramco cyber system was hacked and destroyed by a virus called Shamoun or Shamoon. The Saudis were convinced that the Iranians were behind this attack, but it was never officially proven.

Cybersecurity is not the object of this book and I shall not spend time on something that is quite alien to my competence. But let me give you only one example of the kind of cyberattacks any organization could face: On 10 May, 2021, a cybercriminal gang called DarkSide led a cyberattack on a major US fuel pipeline. The main fuel supply line to the US East Coast was shut down after the pipeline's operator was hit by what is believed to be the largest successful cyberattack on oil infrastructure in the country's history. The attack on the Colonial Pipeline, which runs 5,500 miles and provides nearly half the fuel used on the East Coast, affected some of the company's IT systems. Colonial said it has engaged a third-party cybersecurity firm to investigate the incident, which it confirmed was a ransomware attack, and has contacted law enforcement and other federal agencies.

The examples of ransomware attacks abound and must be countered, but that should be the job of the cybersecurity security expert of the organization although I can only recommend that our new brand of security practitioners put cybersecurity on their to-do list. Maybe not CISSP level, but there are plenty other certifications, a bit less demanding, that can be obtained to show that you know what cybersecurity is about.

After all, physical security and cybersecurity overlap in part and convergence should be the correct attitude.

NOTES

1 To provide an idea of the scale of the terrorist scourge, 171,787 terrorist attacks were recorded worldwide from 1979 to 2017 (Fondapol 2019: 11).

2 This sect was founded in Persia in 1089 by a man called Hassan Ibn-al-Sabbah. This order was the first organization to have theorized the use of terrorism, developing methods of indoctrination, of dissimulation and of organization in the first structured terrorist method in history.

3 In 2020, the GDP of Russia was $1,464.08 billion compared to the 20,807.27 of the United States and the 15,222.16 of China (source International Monetary Fund 2020).

4 In his last book *Le prophète et la pandémie* (2021 – Gallimard), Gilles Kepel coins the expression *jihadisme d'atmosphère*.

5 Retrieved at www.rand.org/blog/2015/07/the-1970s-and-the-birth-of-conte mporary-terrorism.html on 3 June 2021.

6 On 3 October 1980, the rue Copernic synagogue in Paris, France, was bombed in a terrorist attack. The attack killed four and wounded 46 people.

7 The 2002 Karachi bus bombing was one of a series of deadly strikes on westerners in Pakistan in 2002. The blast killed 14 people and wounded another 40. The attack took place in Karachi.

8 On the night of 26–27 March 1996, seven monks of the Trappist order from the Atlas Abbey of Tibhirine near Médéa, Algeria, were kidnapped during the Algerian Civil War. They were held for two months, and were found dead in late May 1996. The GIA was accused of the murder, but there is a suspicion that the Algerian Army was responsible for their death.

9 Euskadi ta Askatasuna is the main independentist Basque organization.

10 The French West Indies in the Caribbean sea.

11 Available at www.start.umd.edu/research-projects/global-terrorism-datab ase-gtd

12 Price JC and Forrest JS (2009) *Practical aviation security: Predicting and preventing future threats*, Butterworth-Heinemann.

13 The detailed list of these hijackings can be found on this Wikipedia link: https://en.wikipedia.org/wiki/List_of_aircraft_hijackings#1970s

14 Part of the article titled Pan Am 103 bombing on the FBI website, retrieved from www.fbi.gov/history/famous-cases/pan-am-103-bombing on 6 July 2021.

15 Retrieved from Wikipedia on 11 July 2021 https://en.wikipedia.org/wiki/9/11_conspiracy_theories

16 ETA stands for *Euskadi Ta Askatasuna* (Basque Homeland and Liberty); it has been struggling with the Spanish central government since its foundation in 1959.

17 Trinitrotoluene more commonly known as TNT, more specifically 2,4,6-trinitrotoluene, and by its preferred IUPAC name 2-Methyl-1,3,5-trinitrobenzene, is a chemical compound with the formula $C_6H_2(NO_2)_3CH_3$. It

is best known as an explosive material with convenient handling properties (Wikipedia).

18 McNicholas M (2016) 2nd ed., *Maritime Security an Introduction*, Butterworth-Heinemann.

19 One such incident unfolded recently in the eastern Mediterranean on 10 June 2020 when a French frigate under NATO command tried to inspect a Tanzanian-flagged cargo ship suspected of smuggling arms to Libya in violation of a United Nations (UN) embargo. During the action, the frigate was harassed by three Turkish navy vessels escorting the cargo ship. A Turkish ship flashed three times its radar lights – an act normally associated with an imminent torpedo attack – and its crew put on bulletproof vests and stood behind their light weapons, it said. Turkey disputes this. It denies trafficking arms to Libya and says the cargo ship, the Cirkin, was carrying humanitarian aid. It has accused the French navy of aggression.

20 Data retrieved from https://dg.dryadglobal.com/what-is-maritime-pir acy#Types_of_piracy on 21 July 2021.

2

Is Our World under Threat?

In this chapter, I will begin with a bit of semantics and define the relation between the words threat, vulnerability and risk. These three words seem interrelated and are used interchangeably by the media, some pundits and our customers. The word threat is itself the subject of a semantic confusion since it designates both the threat-as-agent, these adversaries we fear, and the threat-as-action, that is an event, a bombing, a kidnapping or a plane hijacking.

After having clarified these terms, I will examine the nature of the threat and try to establish limits to what a security practitioner can do.

To close this chapter, I will assess the obvious but often negated relation between threat and politics. A discussion about the cultural aspect of threats will close this chapter.

Threats have an aura of unpredictability and mystery that makes it uncannily fascinating. Social constructivists thinkers would say that threats exist when you decide they exist and disappear the moment you decide they are not real. This is possible, but I doubt you may enjoy a successful career in the security industry if you think that way. I rather believe that threats do exist independently from the security consultant who looks for them, and that they might occur at what you would find a most improbable time, but that they are the outcome of a long process – by the adversary – of target selection, planning, recruitment, training, selection of symbolic

DOI: 10.4324/9781003091080-3

dates – although not always – and that at the moment they materialize, they do so with a definite advantage over you, the security practitioner, for a number of reasons, which we will discuss in a subsequent chapter. There are many reasons for this surprise effect of most attacks, and to paraphrase the famous sentence by Donald Rumsfeld:

> There are known threats, there are things we know that we know. There are known unknowns, that is to say there are things we know we don't know; But there are also unknown unknowns, that is elements we do not know we don't know.[1]

In other words, threats, no matter how hard you work at collecting, analyzing and prioritizing data, will never appear to you in their entirety like assets, which you can measure and rank according to predetermined criteria. As said earlier, there is always an aura of mystery and secrecy in threats. That is what makes them fascinating, but also, for you who have in charge the security of an organization, terrifying and nervously exhausting.

Threats are mysterious. Parts of some threats are obvious, most of their components are elusive. They defy the hardest working of consultants. Threats seems to have their own independent and multiform life. The security practitioner is, when it comes to threat, even when knowledgeable, in an incredibly lonesome and inferiority situation. To start with, in most cases, only open-source data are available to him or her. He or she will never be privy to intelligence collected by government agencies. He will even be more ignorant of what potential adversaries are planning in the utmost clandestinity. The security practitioner has no undercover informant letting him know the degree of preparation of an attack against the organization. Left on their own, security consultants and analysts have to search, collect and organize data and take guesses (not so educated) to anticipate the potential attacks to the facility, plant or other entity they are tasked to protect.

Security has sometimes been defined as the absence of threat. I believe that the pursuit of security is what characterizes human life. Since man lived in grottos, their ultimate goal has always been to protect their families, their clans, their tribe, their country and eventually their values they created and refined through time. At individual level, to live in security is to live away from threats, and when they seem suddenly unavoidable, to be able to mitigate these threats without infringing your security capital. Alas, this definition is very optimistic and very limited since the simple fact of breathing air exposes us to serious threats (of unknown viruses the COVID-19 being the latest and most dramatic example). Threats are everywhere and risk part of everything we do, in everything we make, in any endeavor we pursue, from cradle to the grave. They may not be con-substantial threats, and we might not even be conscious of their existence, they may not all be *security* threats, but threats surround us at all times. They start when you get up, when you walk to the station, when you catch the train, when you start your car, when you go for lunch and do not even end when you switch off your bed lamp. An earthquake, a fire, a lunatic on a rampage are all threats than can materialize while you are sleeping and end your life in a very nasty and brutal manner.

Threats are everywhere and risk, even when minimal, is never really far away. Of course, we know it, we accept it and we even sometimes prepare for it (don't we all lock the door of our flat or our house at night, even in countries reputed safe?). Not to mention burglar bars and alarms in unsecure neighborhoods. Threats, in their many forms, lurk over our existence on a daily basis, and will do for as long as we live. One cannot live away from threat and one has to admit it.

Threat is not, at a personal level, the same thing as a risk. There is a risk that the flight you are taking to go a conference is delayed and that you will have to activate a last-minute Plan B. This is a risk of something unforeseen happening, and we accept the possibility of its occurrence. A risk is not entirely negative. In finance and banking, there are positive risks. A threat always is. A threat is something that will have a detrimental impact on your life, or on those you are tasked to protect. A terrorist wants to hijack the plane you are travelling in; this is a materialization of the threat. The chance it happens is infinitesimal. This is the risk.

Risk is about probabilities. Threat is about actions and agents.

The trade unions block the quay of the train you take to go home; this a threat to your returning home in time for dinner (that you share with many others in that specific case). The plane crashing further due to technical failure is a risk that could normally end your life. You are free to accept it or not – you may choose to travel by train, car or boat). When you do not know if you should use threat in a sentence, replace the word with chance. If it works, then it is a risk. If it is not, you are discussing a threat.

The second thing of importance is that to speak about threat in general is very much like an electoral speech. It does not mean much if it is not related to a target. The threat that a platoon of paratroopers deployed in mountains of Afghanistan or in the shrubs of the Sahel region could con-sider and prepare for is very different from the threat that menaces a group of technicians deployed on a dam or a power station project in a volatile environment, isolated, unprepared and therefore most vulnerable. Both threats may have things in common – the same agents may want to attack them -, but they remain different in essence, because the vulnerabilities of the targets are immensely different. Chances are that the threat for the technicians probably revolves around kidnap and ransom, something that necessitates little resources and that criminals would be very interested in carrying out, while only powerful armed groups would dare tackle a genuine military unit, western-trained and well-armed, able to call reinforcements and perhaps even air intervention, and only in extraordinarily favorable circumstances. It is therefore crucial to always maintain some common sense when discussing threats, targets and vulnerabilities.

Threat is a generic word, but multiform in scale and nature. It is everything and/or anyone that can disrupt your security, your safety, your physical integrity. In our industrial context, threat is anything that can disrupt the integrity and the operational capabilities of the assets to be protected.

2.1 RISK

Risk is somehow a more palatable term than threat and generates much less stress in any audience, client or public. Risk is something one can envision and accept, because the chances that it materializes are subjected to the law of probabilities. We are so built that we accept actions that pose risks, but we feel uneasy when it comes to threat. Why is that so?

I think it is because risk is something that is an integral part of our education and our condition as human beings and risk is a notion that we have integrated with time. We know that there is a risk in crossing traffic light at night, in going to a certain place after working hours, in taking this flight with a very good price but a poorly reputed airline, in climbing that mountain at the wrong season, in sailing in dangerous seas. We are conscious of the risks and we are free (not always though) to accept them or not. This is our choice; we are free to risk our life (not in a professional context though). It may depend on our own evaluation of the threat often mixed with a cost-benefit analysis. Is it worth it hiring these bodyguards and armored vehicle at that exorbitant price for a one afternoon meeting? When was a guy like me abducted last? What are my chances to get away with it? We estimate probabilities (risk is about probabilities, remember). Are we reasonable in doing it? We seldom are. In my country, chances to win the Lotto Big Prize, the weekly lottery, stands at 1 against millions. This is not a good probability. And yet, millions of people each week buy tickets because they want to believe that some superior power, that we can call fate, luck or immanent justice, will designate them as winners. I admit that in this very example, the risk is simply to lose money that might have been useful elsewhere. Sadly, the most financially challenged people are often those who spend the most on these lotteries. What it definitely demonstrates is that probabilities are not always a sufficient element to measure risk appropriately. Emotions play a major role in risk assessment.

The same goes for our personal security. *Because the money is good, I will go and work in this unstable and dangerous country, with fingers crossed, hoping nothing will happen to me and I will come back in one piece at the end of my contract.* By doing so, we evaluate the risk (this is a dangerous country) and our emotions (it would be nasty to call it greed, but honestly, if you are offered three times what you earn today to do the same thing that you do at home, there must be some reasons. Security (or rather the very small guarantee of it) is normally top of the list of these reasons.

So our rational brain says: That place is dangerous and I may (only may) get injured or lose my life, and the emotional side says: I need the money, I am ready to take the risk. In this example, the decision is only partially dictated by probabilities. Emotions, cognitive distortion and wishful thinking have the final say.

In many people's mind, threat and risk are interchangeable words. Our clients and sometimes our employers tend to confuse their significance. Yet they do not have much in common. So how to know when you, the security practitioner, should use risk and when you should use the word threat? This is quite simple: Threat can be (1) a person or a group of persons or (2) an intention or an action that will adversely affect the integrity of your assets (people, property, information). Risk is a probability that a defined threat will materialize.

If one can ask: What is the risk of this happening? One will receive an answer low, high, very high. A risk can be translated in numerical figure (there is a 30% chance of this happening). If one asks what are the threats? One will receive an answer of the type: criminal, thieves or a bomb attack at the canteen. I think this example should settle the semantic issue once and for all. Threats are *dangers* and risk is a *probability* of a threat happening.

For security practitioners, this difference should be crystal clear. It is far less so for the people we work for. For the last 20 years, I have heard almost any combination of the words risk, vulnerability and threat when speaking to customers. The people in C-suite want a security risk assessment (SRA), a security vulnerability assessment, a risk and threat assessment and so on. Refrain from explaining the differences to your audience. It is a waste of your time and makes you pass for a pedant, and damages your credibility. The customer will not listen to you for several reasons, the two most important being that (1) they are not interested in security and (2) you are the specialist and you know what you have to do. This CEO/VP/GM has other things to think about.

In countries where a standard of security applies, there is usually a word to describe this first stage of the risk assessment. Use it. Unless your client wants to be enlightened, do not try to educate them. Just do your job and deliver your report.

2.2 RISK AND THREAT MANAGEMENT

Executives often want to speak about risk management. They think in terms of risk because they are business people, and the chances of something bad happening is really what they are interested in. In the risk equation, they are more interested in the possibilities of an attack than in its consequences. Most of the time, if no authority above them requires a security program, they will feel very comfortable with having none. They believe in probabilities. If they perceive the risk of their facilities being under attack infinitesimal, they would rather avoid spending money on security.

This is why it is important when having a conversation with them to try to bring them on the domain of the threat. You are there on safer grounds. But your audience will not be easy to take with you. Why manage the threat if the chances of an attack are one out of 10 million chance?

2.3 MANAGING THREAT

Can we manage the threat? And does the idea of managing it make any sense? I think that it is worth a thought at least. Dylan Evans, a man who has given much thought to risk and uncertainty, aptly remarks that *"current methods of terrorism risk assessment tend to focus on targets vulnerability, terrorist resources, and the consequences of a successful attack, but neglect the influence of terrorists' values and beliefs"* (2012).

To understand the agents of threat (the persons committing the act), are we going to adopt a kind of social constructivism perspective and try to understand the logics of our adversaries actions? Whatever approach we decide on, it is obvious that we have to do some serious research about what our adversary's beliefs and values are, and why they are articulated the way they are. If we do not use tools to understand the psychological mechanisms of our adversaries, it will be child's play for them to surprise us. Security practitioners have no taste for surprise in their work!

Security practitioners are usually familiar with the five ways to manage risk: risk Avoidance, risk Transfer, risk Spreading, risk Reduction and risk Acceptance. Let us sum up these policies, in one sentence each:

Risk avoidance is simply the avoidance of any risk. To reach risk zero is clearly impossible as it consists in closing the shop, the industry, the facility, the asset and so on. Not doable in our business.

Risk transfer is the idea of transferring the risk to another entity that will provide the service but endorse responsibility should something go wrong. The most used example is the insurance company, but examples are numerous in mega facilities: The cost of running vehicles is high and many companies today prefer to hire a complete fleet of vehicles, with drivers, through a professional entity (Hertz, Avis, Europcar and many more). Food and restauration is another very common transfer of responsibilities and risks. Risk spreading consists in segmenting your production, operationally and also geographically, in order to minimize the consequences of an attack, and avoid the possibility of disruption. Risk reduction is what we do for a living. It consists in preventing attacks and reducing the consequences of such attacks if they cannot be avoided. Last, risk acceptance is a policy favored by many CEOs that consists in accepting a certain level of risk in order to generate as little security expenses as possible. It is of course a direct consequence of what we call risk appetite, that is, the amount of risk that the top management of an organization is ready to accept.

The risk policies are well-known. Yet we are less confident regarding the management of threats. Is it because threat is not about probabilities, or because threats are difficult to circumscribe? Are they just figments of our imagination? When are they credible and when are they simply fantasies? Well, this is a difficult issue and this is not entirely our fault.

First of all, there is this recommendation – almost elevated to the level of fundamental principle – to always consider the worst-case scenario. The reason is probably that it makes calculations of risk easier to produce. Let us take a simple example: During a drive-by shooting, three security guards are standing outside checking vehicles, opening the boom gate and checking the cars. Traditional methods of security or risk assessment will consider that in case of a drive-by shooting, all of them will be killed. This is not a reasonable allegation. It is already complicated to shoot straight when you are a trained soldier, shooting from the passenger seat of an old pickup is likely to cause more fright than dead bodies. And yet we will say three people outside = 3 people killed = very high consequence. Often, the customer frowns when explained this concept, knowing intuitively that it is an exaggeration. But because we are the specialists, and we tell them that it should be done that way, they accept it. This is wrong, because it simplifies our work, but does not reflect the probable reality. The worst-case scenario is used because we do not know how to translate uncertainty into workable figures. As a result, our figures often seem overinflated and our mitigation measures of an extravagant scale (and cost). Yet we, as security people, accept to adopt this worst-case thinking because it serves two purposes, which are more linked to prestige and authority rather than security risk evaluation. First, it gives the customer the feeling that we are more informed about the threats than we really are, and second it allows to build tables with a lot of orange and a bit of red (If all is green – or blue[2] – and yellow, what is the point of paying a consultant?). And it also serves the purpose of keeping the customer in check. A frightened customer is less likely to challenge our conclusions! To illustrate this point, Evans aptly reminds us that "there is something mesmerizing about apocalyptic scenarios. They exert an uncanny pull on the imagination. That is why Bruce Sneire calls 'worst case thinking' is so dangerous. It substitutes imagination for thinking, speculation for risk analysis, and fear for reason" (Evans 2012).

By creating fear in our customers mind, we feel more in control and we tend to shun contradiction. I remember discussing the threat faced by the organization I worked for in Qatar, with my new GM, when the project I worked for turned morphed from project stage to full operations. This happened almost 20 years ago at a time where Saudi Arabia battled with an almost insurrectional situation. The security forces experienced almost daily attacks on people and infrastructure (2004–5). From my side, the purpose of the conversation was to brief the new GM about our security situation, the threats facing our company and explain our current security posture and how we arrived there. He just wanted to know why we were costing so much. I adopted the traditional attitudes of the seasoned security manager: We were in the Gulf, Al-Qaeda (in the Arabian Peninsula) was a serious threat and an attack was not only possible but even probable. This conversation turned very quickly to my disadvantage. I performed poorly on two issues: First, I was quite at pain to express why Al-Qaeda would want to destroy our facility. Second, I had to thread very cautiously about the designation of who would attack our facility. The country was calm, there were no attacks, the only terrorist attack there having been the assassination, on 13 February 2004, of Zelimkhan Yandarbiyev, a Chechen author turned politician, when his SUV – with him inside – were blown to pieces on an open-air parking in central Doha. It was not immediately clear whether the attack had been planned by the Russian secret services or was the result of internal feuding in the Chechen movement (although cui bono balance quickly indicated a Russian implication is now accepted by all, although not officially by the Russian historians).

Be that as it may, Al-Qaeda had nothing to do with it and if that was all our threat, I could muster it looked a bit moot. I did not even believe in it myself. Difficult to convince someone when you, yourself, doubt.

The Muslim threat from other more radical adversaries was not credible, and this did not escape my interlocutor, a born and bred Emirati who had spent his life in the oil and gas industry. They knew their region better than we did. The country was quite good at monitoring the threat against their interests, and they were much better than us regarding the known-unknowns and unknown-unknowns dear to Donald Rumsfeld. The conversation was painful in this respect and the GM kindly put an end to my sufferings and said bluntly: "But Jean, we have far too much security in this company. There are no threats here and I am sure you know it. We must reduce the sail! It is costing us far too much". I knew he was right and I was wrong. Somewhere, perhaps, I wanted to keep this beautiful security machine I had put together with the help of my previous (American) manager – who believed very much in the terrorist threat – for two years. I knew our security was oversized and the situation could not justify such massive running costs. Yes, there were big assets to protect, it was a massive investment, but we were not a target, neither as an industry nor as a country. The project was big and one of the partners wanted strong security, worried by the security situation of the neighboring countries. My GM went to the end of his thinking since he fired me a few months later. There were indeed two major trends in the threat evaluation: One was to consider that the project was located in the Gulf Area, in a period of relative tension. The nature of the project was conducive to varied number of threats as a cross-border, undersea pipeline project that was irking our Saudi neighbors, with hundreds of kilometers of pipelines, several extraordinarily expensive plants, over a thousand employees from everywhere (the subcontinent, the Philippines, but also the United States, France, the UK and Italy). To me, all the potential elements of the powder keg were present! For him, there was no security issue at all, Iranians were pleasant people, we shared an enormous pull of gas that benefited both our countries, our workers were delighted to work for us because we paid well, Saudis and Qataris were brothers and would always find a way to solve their problems in a brotherly way. There was no way that our visions could be reconciled because our cultural approach to similar problem resulted in diametrically opposed conclusions. I always say that, when it comes to threat, it is all about perception. That was a brutal illustration of this point, since it questioned my analysis and cost me a job. And I must say to be fair that 15 years passed since I was told that there was no security threat to the project. And as far as I know, no major incident hampered the technical and financial success of this company (only brotherly quarrels about the right-of-way of the pipeline contested by the Saudis, but nothing major).

The important question one can ask is "who was right?" Facts proved this man right. He chose to downgrade security in order to increase profits and dividends, and I can understand that. He made an intuitive analysis of the situation and decided that supermarket security would be sufficient. Any choice, if one accepts consequences, should be respected. But it poses a fundamental question for security professionals. What is our real value if decision makers make better prognostics than us security professionals?

Of course, one way to exonerate oneself from responsibility is to say that we work on the worst-case scenario and that it is because we have a strong security that no attack occurred. I am not an adept at the worst-case scenario; it is too prone to emotional reactions and generates flawed decisions (see the comment by Evans above), and the previous example refutes this idea that a good security prevents an attack. When a company downgrades its security, it is quickly known in adversary circles and yet it does not lead to an attack. The reason is, I believe, very simple and we tend to forget it too easily. Because our job is to perform risk assessment for numerous clients, we tend to discard the fact that terrorist will rarely attack a library, a shoe factory, a sugar mill or a plastic factory. The probability of attack rests, immensely, on the motivations of the adversary and these motivations, in turn, depend on the symbolic attached to the potential target. Obviously, if we were applying this rule, the number of our clients would melt like snow in the sun and we would very quickly be out of job. Not every bit of truth is fit to be told. This is one of the major points that I will try to develop in this book, that we must endeavor to think in terms of symbolism and interpretation when we start thinking about threat rather than in terms of assets and financial losses. Most of the time, these are irrelevant and unconvincing.

Yet there is always the possibility to say that the time has not come but that our analysis was correct. I could say that in 15 years, circumstances have worsened, the fifth fleet is still hosted in Qatar, Iran – hardly hit by the COVID-19 – is now starving because of American sanctions and crazy with anger at the humiliating assassination of General Soleimani. Everybody can see that they seek revenge. And attack on gas platforms next to their open coastline would look to me as a good start. The Iranian community in Qatar is very numerous, and very well integrated. Yet each of these guys could be a potential ally for a task force bent on infiltrating the country, hosting commandos in their house before a strike. Yet my discourse is not convincing, because Qatar has now established excellent relationships with Iran and Turkey since they were ostracized by their Gulf Cooperation Council (GCC) brethren in 2017 for their support to the Muslim Brotherhood (this feud has recently ended – 5 January 2021 – and a return to normal affairs is ongoing). Probably because of this bias that makes us believe that what is will never change…So not only time has not increased that threat, that seemed so plausible at the time, but also almost obliterated it! This highlights another issue. We can never be sure that a threat we see as an imminent threat exists. We do not know what part of our belief is influenced by the flavor of the day, our own anxiety and experience and whether it is somewhere waiting to strike. We have no guarantee about the reality of the threat – unless it has been specifically articulated in our adversary's policy, and even then, we do not know for certain that plans are being elaborated to strike.

2.4 A THREAT GETTING MORE AND MORE ELUSIVE

Be that as it may, the nature of the threat is changing and we have left the pattern of terrorist leaders giving orders to agents in the field. The last trend is about what the French political scientist specialized in Islam and security Gilles Kepel labels *the terrorism of atmosphere*, a situation where individuals, from their own volution, decide to strike, without having been given a mission, out of sheer conviction, a drive far more difficult to control for a security professional. In Chapter 3, we will discuss the evolution of the threat in the current context. A threat should be specific and time-related. The pretexts have often a longer shelf life than the choices of target, the motivations of the perpetrators, their technical capabilities (the means of action), the value and beliefs they share at the moment they decide to hijack a plane or stab innocents in the street, since these details evolve according to the structure-agent relationship.

Security events should be studied in details. When an undesired security action has occurred, the reasons why it occurred and why it occurred *at this point in time (the why and why now)* should be unraveled, at least in as much details as the action components themselves (modus operandi, number of agents, equipment, preparation, insider's help, chronological sequence of events, access and escape routes, details of action, etc.), which are usually very well covered by the media and the security analyses.

Each new action modifies the threat-as-agent and the threat-as-action. Success will breed new identical attacks. Failures will force the adversaries to rethink their MO and find perhaps new ideas – this process will be detailed in Chapter 3.

The relation between the agent and the structure also applies in the world of security threat analysis. . If the action is successful, it will trigger a chain of copycat attacks (refer the plane hijackings of the 1970s). When the MO is eventually countered, the failures will be analyzed and the planned actions modified accordingly. There is therefore no innocent/neutral attack. Each action – success or failure – generates modifications in the future sequence of actions and in the psychology of the agents. The threat that we display to a customer is a threat at a specific time, and in specific circumstances and security environment, and has a very short shelf life validity. Some companies have analysts drawing global threats for them that are kept for years, adding a few spectacular incidents from time to time, to make it appear informed and relevant. In reality like a can of peas, a threat has an expiry date, even if it appears nowhere.

The second topic for reflection is the political nature of the threat. Depending on our political perspective, values and beliefs, threats appear under a completely different light. People sharing identical values (and biases, and prejudices) will tend to agree on what threats can be, their nature, their type, their magnitude, while people thinking in different cultural planets will not. This explains why security managers deployed in multicultural environments pain to get budgets for their security programs and recommendations. In the regions where I worked for the last few decades, security is about responding to threats, and threats are about some sort of political distribution of power. Should the threat come from one side, a local game of alliances should bring back the balance to equilibrium. It is culturally how things happen, happened and changes are close to nil, in spite of the myth of globalization. Last, this occurs at a level and in circumstances to which we are never, and never will be, privy. In other civilizations where we sometimes happen to operate, we are not perceived as people improving security but as people who represent the interests of some western stakeholders and should mind their own business.

This might be a shock to you right now, but once you have integrated this idea, it will make your professional life and your relationship with your peers much easier.

I will come back on this issue a cultural difference later, as it is a central point in the purpose of this book.

2.5 HOW DOES IT IMPACT OUR WORK AS SECURITY PRACTITIONERS?

Now that we have cleared these definitions of risk and threat, let us ask ourselves how risk and threat relate to/impact on our performance as security practitioners. If you read this book, chances are that you are a physical security specialist rather than a cyberrisk manager.

So what is the purpose of physical security? And how do we add value? I believe that the purpose of physical security is to lower the risk of an attack on assets by devising and then implementing physical security features and measures in order to deter, to detect, to delay and to respond to such attack, intrusion and/or any security breach aiming to interfere with the integrity of the assets we are tasked to protect. This is quite simple. Now, it should also be very clear that the protection of assets should be commensurate with the risk(s) incurred (the traditional equation of risk as the probability of an undesired security event occurring multipied by its consequences).

It is quite common sense that the amount of money spent to protect a piece of equipment, which is not crucial to the operational process, which is easily replaceable and which will not hamper production, should really be minimal, and we all agree with that, don't we?

This is why the risk assessment always begins by the asset characterization in order to differentiate what is critical from what is simply important. The management will probably only accept to spend money on the protection of assets that are critical to the production, so this characterization is crucial. In a previous book – today discontinued – I had defined a critical asset not in terms of its importance in the operational process – that is the traditional definition – but based on the willingness of its owners to pay for its protection.

There is a significant relation between the asset's importance and its possibility of being attacked and there is a difficult balance to achieve there. The reason why I have not decided to dedicate this book to asset characterization is that, from experience, the customer knows better than you what is critical and what is not, and that a consultant is called to work on so many different types of facilities that he cannot master all their processes. But the operational value of an asset is not as important as owners and engineers believe. The value of an asset is moderated by the attractiveness it has to the adversary. A very important asset may be less attractive to an adversary than a building, a silo or a gas tank bearing the logo of its owner because this relatively insipid asset, easily replaceable and not that expensive to fix or replace would look very symbolic when destroyed and being shown constantly on major channel *breaking news*. Politics – and therefore symbolism – is often the main drive behind an adversary's attacks.

The second stage of the risk evaluation is the threat assessment. That is where a good practitioner can really add value. Because, from your correct assessment of the attractiveness, of the threat and the attached vulnerabilities, risk evaluation and security recommendations will naturally develop. Get the first step right and your risk evaluation and your security recommendations will beget respect. Get it wrong and there are chances that your report may not even reach the C-suite.

2.6 WHAT ABOUT THE CONTEXT?

The context could be defined as the situation, a snapshot of the security environment at the moment you receive your brief until you leave your position. The context is a fluid background that changes all the time, and that you must, as a security practitioner, follow very seriously.

Although the standard process for the risk assessment puts assets first and threats second, I wonder whether the first item should not be the context.

The security environment will define the risk incurred and the possible threats that could develop and threaten the facility you have been tasked to protect. The security environment has an important impact on the assets. Let me provide an example: In a region where kidnapping is a traditional/cultural part of the security environment, your employees and their managers are potential targets of the highest importance and make their physical protection as your main task. In a place where this is not really the rules of the game – in some areas of the Sahel, nomadic groups of militants would help themselves at your bush facility with water, food and petrol and would not be interested in abduction – although the possibility of kidnapping for resale always exist. Indeed, this attitude could change overnight if your traditional nomads hear that a more powerful group than themselves is ready to buy westerners at very good price. The relative uncomplicated threat your isolated facility is facing could suddenly turn into far more brutal or violent than the simple confiscation of food, petrol, car parts and tires…

Evaluating correctly the security context when taking up the job should rank first in your preoccupation. Observe, discuss, read and unless you are in an isolated area, in the desert or in the jungle, liaise with the security managers who face the same possible problems as you do. Join the OSAC or the ASIS chapter if there is one, and make it a habit and a priority. I consider this as more important than entertaining good relations with the attaches of the Embassies, who have, more often than not, no idea about what you are doing, what you worry about and, more importantly, what really happens on the ground.

Getting the threat evaluation right is therefore essential to the risk evaluation process. And yet, as we will confirm later in this book, most risk assessment methods are quite ineffective when it comes to measuring the threat.

2.7 TOO FEW AGENTS AND TOO FEW ACTIONS

The number of actions is normally limited to a number of very basic scenarios – apart ISPS who did quite a good job in the past of listing a number of attacks [of defining threats-as-action-, and the number of threat agents to an even smaller number. For most methods, any facility faces only three kinds of threats: the terrorist, the criminal and the disgruntled employee's threats. It is quite a short list: Can we really reduce all the possible adversaries to simply three categories? Biringer et al. complete the list adding religious or political extremists, mentally deranged or the insider employee. Although this list appears very limited, it might be complete. Can a disgruntled employee not become a thief because he is disgruntled? Can he support terrorists for the very same reason? Intuitively, we want to respond there is more in the concept of threat than this short list of caricatural adversaries. Thought must be given to the components of threat and that their interconnections deserve more research than what most methods recommend.

2.7.1 Threat-as-Agent: Nature and Type

In many risk assessment methods, the word threat can mean two things. It can be the actor, the terrorist, the vandal, the disgruntled employee who can represent a threat to the organization. So when asked, what is your most feared threat, the consultant often hears "the terrorist" or "a bomb attack". In other words, the threat can be either the perpetrator or the undesired security event the threat-as-agent (or the threat agent) that is the perpetrator and the threat-as-action, in other words, the undesired security event that we want to prevent. Let us now begin our study with the threat as agent, that we can call the threat agent, or more practically to avoid confusion, the adversary.

2.8 THE NATURE OF THE THREAT

The American Petroleum Institute (API 780) methodology is the most used method in many corners of the world, particularly because the oil and gas industry has always been at the forefront of industrial security. Because it is a solid and versatile method, I will often refer to it in this book. I have used it extensively during my days on the Middle East, and, if it is not perfect, its process is simple, practical and, I believe, quite convincing (let us always bear in mind that the purpose of a risk assessment is always to convince our audience). The API 780 separates the nature of the threat from its type. Studying the nature of threat means listing and defining the threat agents or actors such as terrorists, activists, criminals, saboteurs, vandals and disgruntled employees. Those threat agents are divided into three categories.

2.8.1 External or Outside Threat

These are threats (we may call them adversaries) that will attack the entity entirely from outside.

They are external players who have, at least when they decide on the attack, no prior knowledge of the target and do not benefit from internal complicity. Their task is difficult and few groups will choose this entirely external approach. Being external means that there will be a lot of research necessary to understand the target, evaluate its protection system, guess its vulnerabilities and define an effective mode of attack. This is the stuff of state secret or action services, people who can rely on strong organizations, and consequent administrative support. Selecting an external approach implies observation and reconnaissance trips, undercover penetrations, a number of qualified and trained reconnaissance agents, different actors to carry out the attack and financial means and plenty of time. This is a very expense type of action that requires resources that many activist groups do not have. One tends to think that activists and terrorists fall into this category although post-event investigations almost always reveal that they often benefited from insider's participation, willing or coerced, and that they had some kind of prior knowledge of the target.

2.8.2 Internal or Insider Threat

Gelles (2016) defines the insider threat as

> a person who has the potential to harm an organization for which they have inside knowledge or access. An insider threat can have a negative impact on any aspect of an organization, including employee and/or public safety, reputation, finances, national security, and mission continuity.
>
> *p. 3*

Disgruntled employees, saboteurs, vandals and petty criminals populate this category, but other motives could be considered, and these people could be acting on behalf of terrorists, willingly or under duress.

2.8.3 Colluding Threats

These are threats that combine the two previous types, that is, one *external* threat working with an *insider* for any kind of reason and probably for an unknown motive.

Collusion may be willing or obtained through coercion. An activist group could kidnap a family member of a manager and require that the manager bring dangerous items to the facility or carry out acts of sabotage on their behalf, or grant access to specific areas, in exchange for the safe return of the abducted person. A bank manager could have his/her family taken hostage while he/she opens the bank vaults to associated thugs who are ensured of his/her complicity. Many movies have had this example in their bank heists scenarios. Sometimes, kidnapping or abduction is not necessary since proving that an action is possible is enough to convince the target that they should obey the demands. A good reconnaissance file can therefore do the trick and eliminates a lot of risks for the adversary. The colluding threat is probably the most common type of attack as far as security practitioners are concerned. But it is sometimes a difficult threat to mention in your evaluation document. Often, it is rejected by the organization's management who refuses to admit that any of their employees could act as accessories to crime. One way to unblock this situation might be to spend little time in writing on this kind of threat or reassure the management that a verbal report will be made to a limited audience or make any other arrangements that the management would desire.

2.9 DESIGN BASIS THREAT

I do not find the design basis threat (DBT) an easy to grasp concept. When I started in security, it is one I had problems with. It has been defined as "the attributes and characteristics of potential insider and/or external adversaries, who might attempt unauthorized removal or sabotage, against which a physical protection system is designed and evaluated".

More simply, it could be defined as a profile of the type, number, means of action and capabilities of an adversary.

Developing a DBT is an effective way of staying focused on unwanted events by unsavory people that could harm critical assets. It is not about everything that could happen, but a reasonable assessment of what could be considered as plausible characteristics of a credible adversary. It is never good to consider all that could happen, because nobody can protect everything against anything. For Garcia (2008), the DBT is used as "a management and design tool that helps facilitate informed decision-making by executives and establishes technical requirements for designers". It consists in creating a threat for a specific target – a target-centric threat – and keeping that same threat immovable in order to concentrate on the solutions rather than the problem. Most DBTs I have seen developed were based on history. It generally aggregates all the attacks that have been perpetrated in the past against comparable targets in comparable environments. It often focuses on the terrorist threat – the inescapable budget provider – but it can also address criminals, disgruntled employees and workplace violence perpetrators, or any type of adversary the facility you protect traditionally attracts (artefacts and art pieces if you are a museum, rare and expensive books if you are a library, sacred items of liturgy if you are tasked with protecting a Christian place of worship, vandals and taggers if you profess ideas that contradict the truths of the day).

A DBT traditionally addresses the following five elements: (1) characterization of attackers, (2) potential weapons, (3) preferred tactics, (4) assumed motivation and (5) technical capability.

2.9.1 Attackers – Nature, Number and Type

We have seen above the multiple nature of the adversaries. Our job is to select the most plausible of them. This is, of course, defined by an enlarged context. The context, the security environment surroundings the entity placed under your watch, is not only the facility and the roads that lead to it. The regional security environment needs to be understood as well. The recent incidents, the changes in regional politics, the disruptive events that will impact the security context, the dynamics of the relationship between government and rebellious groups, the internal tensions in the organization workforce, have all to be thought about very seriously and given their right potential. Remember that this context is perpetually in motion, and changes according to the rules and power struggles of people you rarely know and whose decisions are often taken in the greatest secrecy. The chances that you will be informed of the new plan of the terrorist groups roaming in your areas are really slim; organized thefts planned by mafia types groups – external or benefiting from an internal support – will very rarely be brought to your attention. Although they should and somehow, they may.

For guys who are lucky enough to be supported by analysts in London, Paris or Washington – I should rather say Washington, London or Paris – it is reassuring to know that people with high knowledge of your area of operations will be able to warn you about possible changes in threats. Alas, my personal experience does not reflect this reassuring assertion. More often than not, I was the one informing the analysts about what was happening on the ground, and even more often, they took no notice of my warnings, preferring their own information sources, and their selected reading channels. I tend to believe that we, security practitioners, are very much on our own when it comes to threat analysis and I really envy those who feel supported by their headquarters. But it has not been my experience, and the more volatile and stressful the situation, the greater this feeling of lonesomeness.

Now, as a lecturer, I often say to my postgraduate students: *Question everything!* This is also applicable to your understanding of the security environment. If you evaluate this security environment well, you will be able to assess the threat with precision and the risk accordingly. There is not the guarantee of result, of course; nobody could support your conclusion or your recommendations, but it gives you the satisfaction to have understood the political environment better than others, and anticipated the most probable menaces.

Once you think you have assessed correctly the global security context, narrow your scope and think about who could harm your entity. What have been the recent attacks directed against, if any, in the area? Where did they occur? What were the consequences? How did the government react? How is the feeling in the top management regarding threats? What do they fear, what scares them, do they believe that there are brutal adversaries poised to swoop down on the facility, the headquarters, the villas of the engineers, or did they hire you because it was part of a merger, or to satisfy the most advanced partners of the joint venture? My experience in difficult countries is that if you managed to get the job, it is because the management is worried about security. And for them security means mainly terror attacks. When they are worried about theft and robberies, you never get the job because you are too expensive! They always find you too expensive, which is a mistake. A good security manager, very often a keen observer of the workforce and the organizational processes, would find ways to save lot of dollars for a company. But somehow it does not seem to interest the management. In one of my jobs, I uncovered frauds, bribes on uniforms, traffic of petrol booklets that were reprinted and sold at low cost to people external to the company, bribes in almost all sectors of the company. One day, I was called by the new GM – he had been nominated a few months earlier – who asked me what I could do for the company. I explained to him all I had discovered and told him how much money could be saved by the company in a year. No need to say, it paid my own salary several times, but I saw in his eyes that this was of no interest to him. I was here for terrorists and getting my nose in other people's business was really unwelcome and rather perceived as unsavory. Did I want the hides of the HR or the facilities manager? When I mentioned that I knew that some of our engineers had fake diplomas and that security could help HR unmask the fraudsters, I was told that it was HR problems, not mine. And when I proposed a very well worked out security awareness program for the employees, I was stopped in my tracks. No security awareness! It frightens the employees. Well, I went out of his office rather – but justly – dispirited, convinced that my interlocuter would soon fire me and most of my cadres very fast. He did just that, and within the next six months, all the expatriate workforce in security was thanked, sometimes abruptly, and security returned to its supermarket, gate opening and parking surveillance status.

This digression was just meant to remind you that the reason why you have been chosen for the task must never leave your brains and always influence your judgment and subsequent decision-making. Just adapt, you have to reach a delicate balance between effectiveness and survival.

This section of your work consists in elaborating a list of possible adversaries and characterizing them. As said above, the first thing is to evaluate your environment, your security context. But how are you going to do that? Traditionally, security practitioners use a palette of adversaries that resume itself to terrorists, disgruntled employees and criminals. There is nothing wrong with that except that the difference between one terrorist and another can be major and that your job is to provide good value for money. In another word, when you consider the terrorist threat, you must be reasonable. The way most security pros do is to look at similar circumstances and consider what happened in the past as the basis for security countermeasures recommendation.

Bear in mind that the identification of adversaries results from the correct assumptions about the previous phase of the risk assessment called "assets characterization". Unless you have received specific assignments by the management, the assets deemed critical and for which there is no or little redundancy of alternatives are the assets that will serve as the basis of selection for all the elements of the DBT. I have seen practitioners who used to work in a relatively threat stable environment list their threats, without taking any account of what the critical assets to protect were. There is always this danger, for us practitioners, to keep the threats stable, in order to save time and have our table half-filled even before we start thinking.

Before we discuss which adversaries constitute credible threats to the organization, you should keep in mind that any security reflection should be target centric. The target defines the threat and not the contrary. Therefore, the critical assets of your organization will help you create the list of potential adversaries, of agents that will find an interest in stealing, destroying or damaging certain assets that, to them, are symbols of something. Therefore, I will not provide you with a list of the threats you will consider in the threat assessment portion of the SRA because you and your management know what your principal adversaries are. The idea is to start from the target and broaden the circle from the most dangerous and pressing threat toward the periphery and the less pressing menaces.

2.10 A TARGET-CENTRIC APPROACH
AND AN ACUTE EAR

How would you characterize the entity you have been tasked to protect? What is it producing? Which groups of interest find the items you produce immoral, monstrous, unbearable or unacceptable?

I must admit that since I returned to Europe after 32 years spent abroad, I realize that threats on the old continent here are of a different nature. Activists are committed, dangerous and violent. They are so convinced of the justness of their cause that they represent a real danger if your organization is not in line with their ideological diktats. This is particularly true for environmentalists who seem particularly virulent, and feared, while they were practically ignored when I worked in the Middle East and in Africa.

How your mission was defined should help you create a list of credible threats. Remember that you always have to satisfy the people who pay you. If they have chosen a seasoned professional like yourself, it is because they want to defeat a threat they believe in.

So before beginning to work on your SRA, go back to your interviews. Try to remember what were the worries expressed by the CEO, the GM, the VP of HR, the VP of Operations. Once you have been confirmed and sit in your new office of director of security, or whatever your official title is, you should meet with all the people who sit at the weekly management meeting on Monday morning (or Sunday morning if you operate in the Muslim world). If this did not happen, obtain an appointment – officially to introduce yourself – in reality to try to extract from each of these line managers what lies at the back of their mind when it comes to security. These top managers do not always agree on what the real threats are. Some will dare not to challenge the CEO or the GM and will worry in silence. You need to obtain from them what they fear most. And do not forget to ask them whether they have thought about a solution. More often than not, they have! To sum up, listen to people who are not security specialists but who know the organization well. Do not take everything they say as your to-do list. After all, you are the security professional, but offer a benevolent ear to what they have to say. And once you have collected all this information, go back to the fundamentals to answer these questions: What is my mission? What does it say? What was I told when I was interviewed by the board? What is expected of me?

You remember what I said previously about context. Three elements should guide you when you start constructing plausible threats: The contents of your brief, your own evaluation of what your organization produces (materially) and represents, in term of image and reputation, and the security environment (the context, or how you feel about the threat).

The contents of your brief and the context you have to operate in will guide you through the threat definition. Let me expand a bit on that.

When you have received your mission, you were given the context of your operations and the priorities of your action. The context, as always, will determine how you prioritize your actions.

2.11 A CASE STUDY

In 2004, I was hired to provide physical protection for a group of French engineers working on a naval project in one of the ports of one the Sheikhdom of the GCC. Because of the international stature of the job, the security of the engineers was provided by the Navy during working hours. But after hours, engineers were left on their own in a dangerous city at a time where shootouts between police and militants were almost a daily occurrence. My task started when the engineers left the naval base just after lunch, which was located in a rather unsavory neighborhood, adding to the anxiety – and the moment where they crossed the gate again the following morning. This was an enormous responsibility fraught with multiform and varied risks, the main one being that many of the engineers did not believe that the threat existed. Many complained about the bachelor status of the job, since they felt very safe when they went shopping at the shopping mall after work. It is not as if they had been in a camp under siege in the middle of the mountains of Afghanistan, they said. They were living in a big city of several million inhabitants, which had the reputation of being a bit less strict with foreigners than the capital city. In simple terms, they did not feel threatened. As a matter of fact, they were not threatened personally. Victims of terrorist attacks never are, by definition. Simply, the tension between the insurgents and the government were very high, shoot-outs between rebels and police almost daily occurrences, with quite a number of people killed, sometimes in simple cross firings. But because they lived in luxurious compounds guarded by the national guard, played tennis, sun basked by the pool and enjoyed nonalcoholic beers with their shawarma at the restaurant of the compound, they refused to imagine that behind their walls, a battle to death was engaged between the leadership of the country and religious movements that wanted to overthrow them. In Paris, their managers were very worried about the situation. The Karachi incident, where French engineers had been killed by a bomb on their way to the naval base, was in everybody's mind, and the fines imposed by French justice on the company for not having done the necessary to protect their people granted me a job! But a job fraught with dangers because of its unclear and vague limits.

These engineers were very difficult to handle. They were very touchy regarding their advantages and refused to bend to rules – unless threatened to. To my surprise, each engineer had a private vehicle at his disposal. This is, for example, something that was organized before my appointment. The idea behind this was that it was because the attack in Karachi[3] had been made possible by the surveillance made by the attackers on the bus that picked up the engineers each morning at their hotel. When a taxi stopped next to the bus and exploded its charge, 14 people lost their lives. The security decision I could not act upon was that discretion was the better part of valor, and opted for getting rid of the transport. Even such a decision can be discussed. When, a decade before I worked in Biskra, 250 miles North-East from Algiers, during the bloody decade of the Algerian civil war between the Front Islamique du Salut (FIS) and the generals, we travelled to the military base every morning in a bus with a military escort. A 4×4 opened the convoy, followed by a military truck with a half-platoon armed to the teeth, followed by our bus, a second military vehicle with the other half of the platoon closing the march. The government of Algeria took the security of expatriate workers very seriously and during the four stays I did in this helicopter base, we never witnessed an incident, nor felt threatened in any way. A strong military escort taking their job seriously instill in people a certain conscience of threat; it is a deterrent. In the Gulf city port, the management relied on discretion as the best protection strategy, as if being transparent would avert the danger of an attack, a kind of ostrich strategy I did not support.

2.12 UNDERSTANDING THE THREAT

Although one must always be aware that the threat we fear may not be the attacks we will face, it might be a good starting question to ask: What kind of adversary are we fearing? If we are a company where cybersecurity is the ways and means to make/receive/ transfer money, hackers are obviously your main priority. Bank security managers are usually CISSP certified and this makes sense. Although, it would be an error to concentrate all your security forces on cybersecurity only. Cyber and physical should walk hand-in-hand and a good security program should incorporate both. If you are protecting a gold mine, cybersecurity is of course important – because of the physical cyber-enabled attacks – meaning physical attacks where the electronic protection systems are disabled prior to the attack – but physical security and the traditional deter-detect-delay and respond principles do apply first, because it is gold nuggets that are the target, not the transfer online of virtual money.

As a practitioner, you must think wide and identify the adversaries attracted by your organization and its critical assets and final products. When budget is scarce, focus on the most important, and prioritize physical security. If your budget is limited, there is a strong possibility that your IT is not the main concern of your management., and that you deal rather with tangible assets.

2.13 WEAPONS AND MEANS

Another important criterion to measure the threat is the weapons and means that our potential adversaries could be using against us in varied circumstances. Do they carry their actions with small weapons and sedan cars? Are they rather the gang-style or the military type? Do they have the capacity of a militia, or those of bank robbers? Have they stricken on facilities comparable to yours? What were their means of attack? Did they succeed? Why?

This is a list of weapons and equipment that might be used by attackers. Weapons may include the following:

- *Vehicles:* used to deliver explosives, deployed as rams or employed as personnel transport
- *Boats:* for example, inflatable power boats or fishing vessels, used to deliver explosives or transport people and weapons
- *Small arms:* often the AK-47 along with handguns
- *Standoff weapons:* for example, rocket-propelled grenades or mortars, or stingers
- *Accessories:* for example, night vision goggles, satellite phones, binoculars, cutting tools, grappling hooks and computers. These items can be found in almost all types of adversaries, from militia to bank robbers.
- *Explosives:* used to breach barriers or destroy targets; subcategories include person-borne improvised explosive device (PBIED),

vehicle-borne improvised explosive devices (VBIEDs) and water-borne improvised explosive devices (WBIEDs)and all the other possible IEDs

2.14 TACTICS

Tactics is the mode of action chosen by the attacker. A DBT will traditionally consider three different tactics:

- *Stealth:* An attack by stealth can be a penetration done by defeating alarms systems, crawling under unprotected fences (taking advantage of the high rate of false alarms in windy areas), exploiting underground pathways and so on. The idea is that the assailant goes undetected. It is often facilitated by insiders and the purpose of stealth action is dual: (1) obtain information on the organization, its resources and its protection and (2) collect information about the weaknesses of the security program. An attack can also be carried out that way for the purpose of sabotage and/or industrial espionage.
- *Deceit:* Deceit is characterized by gaining unlawful access to the facility under false pretense, either to carry out reconnaissance operations or to participate in an attack. Deceit can go as far as borrowing or stealing items such as uniforms, painted vehicles and ID badges. Assistance from a willing or coerced insider increases the possibilities of deception.
- *Force:* A force attack consists of an attack carried out with lethal weapons – automatic rifles, offensive grenades, vehicles used as rams to breach a security gate and/or often indiscriminate shooting to shock employees and create mayhem. Part of these attacks may be diversions to create a focal point of response while allowing entry by stealth in another area of the facility. Brutal force is what characterizes this kind of attack, and if reconnaissance is necessary, the action itself can be carried out without internal assistance.

Of course, attacks often are a combination of the three different modes. A diversion will be part of the most traditional attack, in order to divert the attention – and the means of the security response away from the real action. I asked one day a security consultant, very experienced and very competent, why he never mentioned complex attacks in his scenarios and

I received that destabilizing reply: "too complicated to quantify". Indeed, when two different simultaneous attacks of different types and/or nature occur simultaneously – a diversion frontal attack coupled with a stealth penetration elsewhere in a facility, the situation becomes difficult to quantify in terms of risk – that is, its possibility of occurrence – but the desire for quantitative security should give way to reality. An attack will not be constructed by the adversary to make the life of the security manager and the response element easy. Just the contrary!

When you plan an exercise with your security workforce – they love it –, if you can find the time and the resources, always plan a multipronged attack and see how it destroys any response plan you had in mind. Napoleon said that no battle plan resists the first shot on the battlefield. You should believe the man who won 40 battles! This should not lower your spirits. It should help you plan better and react better, even if, like most of the security managers I know, you never have to face a major strike!

2.15 MOTIVATION

What are the goals of the attacker (s)? Is it the desire to inflict casualties, damage the environment, harm the local economy and/or send a political message, avenge an unbearable memory or humiliate the government, the management of the organization, you or all three? How deep is this willingness to harm? Note that the motivation can be at the same time to avenge something– the cause or the upstream motivation – and the desire to inflict pain – the result or the consequence. Both could be included in the motivations. To be fair, the motivation portion of the motivation section should rather be the job of the analysts working in the headquarters of your consultancy. We are here in the domain of regional and local politics. Since you have followed my advice, you have now a pretty good idea of the range of political factors that could have an impact on the security situation of your facility. But local open intelligence – namely, newspapers and OSAC and ASIS chapters – often report rumors while analysts in capital cities work day in, day out, on the politics of your region, and therefore have accumulated a wide knowledge regarding the security danger in your area. Consult them if you can, invite them if it is possible. I did it once with two analysts of my consultancy and it created a feeling of trust that improved our mutual relationship as well as the quality of our open-source intelligence. It really is an exercise I recommend, although not always easy to organize.

2.16 TRAINING AND CAPABILITIES

The DBT may assume that only trained outsiders will be used to carry out an attack on a facility. It assumes that some or all will have seen action in hotspots such as Iraq, Afghanistan, Syria, Libya, Chechnya, Algeria and Mali. The attackers are considered competent in small-arms use, close-quarter battles, reconnaissance and security systems. Active insiders would be assumed to have limited weapons training but some ability to collect intelligence.

There is nothing wrong with the DBT when the only threat retained by the threat analysis is the terrorist entity. In areas where armed militant action is expected (Syria, Libya, Sahel and Iraq at the time of writing), armed militants are the major source of immediate concern. Taking onboard threats as thieves, smugglers and disgruntled employees is a luxury that security managers may not be able to afford.

In most cases, using a DBT is fine. It focuses on terrorists and the damage they may inflict. However, it neglects other security issues, like theft, smuggling and workplace violence. In remote construction laborer camps in GCC countries (e.g., Qatar and UAE), the security risk is often linked to personnel issues (salaries, promiscuity, food, antagonistic nationalities, political enmities within the laborers, etc.), which can be addressed if there is a will to do so and which, if ignored, can lead to serious security consequences.

2.16.1 Attractiveness (A)

Attractiveness is an important issue in the SRA process, and amazingly in the evaluation of the threat, it is often neglected. When you lead an SRA meeting, that is, a meeting with representatives of your client's company in order to define critical assets, attractiveness and threats, you will notice that the technical people are surprised when you start discussing attractiveness. Most have never given a thought to the fact that destroying their slug-catcher[4] is a not a sexy prize for a militant. The issue is that you need the technical people to help you fill the boxes of the CARVERI technique – something I use because engineers feel reassured by the simplicity and the coherence of the technique. Attractiveness can be a rich portion of the SRA, and different authors have suggested several approaches that I would like to share with you here.

2.16.1.1 Biringer et al.

Biringer et al. are traditional in their approach. It consists of two steps. First, an analysis of adversary history and intent is performed. The second step is to examine the facility's attractiveness based on three criteria: consequence, ideology and ease of attack. Results are scored 1, 3 or 5, and the total score provides an attractiveness level (from an adversary's point of view) that is simple, acceptable and understandable by nonspecialists.

2.16.1.2 Vellani and the Threat Analysis Group

Karim Vellani and the TAG are strong on threat evaluation but less concerned with attractiveness. In discussing the adversary's target election factors, they summarize their practical approach as follows (Vellani, 2007):

> National monuments and critical infrastructure are terrorists' most likely targets. Areas where large numbers of people gather all make good targets: bus stops, trains, sporting events, and government buildings. Their comments are limited to the terrorist threat, which is acceptable since it remains the main axis of efforts today for most security managers.

2.16.1.3 American Petroleum Institute API 780

For the API 780, the attractiveness of assets should be determined by the SRA team – that is, the people selected initially to discuss the criticality of assets, under the direction of the security consultant, or risk assessor. What it means in practice is that the level of attractiveness of assets will be measured by people who are *not* security specialists: People performing different functions in the facility express their own opinion of attractiveness seen from an adversary standpoint, and a global agreement – by security and non-security personnel – will be sought by the team. This is a consensual process that works well when all stakeholders act in good faith. It gives a feeling of objectivity and impartiality and tells the consultant what people working there think about the threat.

To help measure the level of attractiveness, API 780 provides a table (see Table 2.1) that provides an assessment of conditional probability of the act. Should the adversary have a moderate degree of interest in the asset, for example, the attractiveness is medium, which is classified as a 3. For future risk calculation, it uses a "conditional probability of the act"

73

Table 2.1 Target Attractiveness Ranking Definition

Ranking Level	Descriptor	Conditional Probability of the Act	Threat Ranking
1	Very Low	0.0 to 0.2	Threat would have little to no interest in the asset.
2	Low	>0.2 to 0.4	Threat would have some interest in the asset, but not as much as it has in other assets.
3	Medium	>0.4 to 0.6	Threat would have a moderate degree of interest in the asset relative to other assets.
4	High	>0.6 to 0.8	Threat would have a high degree of interest in the asset relative to other assets.
5	Very high	>0.8 to 1.0	Threat would have a very high degree of interest in the asset relative to other assets.

Source: API 780.

of 0.4 to 0.6. (The attractiveness ranking is transformed into a decimal value to make the risk equation possible.)

This table is fine in principle. However, it does not tell the consultant *why* the adversary would be interested in our facility. This is often the most difficult question to answer for the threat assessor when and if she is asked to present her conclusion to the top management of the organization. The questions business people will ask is always: *Why do you think we could be selected as a target?* The consultant usually avoids responding directly to this question, and beats about the bush, providing unsatisfactory answers to a most important question. It is often simpler to tell the truth. No, sir, there is no specific reason why you should be chosen as a target (unless there is an obvious one, of course). This is not a reason to neglect your security and attract attention to obvious lack of deterrence capabilities reflecting a poor security commitment. There is no need to panic. Unless there are specific reasons to expect an attack, the facility is a no more risk than the facility next door. But you should be prepared, and all discourse along the line of 'rather safe than sorry'.

74

The risk assessment is about just that. Providing a picture of the potential threats, vulnerabilities and risk and suggesting reasonable measures to deter would-be attackers. Do not try to be too emphatic, or dramatic, and do not cite figures from countries at war when you work in a country at peace. This temptation is to be avoided at all costs! During the war in Iraq, many consultants working in the GCC sheikhdoms used to cite the number of attacks carried out against US forces, the number of pipelines destroyed, the number of people assassinated and so on. If you use these figures in countries like Qatar or the UAE, you not only make a fool of yourself, but you irritate tremendously your local audience who happen to be the decision makers in most projects. The secret to credibility is reasonableness. If you are realistic and level-headed, people will trust you and listen to your speech. If you overdo it, they will switch off, politely most of the time, and you can forget your contract. Instead of bombarding them with terrifying figures that have nothing to do with the reality they live in, insist on your cost-benefit analysis, and highlight benchmarking with comparable organizations. No CEO wants to have the cheapest security in the industrial city. For decision makers, what the neighbors/competitors do matters.

The CARVERI method of target attractiveness (explained in detail in the vulnerability section that follows) is one way of answering the question "Could it happen?" It does not define attractiveness but examines how vulnerabilities can prove attractive to an adversary.

Attractiveness is adversary-specific. One asset may be attractive to a terrorist, while another may attract criminals. In other words, attractiveness is a relation between an asset and the desire this asset creates in the adversary's psyche. For example, a tank farm will probably be an attractive target to an activist. His desire to attack it is exacerbated by his anticipatory vision of the tank (with its company's name and logo visible) burning with black smoke, with a "Breaking News" subtitle next to a CNN logo. By contrast, a criminal may be spurred to action by the presence of new computers in an administration building poorly protected. He envisions improving his life by selling the stolen items. A disgruntled employee may be more attracted to sabotaging the company's supervisory control and data acquisition (SCADA) system and create havoc and panic in the operational teams. Again, the attractiveness of an asset varies according to adversaries' desires and the opportunities to act.

What makes API 780 somewhat practical for the consultant is that if the attractiveness rating is ranked lower than 3, the threat (as-agent)

75

is discarded for the remainder of the study. In other words, if only the terrorist threat scores 3 or more, only the terrorist threat will be studied thenceforward.

The result is that most of the time, and particularly in volatile environments, the terrorist threat remains the only selected candidate for study. That leaves out high-probability/low-consequence events, such as thefts, smuggling, vandalism and other petty traffics. Sad really, because these threats are very real and interesting to tackle. When the terrorist threat recedes, which will happen probably sooner than later, this is where security managers will have to transfer their skills, because fighting crime within the organization might be less prestigious than working on anti-terrorism countermeasures but is worth it.

An attractiveness ranking is an educated guess. Saying an adversary has a relative or mild interest in an asset without explaining why does not look good. We need to devise a more convincing way to measure attractiveness.

2.17 MEASURING ATTRACTIVENESS

One approach is to create a table listing the desires and expectations of different types of potential adversaries. We could list five items that represent the desires or expectations of each threat. This choice would still be subjective, and it seems unlikely that one could list all the motivations of a criminal, smuggler, activist, saboteur, vandal or terrorist. However, it may be worth trying.

When measuring an asset's attractiveness to a specific threat agent, the highest score must be kept for further study. If an asset is not attractive to a terrorist or a disgruntled employee (scoring 1) but is irresistible to a criminal (scoring 3), its overall attractiveness remains a 3. That means the asset needs to be protected against that particular adversary. The fact that it may be a high-probability/low-consequence threat is not relevant.

2.18 TRADITIONAL THREAT ASSESSMENT

The threat assessment is the second most crucial part of the SRA. Threat assessment aims to measure the vulnerability of the site – or assets – against their potential threats (both threat-as-agents and threats-as-action).

The threat assessment is normally a five-step process:

1. Identification and evaluation of potential threats
2. Threat ranking
3. Asset attractiveness for each threat (including the CARVERI method or any method you feel comfortable with)
4. Attractiveness ranking for each asset–threat pairing
5. Calculation of the unconditional likelihood

A good threat definition establishes the level of performance required from the security program (or plan) in terms of technical and human capabilities.

The countermeasures that will protect the facility will flow from a correct evaluation of the threat. If the threat is underestimated, the facility may be at risk of becoming an attractive target. If the threat is overestimated, management may feel overwhelmed by its complexity and magnitude and be reluctant to spend the necessary funds. In other words, the assessment of threat actors (agents or adversaries) must be credible, and their actions (threats-as-actions) must be plausible enough to generate a response – a security program – that can be endorsed by all and funded by the executive management.

From the customer's side, there are basically four causes of concern that can be summarized into four questions:

1. Are we a potential target?
2. If so, who are our adversaries?
3. What threat are we facing, and which forms could attacks take?
4. When will the attack (s) occur?

The problem is that answering these questions requires competencies that the consultant may not possess. The consultant is not always an analyst and does not always have the academic knowledge necessary to answer these questions with confidence in front of decision makers born and bred in the country. Still, the consultant probably knows what an adversary could do to the facility.

Clients can usually answer the first and second questions. The third question can be answered through open-source intelligence obtained through the Internet and through fellow security professionals and organizations like OSAC (the U.S. State Department's Overseas Security Advisory Council), the Security Institute or the local ASIS chapter.

Consultants must develop a taste for security snippets in their area of activity and try to improve their knowledge of local politics, geopolitics and the regional balance of forces. It may be useful to join security interest groups within our professional security organizations in order to gain more knowledge.

The fourth question – when? – is, of course, beyond the capability of most analysts, even those working in government intelligence agencies. Cynthia Grabo (2004), a U.S. government intelligence analyst for almost 40 years, wrote in her seminal book that

> Nothing is more exasperating to members of the intelligence profession than to be charged with failing to predict coups and assassinations, which they rightly consider "acts of God" somewhat less predictable than tornadoes, avalanches, and plane hijackings. It is ridiculous and grossly unfair to expect the intelligence system to anticipate such acts, which are plotted in secrecy and sometimes by only one individual.
>
> *p. 94*

We can safely extrapolate this judgment to the realm of security consultants trying to anticipate probable actions by terrorists and ascribe a timeframe to it. As a reminder, consultants do not have access to an extensive government apparatus and most of the time have to rely on open-source intelligence and their own intuition (seen as a mix of experience, sixth sense and observation skills). Still, I believe that they can produce adequate threat assessments. D. H, then editor of a Middle East intelligence review, told me while I was interviewing him in London as part of my dissertation process (2011):

> Although intelligence information is weighted much more than open sources, it is still susceptible to far more manipulation than open sources. … [When working on a situation,] you go through the same process and try to build the big picture. Intelligence is one part of that. If you take that away, I think you can still build a fairly accurate picture. I would argue regarding what is happening in Libya and what is happening in the Arab world, it would not be much different from assessments being made behind closed doors in Washington. I would also argue that even if we do not have access to this [intelligence] information, we can come up with assessments that are reasonably similar.

This should be a strong and reassuring message for most consultants. Establishing a credible threat is difficult but feasible – at least for the first three questions. The fourth one, when? is beyond the reach of analysts and consultants alike. As Grabo (2004) wrote, "Any forecast of the precise timing of attack carries a high probability of being wrong" (p. 118).

This confirms, in a way, D.H.'s statement that open-source information provides enough data to produce satisfactory threat assessments.

2.19 THREAT IDENTIFICATION

The consultant's first task in this second stage of the risk assessment is to identify the threats. In the previous stage, the consultant characterized the potential targets, especially which assets were critical to the operation. In this second stage, the consultant must decide who (threat-as-agent) would want to harm the target. This research can be done via three methods:

1. Develop the threat from historical or intelligence data.
2. State the threat via policy promulgated by a recognized organization, such as the client's firm, your own security consultancy or a government – or an analysis of the validity of these three sources.
3. Create a range of potential threats that your client will agree with.

The next step would be to identify which parts of the facility the adversaries could target. The ASIS/RIMS standard summarizes this by using a dual-oriented threat (2015):

> "Threat from" is based on the nature and attributes of the threat, and how the threat may cause harm and uncertainty. "Threats to" considers the locations of the potential assets and services. In assessing the threat, the nature of the threat should be considered (malevolent, naturally occurring or accidental). For a malevolent threat – which should be the only one concerning us here – the assessment should consider "who/why" (e.g., a description of the adversary), "what" (e.g., the material used by the adversary) and the "how/where/when" (e.g., the characteristics of scenario and related tactics). Threat is assessed by evaluating the combination of motivation, intent, and capability of an adversary to impact priority or critical asset, function, activity, or capability.

2.19.1 "Threats From" or the Nature of the Threat

Several authors give different images of the threat. What the client needs to know is who these agents are and how they can harm the facility. In

Figure 2.1 The elements of threat (ASIS_RIMS).

Figure 2.1, we see the threat characterized by two major elements: motivation (split into their desire to act and their self-confidence) and the capability to act (summed up in knowledge and resources).

2.19.2 API 780: Define the Nature and Type of Threat

For the API 780, threats are considered as agents or adversaries and can be terrorists, activists, disgruntled employees, criminals, vandals and so on. Moreover, they can be divided into three major types: external, internal and colluding.

In the Middle East, for example, bomb attacks by terrorists are the only threat that seems really interesting to the executive suite. Less spectacular threats are often discarded out-of-hand by management as being insignificant in terms of loss. I disagree with this approach. From my experience, the three biggest threats to any company or facility are theft, fraud and smuggling. Neglecting these high frequency–low consequence security events is a bad idea because leniency in this domain gives a poor image of security, and facilities perceived as weak may be selected as targets over better-protected ones.

2.19.3 The Nature of the Threat

You may choose to consider only the DBT, which is the threat measured as the sum of the plausible adversaries. This threat traditionally includes three types of foes:

The terrorist, who can be an activist or a militant promoting any political, religious, environmental or other cause, and who is ready to use terror to reach his or her objectives. I believe that the terrorist as we see it today will soon be replaced by the activists – climate, vegans, gender and so on who show a very high level of motivation coupled with a taste for brutal means of action. Rarely lethal nowadays, but I think they will become a dangerous adversary when the terrorist threats recede.

The saboteur, usually a disgruntled employee or a contractor, who seeks revenge by sabotaging parts, stopping a production process or entering wrong data in computerized systems. The saboteur's motivation is strictly personal, and he or she does not want to be unmasked. The saboteur wants to keep his or her job, but get justice.

The criminal, this adversary is the most difficult to portray. The criminal can be an outsider targeting a facility to steal assets for resale. The criminal can be also an opportunistic criminal, a normal employee who acts on an opportunity for theft with a negligible chance of being caught. Opportunistic crime is common in very big organizations where field personnel and white-collar employees are very much left on their own. A good security program will help deter and detect these potential petty criminals, but they usually are by far the most numerous of the three. Lenience regarding petty theft and embezzlement could lead a dishonest employee being approached by serious adversaries and coerced into cooperation.

2.19.4 Type of Adversary

Adversaries are defined as insiders, outsiders or colluders, whether willing or coerced.

One immediately sees that reality is not as clear-cut as this. Terrorists seldom act without internal support. They often obtain the information necessary to plan their attacks by approaching sympathizers or members of their family. Statistically, there is a high chance that security personnel may be approached and offered compensation for assistance, for information or for turning a blind eye to reconnaissance activities.

The guard force is both a shield and a weakness. You need to trust them and at the same time regularly test their loyalty. They may be among those who are disgruntled. When I was director of security in an oil and gas company in the Gulf, I convinced management that recruiting

Indians to guard the headquarters and the facility would be a mistake. Indians employed in security positions are despised in the Gulf and fear losing their jobs on a native's whim. It would be unthinkable for them to challenge an Arab for not wearing a badge. Therefore, I convinced my management to let me recruit in North Africa, where I knew the guards could claim a military background and, with management support, could tell employees what to do without fear of losing their job. And it worked for a time…

2.19.5 Adversary's Intentions

Evaluating the adversary's intentions is obviously difficult. How can a security consultant figure out the adversary's intention when well-funded government agencies often fail to do so?

2.19.6 Adversary's Motivation

Motivations might be easier to apprehend. In Nigeria, people of the delta, who see the oil extracted by foreign companies, without enjoying its benefits, want a bigger share of the oil revenue, for example, but this obvious fact is not especially helpful or significant for the security practitioner. I have some concerns about private intelligence providers, who may tend to overdramatize undesired security incidents. The security consultant must apply reasonableness when trying to evaluate the adversary's motivation.

2.19.7 Adversary's Capability

We are on more stable ground here. When police conduct raids, they regularly find caches of arms, ammunitions and explosives, but that does not strictly mean the people raided had the capability and skills to use the equipment in a complex attack. Obviously, when militants return home from a theater of operations (such as Iraq, Afghanistan, Libya or Syria), the home country may face some risk, which the security consultant must take into account. Still, the adversary's capabilities must be considered an educated guess.

Regarding the internal threat, we need a good knowledge of a facility to know whether employees nurture a grudge against management, or whether it would be possible to take hostages. One approach is to classify employees according to race, ethnicity, clan and tribe to gauge the amity/enmity ratio within the work force. Not a very politically correct approach, but one that makes sense. You just do not need to advertise that you are doing it. Keep it a confidential approach.

The notion of the adversary cannot be separated from the notion of threat. The threat is what threatens the running of operations, and it can be perceived either as the perpetrator itself (the threat-as-agent) or as the undesired event (the scenario or the modus operandi the agent will use). In API 780, agent and threat are used interchangeably. Only the context suggests whether the methodology is discussing the agent or the action. Next comes probability, which is the product of these factors:

1. Target attractiveness (which can be obtained through numerous methods, such as CARVERI)
2. Adversary intent, motivations and capabilities
3. Specific vulnerability (in other words, the vulnerability of a specific asset measured against a list of relevant undesired security events)

Consequence is the result of the undesired event, should it take place, in terms of destruction, stopping of operations, business implications and other factors, quantified in lead time and U.S. dollars.

2.20 THREAT EVALUATION

Several authors have given thought about the threat evaluation and I would like to cite a few here, that I have used when I worked as a consultant, choosing the one that seemed the most appropriate to the situation I was facing. This is in fact what I suggest. Avoid sticking to one method only. The more methods you know the more flexible you will be in your evaluation, and flexibility is really what one needs in extreme circumstances.

2.20.1 Biringer et al.

For Biringer (2007), threat analysis consists of five steps:

1. Collect information on the potential threat (threat-as-agent).
2. Derive an adversary spectrum for a given application.
3. Describe adversarial capabilities.
4. Estimate the likelihood of attack for specific adversary groups for a given asset.
5. Define the adversarial threat for a given entity.

The challenge is to create an adversary spectrum that is acceptable to decision makers. Although Biringer describes adversaries as internal, external and colluding, the full spectrum of adversaries may include terrorists, criminals, extremists (a softer version of terrorists), vandals, foreign intelligence personnel and psychotics, though the last two are usually out of scope for a security consultant.

In evaluating the adversary's capabilities, the consultant may need the following items of information:

- motivation
- tactics
- intelligence-gathering means
- targets of interest
- expected number in group
- equipment
- transportation
- weapons
- explosives
- technical skills and knowledge
- financial resources
- potential for collusion with an insider

All these items are vital for creating a DBT that will be the reference against which to measure possible threats. How can the DBT be developed? According to Biringer,

> historical adversary data would not necessarily predict whether an adversary group would attack a particular asset/facility. Adversaries, particularly those motivated by ideology, have very subjective reasons for attacking a particular target and they gather data, conduct surveillance, and rehearse until they are confident of their success.

The security manager should try to keep his evaluation of the threat at the projection or extrapolation level.[5]

Biringer's approach to measuring the threat is interesting in that it first establishes an adversarial threat summary, where the following criteria are explored: type of adversary (terrorists, criminals, vandals, etc.), number of adversaries, equipment, vehicles, weapons, motivation, tactics and targets of interests. Instead of starting from the asset and measuring whether it can be of interest to adversaries, Biringer prioritizes the threat according

Table 2.2 Threat Evaluation table by Biringer et al.

Adversary Capability	Adversary History/Intent	Relative Attractiveness of Asset to Adversary
Access to region	Historic interest	Desired level of
Material resources	Historic attacks	consequence
Technical skills	Current interest in site	Ideology
Planning and	Current surveillance	Ease of attack
organizational skills	Documented threats	
Financial resources		

Source: From Table 4.2 of Biringer (2007, p. 63).

to the nature of the adversary. Instead of saying the power station could be destroyed by terrorists, this method would say that terrorists could have an interest in destroying critical infrastructure items, of which the power station is one.

The capability of the threat is then studied according to the following (Table 2.2):

If the capability is proved, the analysis goes to the next level: the adversary intent. The same procedure applies and the analysis continues only if the adversary intent is confirmed. This is an interesting process, but its essential drawback is that it is gives capability precedence over intent and motivation. In other words, if an adversary does not currently have the means to carry out an attack on a facility, the adversary will not do it. However, that belief may be mistaken. Where there is a will, there is a path. With intention and motivation, the adversary can work to obtain capability.

2.20.2 TAG Risk Assessment Process (2007: Vellani)

The threat formula expressed by Karim Vellani is traditional in its approach. It simply says that Threat = Intent + Capability + Motivation.

Vellani considers historical sources as a primary foundation for risk assessments, with crime analysis as a quantitative measure of the threat assessment while the terrorist threat analysis is normally qualitative. The TAG risk assessment process includes these steps:

1. Threat identification: Identify potential adversaries and their characteristics (type, intentions, motivations and capabilities)

2. Asset classification: Identify targets and determine their vulnerabilities
3. Consequence/criticality analysis

In Vellani's approach, identifying potential adversaries is the distinguishing point. In other words, are there people who may want to harm our operations? Who are they? Which of our targets can they be interested in? What would be the consequence for our business if they successfully destroyed, damaged or sabotaged these assets?

2.21 THREAT EVALUATION STEPS

As we can see, the various approaches, if not identical, are at least comparable and can be summarized in these stages of threat assessment:

2.21.1 Identify the Nature of the Adversary

This means understanding who are the potential adversaries of the project. We tend to focus on glamorous high-end threats, yet other threats may be equally damaging. Sabotage by disgruntled employees can bring great harm to the production process, and vandalism and tagging can scare customers away while creating an unpleasant work environment.

Many court cases have highlighted the employer's responsibility for personnel security. Consequently, most CEOs prefer to invest in security than to pay massive settlements after the unthinkable occurs. When you designate adversaries, remember that some are structural adversaries, while others are just opportunistic ones. The distinction has ramifications for security. Basically, the politically motivated adversary is a structural enemy, while thieves and disgruntled employees may simply be opportunistic.

2.21.2 Identify the Type of Adversaries

The first type is external. This means that from the preparation to the execution of the attack, the adversary has worked entirely from outside, without support from any insider. The second type is internal. This definition points toward either a disgruntled employee or a criminal element in the workforce. The third type, the colluder, refers to collaboration between the attacker and an internal accomplice, who provides information to the adversary, uses his or her position to introduce items in the facility or helps the attacker become oriented within the facility during the attack.

2.21.3 Identify the Nature of the Potential Attack

The philosophy of knowing thy enemy helps the security manager prepare for the unexpected. An attack can take at least three forms: overt, covert and stealthy, or any combination of these.

The overt attack is the brutal frontal attack – sometimes coupled with a diversion – aimed to apply force to a target and bring as much violent damage as possible, material and human, in a shock-and-awe fashion.

The covert attack may itself be a mix of spectacular attack and sabotage. The purpose is to obtain a result through surprise. Instead of starting at the gate or at the perimeter, the covert attack may start inside the facility and adversaries may want to reach (1) assessment and decision centers such as the security control room; (2) the central control room to disrupt or stop production; (3) the administration building to kill, abduct or kidnap the facility's leadership; or (4) the process area to destroy pipes that distribute finished products. In a covert attack, it is likely that a response can be made only after the damage has occurred.

Preventing a stealth attack is difficult, and when such an attack succeeds, it is cruel proof that the protection program was ineffective. Unless security receives information in advance, a stealth attack cannot not be discovered until the damage is done. Often, adversaries have already left when the attack is discovered. Furthermore, diversion attacks – overt – may have mobilized the response force somewhere away from the real damage. Such actions usually take place at night, often on remote targets such as pipelines, pump stations, manifolds and platforms, and preventing them is often mission impossible.

As for preventing these attacks, a physical security only approach will fail. What is needed is an all-encompassing security program that includes human resources security, security awareness and any other security activity that supports a security culture.

To measure the threat, it seems obvious to start with an analysis of past security events. What happened before could happen again. The downside of the historical approach is that attacks are few in number and may not accurately reflect the current menace. Listing incidents that occurred five to ten years ago does not impress clients. Some consultants point to the modus operandi of other armed groups in neighboring places, but again, it fails to convince. What happens in a war-torn country is obviously different from what happens in an industrial area in a country that is basically at peace and under control. In strong, solid countries, the adversary does not have a safe haven for preparing and setting IEDs.

In summary, the safest bet is to draw up a list of incidents related to similar companies, in similar countries and comparable circumstances. (Alas, there is always a first time, a first plane hijacking, a first 9/11, a first marathon bombing, a first Paris carnage.) A consultant is not really equipped to forecast what form the threat will take. Sticking to historical antecedents is not perfect, but it has the advantage of being factual and unquestionable.

2.21.4 Create a List of Possible Modi Operandi

A few years ago, senior consultants in a company I worked for in the kingdom of Bahrain decided to create the following list of attacks that could be carried out in our area of operations:

- Use of weapons
  - Small arms (handguns, AK-47s, grenades, etc.)
  - Direct shooting
  - Stand-off attack
  - Complex attack (meaning coupled with other types of weapons, such as IEDs)
  - Light weapons (mortars, RPGs, etc.)
  - Direct shooting
  - Stand-off attack
  - Complex attack (with diversion attack)
- Use of explosives
  - Person-borne bomb/IED (suicide bomber with high explosive)
  - Vehicle-borne bomb/IED
  - High explosive
  - Low explosive/gas cylinder
  - Placed or thrown bomb/IED (excluding petrol bombs)
  - Package/mail bomb/IED
  - Airborne bomb/IED
  - Seaborne bomb/IED
  - Bomb threat
  - Hoax bomb
- Use of vehicles
  - As a weapon

- As a means to carry people and equipment for an attack
- Hijack
- Aircraft as weapon
- Damage
  - Arson (including petrol bombs)
  - Breakage
- Biological attack
  - Water
  - Air
  - Powder
  - Food
  - Land contamination
- Chemical attack
  - Water
  - Air
  - Food
  - Land contamination
- Nuclear attack
  - Explosive
  - Radiological
- Carrying or hiding equipment for illegal use
- Blockage of key routes/access to site
- Kidnapping/hostage taking
- Robbery/burglary/theft
- Civil protest/unrest
- Press intrusion

This exhaustive, somewhat over-the-top list, may help readers create their own lists of possible threats.

2.21.5 Rank the Threat

API (2013) provides the following scale to measure threat rankings against an asset (Table 2.3):

2.21.6 Evaluating the Likelihood of Attack

The likelihood is not to be confused with evaluating the time of an attack. In a risk assessment, we discuss whether undesired security events can materialize on your plant or facility, but not when they will. The ASIS/

Table 2.3 Threat Ranking Table – API 780

Threat Level	Description
1 – Very Low	Indicates little or no credible evidence of capability or intent and no history of actual or planned threats against the asset or similar assets (i.e., no expected attack in the life of the facility's operation).
2 – Low	Indicates that there is a low threat against the asset or similar assets and that few known adversaries would pose a threat to the asset (e.g., ≥ 1 event is possible in the life of the facility's operations).
3 – Medium	Indicates that there is a possible threat against the asset or similar assets based on the threat's desire to compromise similar assets, but no specific threat exists for the facility or asset (e.g., ≥ 1 event in 10 years of the facility's operations).
4 – High	Indicates that a credible threat exists against the asset or similar assets based on the knowledge of the threat's capability and intent to attack the asset or similar assets, and some indications exist of a threat specific to the company, facility or asset (e.g., ≥ 1 event in five years of the facility's operations).
5 – Very high	Indicates that a credible threat exists against the asset or similar assets; that the threat demonstrates the capability and intent to launch an attack; that the subject asset or similar assets are targeted on a frequently recurrent basis; and that the frequency of an attack over the life of the asset is very high (e.g., ≥ 1 event per year).

RIMS Risk Assessment standard suggests several ways of approaching this issue. The first one it suggests is a method that professional forecasters call judgment call. In this approach, the subject matter expert provides an input based on an analysis of events.

Garcia (2006) provides an interesting tool to estimate the likelihood of attack. She notes that historical data can be used to define not only the adversary but also the probability of attack. She writes that because major assets will need protection anyway, it might be good to approach their protection through the concept of conditional risk. Garcia has suggested a simple but effective way to measure the probability of attack (P_A).

Garcia (2006: p. 320) also provides a good worksheet for measuring the attractiveness of the facility for the terrorist threat. The method is logical and effective. It follows the following sequences:

One must start by specifying an undesired event (threat-as-action) and a specific threat agent. In other words, establish a possible scenario of attack and a portrait of the potential perpetrator (the adversary).

Four questions will be asked, and the answer will incrementally define the level of probability of the undesired event specified materializing.

Question 1: Is the threat present (in that case, the threat agent is meant)? If one cannot identify possible adversaries in this specific context, then the probability of attack is very low. If your analysis point toward a possibility of existence, you should move to the second question: the capability of the threat.

Question 2: Has the threat the adequate resources to carry out successfully the undesired security event?

In case of negative answer, the probability of attack is low. In case of a positive answer, we move to the next question dealing with the intention or history.

Question 3: The intention can be compared to the motivation factor described by the ASIS/RIMS method that considers that *desire* and *attractiveness + confidence* create motivation. Although, one could argue that intention and motivation are slightly different things. Motivation can be defined as a reason or reasons for acting or behaving in a particular way, while intention is a mental state in which the agent commits themselves to a course of action. In both cases, what matters to the security analyst is that if the threat exists and the motivation exists, one can safely argue that the intention is present and should consider it as a plausible pat of the equation. If the answer to this question is no, the probability of attack is still medium, since it might be extremely difficult to answer this question with certainty. If the analyst considers that the intention might be present, therefore if the threat agent has a history of comparable attacks or can be expected to have motivation to act, we move to the next and last question, which is another difficult question,

Question 4: Has the threat targeted the facility?

This is of course the most difficult question to answer and this is where we enter the realm of prognostication and where you will have problems to justify a positive answer to this question. Be that as it may, the answer to the previous question has already provided a high probability of attack and should be enough to start building the security program. A positive answer to this question is possible, if you manage to have informants within your organization and without becoming paranoid, any hint at a possible attack should be taken very seriously. This method has the advantage of being parsimonious – only four questions to ask – but is limited by the capacity to answer definite answer and be able to justify them.

Let me remind you again that the probability of attack does not (because it cannot) provide the timing of attack.

Once equipped with the nature and type of threat, the scenarios and likelihood of attacks, the security manager/consultant is ready to move to the next step of the SRA, the vulnerability assessment.

Meanwhile, keep in mind that the threat evaluation is where the risk assessment will succeed or fail. If you are too conservative, your mitigation measures will be turned down on the basis that if the threat is low, there is no need to install these expensive security systems. By contrast, if you fall for the glamorous threat of high-level terrorism, you may lose credibility. The people you are dealing with have a pretty good idea of which threats they are *really* facing. You are not expected to give them a lesson in geopolitics and the situation of international terrorism. You are there to provide cost-effective solutions to mitigate a plausible/possible risk of attack against their main source of income.

2.21.7 Evaluate Attractiveness

An asset may be critical (to a process) and yet not automatically become a target. Only when an adversary finds an asset attractive does it become a target and need special protection.

The API 780 is vague when it comes to measuring the attractiveness of an asset. It suggests that attractiveness depends on the following factors:

- Usefulness of the process material as a weapon or to cause collateral damage. Explosives used in the mining industry would fall into that category.
- Proximity to a national asset or landmark. This is a bit unclear. Does it mean a target close to a landmark faces higher risks than one farther away? This is possible but not a major factor.
- Ease of attack, including ease of access and degree of security measures (soft target). The target's vulnerability is indeed important, but not so much as the significance or symbolism of the target.
- High company reputation and brand exposure. This seems possible but cannot be confirmed. Most facilities attacked in recent years have been industrial sites or government buildings. The purpose of the attacks was to harm the center of political decision-making and the main source of income supporting unpopular governments (oil

and gas in Saudi Arabia, tourism resorts in Egypt and Tunisia and embassies the world over).

- Iconic or symbolic target. This criterion is influenced by the 9/11 attacks, but iconic and symbolic targets have a greater chance of being destroyed by accidental fire than by terrorists.
- Chemical or biological weapons precursor chemical. This criterion seems less important and less likely than others.
- Recognition of the target. Nothing is more puzzling to a novice than an industrial site such as a gas plant. The fact that it looks like a medley of colored pipes going in senseless directions may be its best protection against attacks by amateurs. Please note that Recognition is one of the seven criteria of the CARVERI method and has an extreme importance.
- API's target attractiveness ranking is based on the following table (Table 2.4):

This is a subjective way of measuring the attractiveness of an asset, but attractiveness is not only subjective by nature but also a weak one. Better methods would be appreciated, and probably exist.

Table 2.4   Threat Attractiveness Criteria (API 780)

Ranking Level	Descriptor	Conditional Probability of the Act	Threat Ranking
1	Very low	0.0 to 0.2	Threat would have little or no interest in the asset.
2	Low	> 0.2 to 0.4	Threat would have some degree of interest in the asset, but less than in other assets.
3	Medium	> 0.4 to 0.6	Threat would have some degree of interest in the asset, but less than in other assets.
4	High	> 0.6 to 0.8	Threat would have a moderate degree of interest in the asset, relative to other assets.
5	Very high	> 0.8 to 1.0	Threat would have a high degree of interest in the asset, and it is a preferred choice relative to other assets

2.22 THE CARVER + I METHOD (AKA CARVERI)

The CARVERI technique is not part of the API methodology and does not measure attractiveness *per se*. Instead, it measures the easiness of attack and the potential consequences of such attacks of an asset as a target, from an assailant's perspective.

CARVERI measures the operational attractiveness of an asset, not necessarily the political attractiveness. It tells whether the asset has all the characteristics that will make an attack on the asset a success. CARVERI has the advantage of being easy for non-security people to understand.

The method, then called CARVER, was developed by U.S. special operations forces to analyze an enemy's critical infrastructure to identify a node against which a small, well-trained force could launch an attack. The last criterion, I, for Insider, is a later addition from the industrial security field. Some security specialists also use an eighth criterion, called shock.

The values inside the matrix are shown in Table 2.5.

Although the original CARVER method was based on a 1–10 scale, I find it easier to use this CARVER + I technique applying a 1–5 scale, simplifying calculations and putting it on par with the rest of the calculations used in traditional risk assessment methods.

Only existing sites should be evaluated with this tool. You cannot understand how attractive an asset is unless you know what it looks like. The following case studies illustrate that point:

Table 2.5 The CARVERI Criteria

Criteria	Scale
Immediate halt in output, production, or service and target cannot function without it.	5
Stop output, production or service within one day, or 66% reduction in output, production or service.	4
Stop output, production or service within one week, or 33% reduction in output, production or service.	3
Stop output, production or service within 10 days, or 10% reduction in output, production or service.	2
No significant effect on output, production or service.	1

Table 2.5   Cont.

13. Accessibility	
Criteria	**Scale**
Easily accessible; stand-off weapons can be employed.	5
Potential target is inside a perimeter fence but outdoors.	4
Potential target is inside a building but on ground floor.	3
Potential target is inside a building but on second floor or above, or in basement, requiring climbing or lowering.	2
Potential target inaccessible, or accessible with extreme difficulty.	1

14. Recoverability	
Criteria	**Scale**
Replacement, repair or substitution requires one month or more.	5
Replacement, repair or substitution requires one week to one month.	4
Replacement, repair or substitution requires 72 hours to one week.	3
Replacement, repair or substitution requires 24 to 72 hours.	2
Same-day replacement, repair or substitution.	1

15. Vulnerability	
Criteria	**Scale**
Vulnerable to long-range laser target designation, small arms fire, or charges of five pounds or less.	5
Vulnerable to light anti-armor weapons fire or charges of five to ten pounds.	4
Vulnerable to medium anti-armor weapons fire, bulk charges of ten to 30 pounds, or very careful placement of smaller charges.	3
Vulnerable to heavy anti-armor fire, bulk charges of 30 to 50 pounds, or requires special weapons.	2
Invulnerable to all but the most extreme targeting measures.	1

16. Effect	
Criteria	**Scale**
Overwhelmingly positive effects and no significant negative effects.	5
Moderately positive effects and few significant negative effects.	4
Neutral – no significant effects.	3
Moderately negative effects and few positive effects.	2
Overwhelmingly negative effects and no significant positive effects.	1

(*continued*)

Table 2.5 Cont.

17. Recognizability

Criteria	Scale
The target is clearly recognizable under all conditions from a distance and requires little or no training for recognition.	5
The target is easily recognizable but requires a small amount of training for recognition.	4
The target is difficult to recognize at night or in bad weather or might be confused with other targets or target components and requires some training for recognition.	3
The target is difficult to recognize at night or in bad weather. It is easily confused with other targets or components and requires extensive training for recognition.	2
The target cannot be recognized under any conditions, except by experts or insiders.	1

18. Insider

Criteria	Scale
Little knowledge of the operational process would be required and only limited access to the critical site needed, for example, cleaners.	5
Some knowledge of the operational process would be required and only general access to the critical site needed, for example, administration staff.	4
Some knowledge of the operational process and essential services would be required and full access to all operational areas of the critical site needed, for example, maintenance staff or third-party contractors.	3
Specialist knowledge of the operational process and understanding of the essential services would be required and full access to all areas of the critical site needed, for example, engineer or IT administrator.	2
Specialist and complete knowledge of the operational process and essential services would be required and full access to all areas of the critical site needed, for example, site manager.	1

Case Study 1. On the western side of a facility, a tank farm can be seen from afar. There are eight major tanks there, containing millions of gallons of hydrocarbons. Seven are painted light blue. The eighth is painted in bright colors, and the brand of its owner is painted in gigantic letters.

96

During reconnaissance work, starting with a Google search and followed by physical observation, this eighth tank will attract the observer's attention. Same size, yes, same contents, maybe, but why is it the only one painted with the brand name? This tank has several advantages for an attacker. The action team carrying out the attack will have no problem identifying it. It also scores in terms of shock: if destroyed, the image of the black smoke emanating from the smoking tank with the logo still visible will do very well as part of the political campaign against the exploitation of the great petroleum groups. An attack on that specific tank will yield more results than an attack on the anonymous tank right next to it. This is the CNN breaking news effect. The consultant needs to see the asset with their own eyes to integrate it into the matrix and recommend appropriate countermeasures.

Case Study 2. You are performing a risk assessment on a gold mine. Mines use a lot of commercial explosives, and explosives are gold to terrorists, bank robbers and other villains. Often, the main outdoor explosive storage magazine is set in a remote area within the facility or separated from it by a few kilometers. Explosives are regularly transferred from the explosive storage magazine to the mine itself, where underground storage magazines keep them in stock for day-to-day use.

The outdoor explosive magazine is usually well protected, with heavy fencing, CCTV surveillance, good lighting, and an appropriate guard force. The second explosive magazine, located in the mine, underground, usually has only a reinforced gate, a light, and a CCTV camera covering the door, with no one to physically present protect it.

In theory, both harbors very valuable items for adversaries and one could think that recommendations for protecting both would be very similar. However, if we apply the CARVERI matrix to both magazines, we reach different conclusions.

Criticality: Although one ignores whether the explosive will be used on the facility or elsewhere, criticality gives us the same reading for both magazines. According to our scale, it would be a very high severity, just because the theft of explosive is a worrying phenomenon. We would rank it at 5, on those grounds, for both magazines.

Accessibility: The first explosive magazine is located outdoors, in a fairly remote area, and would constitute a relatively accessible target for trained adversaries. It would rank 4 or 5. The underground magazine is inside the mine, within the facility itself. The team would need to gain access to the site, defeat several lines of defense, and find the underground magazine. That would be quite a feat if no insider was involved. The underground magazine would probably rank 1.

Recoverability: The right answer to this would probably be given by the security manager who would have a better idea of the time necessary to refurbish the explosives magazines—in case of theft only. The delay is expected to be nearly identical, perhaps 72 hours. We would rank both assets as 2.

Vulnerability: Vulnerability is another element where a significant difference will show. The explosives magazine, located outdoors, would indeed be vulnerable to long-range laser target designation, small arms fire, or charges of five pounds or less. The outdoor asset ranks as a 5.

The underground magazine would not. No anti-armor gun could be used for lack of space and visibility, and only specific explosive charges would be practically used against the door. The asset vulnerability can be rated a 2.

Effect: The effect of the theft would be identical. It would be a shock in both cases and a serious security issue, at all levels. We give both assets a recoverability score of 3, for lack of better information.

Recognizability: The outdoor magazine is clearly recognizable under all conditions from a distance and requires little or no training for identification. A Google search would help locate the spot, and a reconnaissance expedition, by day and at night, would eliminate confusion in identifying the target. This is an unambiguous 5.

The underground explosives magazine is difficult to locate, cannot be researched on Google, and is impossible to detect by a reconnaissance team, unless the help of an insider has been secured. The underground magazine would rank as low as 1.

Insider: The outdoor target is easily recognizable, so insider help is not needed. The outdoor asset would score 5. An attack on the underground asset would require inside assistance, so it scores a 3.

If we now summarize our results, what do we get? The outdoor magazine scores 30, and the underground magazine scores 17. Thus, the outdoor magazine represents a much more attractive target than its indoor counterpart. While both are critical and somewhat attractive targets, the CARVERI method provides a way to differentiate their attractiveness to adversaries. I recommend incorporating the results of the CARVERI evaluation into the target attractiveness ranking definition or process.

Chapter 1 has listed a few of the terrorist attacks mainly originating from the Muslim world and targeting the western civilization. They constitute only a fraction of the terrorist attacks in the world, but they are the ones that our reader is interested in. But what, I hope, has been demonstrated in this chapter is the obvious link, between threats evaluation and political analysis. Threats do not occur *sui generis*. Threats, and its corollary terrorism, are just means of expressing a political anger, weakness and frustration, in the face of an adversary that has no intention to relinquish an ounce of power and will not be defeated by traditional means. The multiplicity of causes in the modern world and the relative monopoly of legitimate violence enjoyed by states make this type of action the definite choice for many politically motivated groups and even individuals (the infamous lone wolves).

Of course, there are several levels of potential threats, from the government challengers (strong entities, movements), to the bunch of illuminated individuals, who want to leave their name to posterity, and end up in a firework while being killed by the police. The security practitioner has to face the whole spectrum, from the alternative government candidate to the asocial lone wolf, and of course, the mitigations measures need to be adapted to the most probable threat. I believe that our security practitioner should take a bit of reflection time before acting, and meditate about which threat he or she is most likely to face before discussing what damage they (the threat as agents) are likely to inflict to the assets under consideration.

You might think this goes without saying, but I have witnessed for many years consultants who establish their risk assessment without really thinking about the real nature of the threat, other than saying "we have the terrorist, the criminal and this disgruntled employee". Yes, we may have those, but depending on where we are, what we produce and how attractive we are to some malevolent people, some threats will be more plausible than others.

Instead of taking the threat as a given, we should start with our facility/potential target and see how and why we might be of interest to someone. Threat agents do not attack targets for fun. They do it for a purpose, always political or political cum economical, and a lot of thought is spent, on their side, trying to find the ideal target.

We should therefore start our study from a parochial approach, and from there, see the biggest picture.

2.23 THREAT AND THE BUSINESS OF SECURITY CONSULTANCY

This assertion will surprise some readers, particularly the security student community, but I have noticed that out of the whole risk assessment process, threat is perhaps the most neglected, or to phrase it differently, often overlooked by risk assessors. Threats, for many, is more a tick in the box than real thinking. The reason is simple enough. Risk assessors work hard on projects and they do not really have time to think thoroughly about the specific threats. I know that template – particularly the threat template of the API780 says otherwise, but consultants do fill these boxes once for all, because the purpose of the risk assessment is not to discuss the threats but to suggest recommendations and mitigation measures. Customers do not always appreciate security analysis that do not give a virtuous image of their communities, and some countries are very reluctant to share any security information with exogenous consultants. Furthermore, risk assessors are always pressed for time, because technicians and engineers are waiting for their work to start the design and AutoCAD people are also waiting for the risk assessment outcome to start producing drawings.

In a security consultancy, everybody is under pressure. Always. If you are not, your consultancy is not going well!

In our work, there is a lot of cut and paste, – how long do we spend trying to trace the names of previous companies that might have been forgotten in one of our tables or analyses? – documents and drawings must be produced fast... Said simply, changes in threat assessment implicating changes in technical design might not always be welcome. That sounds terrible, does it not? Not really, in fact. Consultants often work in similar or very comparable security environments. What matters is that the threats that you are listing and developing do not go against the beliefs of your customer. Even neighboring countries in the same regional security hub mays have very different perceptions of threats. If we consider the security threats against the state of Qatar, the Emirate of Abu Dhabi and the kingdom of Saudi Arabia, for example, the security consultant should understand exactly what threats will seem plausible to their audience, which ones will be accepted and which should absolutely NOT be mentioned, even in passing!

This means that our consultant may have to discard threats that will not be accepted by the customer. Their threats will not appear in the report since they do not exist. Yet the security consultant shall keep these threats in mind at all times, particularly when offering security mitigations measures that must also apply to these "unsaid" threats. We are here again in the middle of the cultural aspect of threats definition, and the security consultant evolving in a different cultural environment should take time before writing security reports for their management.

Yet threats are the cornerstone of any risk evaluation! But defining them can be a difficult exercise because not every bit of truth is fit to be told and eventually, you still want to produce the best protection program for your client!

2.23.1 The Cultural Aspect of Threats

Speaking about our world is of course an unprecise and dangerous formula. The world is not ours, there are many other worlds as rich and unique as ours elsewhere in the world, and ours is probably very different from the world of a peasant in China or an African gold miner in South América. When I say our world, I am, to my surprise, echoing the words of George W. Bush "they hate us for what we are". And what we are is what defines our world. It is how we conceive the world, the values we believe in and the actions we are ready to take to preserve it. By our world,

101

I mean the democratic Christian West. Europeans and Americans may differ, a Pole may feel very different from an Australian, but our values are, if not identical, at least comparable. We are Christians and this is what characterizes us, whether we are believers or not. Our Christian roots have guided our societies and remain a moral compass that explains our choices, our actions and the limits we choose to circumscribe these actions within. I do not need to list these values and explain them. I cannot resist the envy to paraphrase Justice Potter Stewart who, in 1964, during a trial about hardcore pornography, which the council of the accused said was impossible to define with precision, replied "I shall not today attempt further to define the kinds of material I understand to be embraced... but I know it when I see it ..."

Culture, more than anything else, is what differentiates us. And it also differentiates us in the world of industrial security since, being part of the international western epistemic security community, we are asked to develop security programs for major projects in other parts of the world, where culture and values are different. I could recently feel this gap when I was asked by a European continental consultancy to check the proposal they made to a Saudi prospective client. Nowhere is the importance of culture in security more visible than when a western consultant is asked to work on the security aspect of a project in a country, or countries, of a different culture (in the Huntingtonian sense of the word). Bear in mind that I had just recently relocated to France after 17 years spent in the different Gulf sheikhdoms. My recent return and the experience gained over there were of course the reasons why I had been asked to help!

This document I checked was very well-written and well documented and yet rather inappropriate or unsuitable. My long experience with the targeted audience told me that the document would not be seen favorably by the final customer. Why? Not because of the presentation, or the contents or the very serious approach that had been chosen by the consultancy. No, the red-light flickered when I started to read the *threats* section. Simply because the threats facing the customer had been assumed and written from a western perspective. We are evolving so much in an environment, a context shaped by the media, the press, the conferences we attend, our professional discussions with colleagues who all share comparable assumptions that we forget that people, elsewhere, can think differently.

Our assumptions need some adjustments: We believe that terrorists are bad people, for example, while they may not appear as such to some of our customers. I do not mean, for example, that when we operate in the Middle East, our Middle Eastern clients do not want to defend their property against terrorist attacks. This is not what I am saying. They are business people or high civil servants with interests, and like for all human beings, their own interest comes first. So they count on us to understand the situation, list the correct threats and protect their environment against major attacks. But they want us to do so with respect and avoid being contemptuous regarding the motivations of what we call the adversary. In the Middle East, most Muslims are sensitive about brotherhood, do not consider that their deviant brothers are to be insulted and trust that the distance between them and their cousins is not exaggeratedly wide. Calling threats the way we traditionally do does not go well with people of a certain culture. We must exert our sensitivity, we call it tact, about the way we say things, because the cousins of these decision makers, although misled, are Muslims…and we are not. Some of you will shout in anger, and say we call a cat a cat. May be, but when your audience is made of cats, you have to exert some kind of caution and show respect for the sensitivities of your hosts.

When I landed in Saudi Arabia in 2004, working on the famous naval project, it took me some time to interpret reactions, body language and understand that people in the region were not seeing the "terrorists" the way we saw them. First, the motivations of the terrorists are, most of the time, supported by our clients. The supremacy of the West over world affairs, and particularly vis-à-vis the Muslim world, is perceived as unfair and unacceptable for most Muslims. Muslims should dominate the world since this is what the prophet said. Any subservience of the Muslims to any non-Muslim authority is unacceptable and this will not improve, democracy or not democracy... So, what we call the terrorists are fellow brethren who have erred. What they disagree with is the method they used, not the motivations behind the technique. Terror is a method, but it is a method that is used mainly at a last resort! But look to us as the more logical and probable threats, were not what the customer wanted to hear. I said wanted to hear because of the reflexivity code that I respect. I cannot pretend to know what happens in a customer's mind. I ignore how it was formatted, I do not know exactly what their values are, how they perceive us and how they measure our communication with them. Reaching total trust is illusory. What can be achieved, though, with a lot of effort, though, is establishing a link. When people of different cultures speak to each other, trust is seldom there, particularly at the beginning. Often the confidence barrier is never raised. And yet, with time and experience, one can encompass the great lines of a culture, understand the narratives that

103

have formatted their interlocutors, grasp what they would consider as acceptable, possible, tolerable or definitely unacceptable. This can only be achieved if one shows interest in the other's perspective. This is why some ambassadors do very well in complicated places. They stay themselves, respect their hosts and manage to create a bridge between two distanced mindsets. Others immerse themselves in the other's culture, thinking it is what is expected of them. This is not a good idea. "Going native" is almost always perceived as a weakness. When I travelled extensively in West Africa in 1990s, I met regularly Europeans dressed in African garbs, sharing their time and drinking beer with Africans, looking almost like albinos Africans. I do not think that they were respected. Their lives must have been complicated and their efforts misunderstood. I lived 17 years in Africa. I travelled extensively in Western and Southern Africa. I dressed like a mzungu – a white man – and was always well-received and respected. I knew my hosts, and I behaved in an appropriate manner making a point not to offend them. This was enough to guarantee safe travels on the continent. I digress but what I mean is that other culture's individuals are always ready to accept is that you are what you are, you have your values, principles that might be different, and they accept that. What they want is that you understand that they have values as well, and principles and that if there is a bridge between theirs and yours, then a collaboration is possible. But this has also limits. For example, many Muslims have, most of the time, no issue with you being a Christian (I apologize if the reader is not one), they usually try nicely to incite you to consider converting to Islam, but if you stand your ground, they will accept it and even admire that. Do not forget that in their creed, apostasy is punished by death. But what they cannot understand is if you say: "Sorry, I am an atheist, I do not believe in God!" I have seen westerners doing that in Gulf social environment. The apparent modernity of their hosts, most of them educated for a few years in the United States or the United Kingdom and aware of our idiosyncrasies, can create a feeling of intimacy conducive to confidence making that must be avoided at all costs! There is no worse catastrophe than claiming agnosticism! You cannot survive such a declaration. Cultural understanding and common sense are what is needed to draft a correct threat assessment. Be aware of your host/client no-go areas, and have a reasonably correct ideas of what should or should not be said or written. I experienced this once when I was chosen as a security director for a project where the main partners were American, French and Emiratis. There were three different approaches to business and to security that were almost impossible to reconcile. Although the relationship between individuals from these three main entities was good, the trust as culturally different partners when major decisions had to be taken was fragile. Small things, acceptable in one culture, and unacceptable in another, made life at work heavy and mistrust within the organization rife.

To come back to the example cited above, the western consultant selected five major threats, four of them very traditional, and a fifth that was an absolute No Go! What was this threat? It was simply *violent and public manifestations against the government*. I was surprised to read this, since this consultancy had already some experience in Arab countries, and should have been more cognizant of some specific traits of the Arab political culture. It is not that demonstrations in the GCC turning violent are unheard of. Expatriate workers from the subcontinent have gone on strike several times, in Dubai, in Abu Dhabi, in Qatar to protest against their appalling working conditions, unpaid or overdue wages and the privation of their right to move outside of their place of work. These actions are usually dealt with brutally through termination, except when the media are aware – like in Qatar during the construction of football stadiums and other facilities for the football World Cup.

So the rarity or the occurrence of the event is not what matters there. What is not an acceptable proposition is to suggest that the government would not be able to detect, delay and deny such occurrence. It is an insult to their capabilities to maintain order in their own countries. All Arab governments consider authority and the maintenance of order as their supreme (and principal) duties and any attempt to doubt their authority is simply offensive.

A better knowledge of the Arab mentality would have avoided listing a threat that, although it is a very reasonable and possible threat, is culturally perceived as an insult. The underpinning message is that the government would not be able to prevent a massive demonstration in its capital city! In other words, the threat assessment contains a strong suggestion that the customer, or their government – is incompetent! You do not get contracts by insinuating such things. But my employers on this project were not at all conscious of this element and did not understand that it would probably disqualify them from the bid. They were applying the same threat spectrum they would use in Europe or in Africa, the location where they generally operated and did not integrate the cultural element variation in their study.

It might surprise you that assets, are, also, in some ways, a cultural concept. While Europeans consider people, property and information as the three families of assets, and ASIS and others say that the most valuable asset is the individual, one cannot deny that the value of human beings in some countries is quite cheap. Unskilled workers – I wanted to use the word indentured – also reply to the law of offer and demand. When the demand is huge, the intrinsic value of these workers diminishes by as much. Families of people you pay almost nothing will always accept a little bit more than nothing and be satisfied with it. What kind of appeal could they lodge and where? But of course, all this should appear nowhere in writing. People, particularly when unskilled and easily replaceable, have a relatively low cost.

In the Arab culture, but also in Africa, information has tremendous value. In a culture of honor, where contracts used to be verbal and where a word is a word, there seems to be, nowadays, a fascination for contracts, files, assessments, audits, standards and IT secrecy. A loss of information equals a loss of face. I guess that the proximity with American advisors has probably modified the Arab mentality at least in the GCC. The same goes for all cultural groups that share identical values, suffer the same complexes and prejudices against other cultural groups and express their pride in similar manners. It is not a surprise if more business schools offer courses where relations with other cultural entities are taught: how to deal with Chinese or Japanese customers, for example. Threats follow the same route, threats are culturally tainted and are perceptions that react, like chemical products, to certain social stimuli.

To conclude that digression, I would say that the world we are living in is definitely not to everybody's taste, and that we can reasonably assume that, for some time to come, it is under threat from an existential adversary who considers that it is their duty to defeat us and replace our world with their own system of values and their peculiar justice.

Being conscious of that will of course have an impact on the way we organize our work, how we conceive and how we organize it. We will discuss that in time later in this book.

NOTES

1 "There are known knowns; there are things we know that we know. There are known unknowns; that is to say, there are things that we now know we don't know. But there are also unknown unknowns – there are things we do not know we don't know".

Declaration by Donald Rumsfeld on 12 February 2002, before the invasion of Iraq.

2 In many risk assessment methods, green is replaced by blue, to show a low level of risk. The idea being, of course, that since there is no zero risk, no situation can be painted as green.

3 On 8 May 8 2002, a bomb attack killed 14 people of which 11 were French engineers of the Direction des Constructions Navales working on a submarine project. The bus that transported them had been pulverized before the Sheraton Hotel by a VBIED disguised as a taxi.

4 A slug catcher is a piece of static equipment in the form of a vessel or piping network. It contains sufficient buffer volume to handle the largest expected slug from the oil and gas pipeline systems or flowlines.

5 An extrapolation is a statement of what is expected to happen based only on past observations (Clark, 2007, p. 196). A projection predicts a range of likely futures based on the assumption that the forces that have operated in the past will change (p. 200).

3

The Globalization of Threats

Threat has obtained a globalized status. There is not a place in the world where a terrorist attack cannot occur. Although terror attacks in a region can reach unbelievable proportions (Afghanistan, Iraq, Pakistan, etc.) with an incredibly high number of casualties, in an industrial or corporate security context, a single loss is perceived as an unacceptable incident.

3.1 A NEW TREND IN THE NATURE OF THREAT

There is a new trend regarding the nature of threat. In the recent past, one considered threats as individuals who willingly wanted to harm the facility, or harm the people working in the facility. I think we have to alter that definition if we want to stick to the way our societies are evolving. We have seen recently a number of random attacks on people, indiscriminately chosen and murdered for reasons that often belong only to the brains of the assailant. Successful terror stabbing attacks on bridges in London, in churches in Nice and elsewhere show that the threat to one's employees is on the rise, not because they are one's employees, but simply because they might be at the wrong place, at the wrong time. Does this impact our job as a security manager? Although you cannot provide 24/7 protection to your employees, their demise, murder, abduction or beating will have an impact on the reputation of the organization and the feeling of safety in the enterprise and, although it seems utterly unfair, the management will probably hold you responsible for the attack. How can we approach this issue? I see two ways of doing that. The first one would be to enlarge/increase the area of physical surveillance of your facility. If you protect offices in town, increase the surveillance area at the periphery of the walls. Use CCTV to monitor the perimeter, check the opposite sidewalks, check the stationed cars and so on. Augment the physical area surveillance and have intervention plans in case of suspicious behaviors. It seems simple, but it is not. What if the security officer on duty remarks a car with three individuals parking regularly close to the main entrance of the facility. There is probably no law that prevents someone from parking on the other side of the road. Yet, this is inacceptable situation. What should you do? Your action plan in such a situation will depend on the location of your facility, on whether the police can be considered as a partner or not, what the legislation of the country says and many other factors that make the choice of responses a complex issue. Simply taking pictures of the car and its occupants will demonstrate that you have identified them as a reconnaissance unit. Or you might want to keep observing them and try to get the faces of as many reconnaissance agents as possible. As you can see, such a situation is difficult to manage and should be brought to the attention of the CEO as soon as it is detected. Such a situation should involve quickly government agencies that have the means and the intelligence that you normally do not possess.

To complement the action plan that may become the main occupation of the security department, you might want to create an awareness program. It is now perfectly acceptable to organize awareness sessions for personnel deployed or traveling abroad in unknown countries. The do's and don'ts, the prudence and caution and a few emergency conducts and telephone numbers to call in case of doubts, but awareness programs can be created for a facility, a headquarter or any other entity.

I believe that generic security awareness sessions should complement the traditional inception or welcome speech to new employees. It has often been objected that talking about threats to new employees would have a bad impact of their appreciation of the safety within the organization, but I believed that the way the message is carried out is crucial. This difficult talk should be the prerogative of the security manager themselves, and if well done, it rather creates a feeling of trust and solidarity rather than defiance. Also, when a new threat appears, like the vehicle-ramming attack in Nice[1] causing the death of a large number of indiscriminate and innocent people, it would be good to do some kind of awareness for employees – places to avoid, things to look for before entering a pedestrian area, how to observe the traffic, how to think about escape routes and so on. This would benefit the employee and their family at the same time. Let me tell you an anecdote. In 1984, aged 27, I passed the selection to be trained as an agent of the service action of the DGSE. I perfectly remember that the first transparent of the first session about security to be projected on the wall contained a simple sentence that stayed with me for the rest of my life. It said: *Security is a state of mind, a way of life, a sixth sense.*

Why not try to help our employees acquire this mindset? Nothing bad could come out of that. Of course, to provide awareness sessions approved by the management might prove a more difficult matter than anticipated. You need to know that. All seasoned security managers went through it, and many gave up on instructing their fellow employees, unable to commit too much time on these uphill battles.

Anyway, what we must try to avoid is this bad habit of favoring some threats to the detriment of others. The classical example is: In our facility, we are fearing terrorists, and exclude petty criminals, vandals, saboteurs, industrial spies from awareness sessions. It is never a good policy as it gives the employee the feeling that the terrorist attack is imminent (otherwise why discard the other threats?). We must avoid pointing at too specific a threat, because it sends the wrong message and the management will never accept a set of sessions that could scare the employees. It can be a better idea to mention all the threats starting with the high probability-low impact one (theft, bribes, cheating with badges, tailgating, etc.) and grow casually toward sabotage, industrial espionage and terrorism. Your tone, your approach and your empathy with the employee will make your speech appreciated.

If you want to create awareness session, it is because the security situation requires it. Therefore, the message must be delivered as softly as possible, with a lot of pedagogy and sensitivity. Awareness is meant to make employees aware, not send them into a panic frenzy and initiate a wave of dismissals. I have seen once, while I was preparing an evacuation plan in South Korea, that my working on this plan created more anxiety than reassurance amongst the employees. I must say that this happened in Seoul – which is not located very far from the 38th parallel[2] and that the North Koreans had been behaving very naughtily for some time and that the organization thought that it might be a good idea to have a plan, just in case. It was a sound precaution, but fortunately and to my knowledge, the organization is still in the banking sector in Seoul, and employees are still enjoying the very pleasant Korean lifestyle, until the next crisis…

111

The emergence of lone wolf attacks or attacks by psychologically disturbed people against civilian population is definitely a new trend in a Europe harboring increasing exogenous populations from Africa. Are these new trends here to stay? Are they of particular concern to the security practitioner? If security awareness for employees seems the correct response to an increasingly dangerous and multiform workplace violence, it runs the risk of being stopped by the top management of the organization in order to not discriminate part of the workforce. What tools do we have as security practitioners to fight this problem? How can we protect without stigmatizing?

Last, the issue of the 5th column in our offices and workshops will be discussed. The recent attack in Paris by an IT specialist, recently converted to Islam, working for the government, habilitated secret defense, who murdered four of his fellow employees while at work poses an important question, and we will try to answer it with reasonableness.

3.2 THE GLOBALIZATION OF THREATS: FROM THE GLOBAL TO THE LOCAL THREAT

In May 2020, I was invited to present a course at the *Military Academy of St-Cyr Coëtquidan* for their War Studies department. I had contacted this venerable institution, created by Napoleon on the same year as West Point Academy and the Royal Military College of Sandhurst, to propose a course on international security. I contacted Prof. GG on the phone and discussed my syllabus. Prof GG was clear that, because of COVID-19, the course, which was aimed at international cadets and delivered in English, might be cancelled, as many military schools were still uncertain about reopening in September 2020 due to the pandemic.

I was not to miss out such an opportunity to reflect on a topic that was at the core of my intellectual interests and that I find somewhat theoretically underdeveloped. I was given the chance to establish a link between international security between states, and the practical aspects of industrial or critical infrastructure security. I could spend time thinking about the link between politics, balance of power, critical infrastructure and the practical protection of their offspring's, pipelines, sea cables, nuclear and industrial facilities, oil and gas facilities, desalination plants, corporate headquarters, all industrial assets security practitioners are normally tasked to protect.

But before I started thinking about the syllabus, I decided to take a week to let the whole thing sink, leave my subconscious do the research work and put all that in order. This interesting request coming from the War studies of the top French military establishment was worth some thought. It is interesting to note that the Head of the War Studies is an academic, not a former officer, with probably a very limited knowledge of industrial security.

What surprised me is that Prof. GG expressed more interest in industrial security, critical infrastructure than in international security. He saw a link between what the cadets wanted to learn about and thought that the international relations (IR) approach to security would be less interesting than an industrial – practical, hands-on approach. It was the first time I was asked by an academic institution to prepare a course on the practical aspects of security, and I was, at first, uncomfortable. But I found the challenge exciting. Wearing the double cap of an academic and of a practitioner, I had the possibility to consider security from the global – the traditional field of the academic and the analyst, to the local, the area of competence of the law enforcement people and other security practitioners. With reflection, it appeared quite a brilliant idea to present a chain of logic between the security of states and the security of their critical assets, since the later could become a target as a consequence of the choices of the former. Furthermore, cadets would probably have to deal with some aspects of security in their career, from external military operations to peacekeeping, protection of industrial assets abroad – pipelines, factories, oil and gas production sites – and for many of them – industrial security as a second career. I could see a parallel in the career of these young men and the competences necessary to be a good officer, and later, to be a good security practitioner and manager. I also came to the conclusion that, even in the course of their military career, they would possibly be tasked with protecting critical infrastructure assets, such as pipelines, subsea cables, industrial areas, oil and gas facilities and so on. I remembered that when I was working in the oil and gas industry, I had had the occasion to visit a major oil extraction site in Hassi Messaoud, Algeria, and had observed that the site was protected by units of the Algerian army and special forces. Later, again in Algeria, I worked on a project in a helicopter base, and we were protected again by units of the army. The missions of the military can be so varied...Understanding how industrial security works, how security risk assessments are constructed and he different risk strategies would give them a good understanding of security and might improve their understanding of the principles of protection of industrial sites.

But as soon as I started putting the course together, I became conscious that it was a mistake to consider the threat from the global image down to the job of the security manager on an industrial site or working on part of the critical infrastructure. It supposed that there were major issues (political and security issues) decided upon at international level that cascaded down to the level of the man of the field. But this is not always the case. Sometimes, a security issue on the field, left in the hands of a site security manager, can take such proportions that they become international issues. Security is fluid and permeates all layers of social material from top to the bottom, but also from the bottom to the top. This is why, before I could clearly see the plan of this course, I renamed it: *Security: from the Global to the Local…and Back!*

All these aspects will be covered in Chapter 3 in more details.

3.3 SECURITY AND NON-SECURITY THREATS

The first thing the security practitioner learns is to differentiate between what is a security threat and what is not. A security threat is a threat that is man-made in origin. A theft is a security threat, a bomb attack is a security threat, a drive-by shooting, a VBIED or a placed IED, the sabotage of equipment and/or systems, the kidnapping of key people, the assassination of innocent people, all these are security threats because they result from a human decision.

Anything that happens by accident and without human interference is a hazard. This is why it is important to refute the use of the word hazard when we talk about security (most security risk assessment methods still use the word hazard and I think they should not).

The only undesired event that can belong to both security and non-security event is fire. If it is human triggered, then it is *arson* and it is a security incident. If it happens by negligence or lack of surveillance or it simply happens, then it is a *hazard* and should not be listed in our security threats.

In simple words, only firemen will tell us whether the fire was started by a person or if it resulted from an electrical accident or anything of the sort. In itself, it is neither until the fire specialist has spoken.

This is quite simple, and must be kept in mind by the practitioner looking to establish its list of security incidents.

3.4 GLOBAL THREATS: WHAT DOES THIS MEAN?

Global security threats are the threats that occur in the struggle for survival of the 193 member states of the United Nations assembly that populate the globe. If Realist thinkers are to be believed, the ultimate goal of a nation is survival. This is fine for the existing ones, but others, who feel like nations, do not have a state and want to have one. The Kurds, the Palestinians, several Russian enclaves are the famous among many. Poles were deprived of a state several times in their history. When South Africa became the Rainbow Nation in 1994, some Afrikaners dreamt of creating *Oranja*, an Afrikaner enclave within the new country. Of course, this dream could not be tolerated by the ANC, and was not really shared by most South Africans tired and weary of so many years of guerrilla, danger and tarnished reputation. Most were ready to let go and Mandela benefitted from this weariness and did not abuse it. The homelands disappeared, the dreams of a new Trekker staat vanished in the wave of optimism that swiped the Rainbow Nation and the old Republic became one single country where many ethnic groups had to make do, with a relative success. At that level, security threats do exist, but they are usually dealt with by state security (army, secret police, intelligence, etc.).

The security practitioner is rarely involved in this type of national security (sometimes an advisor for local polices, or intelligence services, but these are very specific situations that we will not discuss in this book). The security professional does not work for the state, but for the industry. The difference becomes blurred, particularly when the security practitioner works in critical national infrastructure entities. He then works for companies, often government owned (at least partly and mostly in Europe) who provide services for the well-being of a population. But although the company may be statal, the security professional is on the payroll of that specific private entity and usually reports to a member of the board of this company or to the board themselves.

The means are also different. The security practitioner is often very restricted in the tools he can use to improve the security posture of a site, factory, building. Private companies must generate profits and security is often (always?) perceived as a cost center and closes the list of beneficiaries of the annual budget. Although, we security people are adamant that security is the ultimate enabler, spoiled CEOs and presidents often refuse to acknowledge it – usually dismissing the reality of the risk since they have been in the industry for a long time and never had to face single attack from anywhere, and so on – all arguments difficult to counter, by definition... There are as many situations as there are companies and security departments, but it is important to understand that the horizon of the professional is limited to the site he has to protect and the latitude offered by the board of directors (unless of course industrial security is organized at

115

ministry level and/or standards have to be applied, mainly in major companies or in a very limited number of countries).

3.5 LOCAL THREATS

Many practitioners I know, often because in our industry time is of the essence, take local threats as granted. A number of accepted, standardized threats are integrated in their security risk assessment and will stay there – in their template – for a very long time. Only a resounding successful attack with a new modus operandi will succeed in inflating the list of accepted threats (like drones, the new flavor of the day, or random stabbing or hostile vehicle attacks). Taking a threat away from the list will also be a complicated exercise.

What is, alas, bad news, is that a local threat (both as-agent and as-action) is, in reality, almost impossible to disentangle from a global treat since the latter will trigger the organization and implementation of the former. What we tend to call disparagingly the local threat is, most of the time, the end result of a political decision taken at a global level, by someone – or a group of someones – somewhere who, for political gain, decides to target the facility among perhaps other targets, placed under your protection, with the goal to harm, directly or indirectly, the company and what it represents. This means that you must be very aware of what your company represents, in terms of image, reputation and power and check what happens at the global level that could impact the security situation and become aware of related signs.

The choice of your facility as a target is not a random choice but a well-planned and well thought selection process. Someone, or a group of "someones" will decide that attacking your facility will serve best their purpose and have a resounding shock effect that will serve the cause. Your job is to guess about who these someones could be and why they would find the facility you protect attractive. What the company represents is therefore key. You know about that. Remember. When you accepted the job offer, it is because you had a good idea of what it would mean to work for this company. What were the reasons: Old company with international outreach? Company working in sharp sectors (army, defense, military manufacturing industry)? What seduced you in the first place is probably what attracted the people who intend to make your life as a security manager a misery. Think back and take notes about the pros and cons of the firm. The list of pros would probably be close to the list of reasons why

116

someone wants to attack it, or kill people who work for it. After all, killing an employee of Haliburton or any other majors when they get back home at night is not such a difficult task and will have a resonance almost as big as attacking a facility, but with much better chances of success! Now, you must come to the second question about the target selection. You have studied the *why*: because it represents American, western, Australian interests, because it will paralyze the company for a while, because it will tarnish the reputation of an enemy of a specific 'God', because it will highlight the weakness of the government, the list is endless, and it is important that you establish a list of 20 reasons why you could be targeted by adversaries. Why 20? I borrow this idea from Dobbins and Pettman's fantastic book: *What Self-Made Millionaires Really Think, Know and Do.*[3] These authors propose a number of techniques to improve your creativity and the 20-proposition principle is one of them. What do Dobbins and Pettman say about it? "Of all the techniques for solving problems (…) the 20-ideas method is probably the most powerful and the most widely used. The key to using this method is forcing yourself to come up with 20 ideas. Managers often find that ideas 17 to 20 are the best. This method can be used alone or in groups and unfolds as follows:

1. Write down the problem, challenge, opportunity.
2. Generate 20 possible answers. Force yourself to go the distance and create twenty solutions. It is usually the last few ideas who are the best ones.
3. Select the appropriate answer and take immediate action" (Dobbins & Pettman 2006: 18)

The item 2 is the most important point. The authors assert that usually the last items of the list are the best and the most important, because they have requested a renewed effort of imagination after all the simple things have been exhausted. I have total faith in D&P recommendations and had often resorted to their advices and guidelines when I worked in corporate security.

3.6 IDENTIFYING POTENTIAL ADVERSARIES

Once you have thought about the reasons why you could become a target, the second reflection flows from the first. The identification of potential adversaries, or threat agents, is a logical consequence of the previous exercise. Who could have an interest in harming the organization, its employees or its reputation (people, property and information)? Particularly if you protect a company deployed abroad, look back for similar organizations, positioned in comparable surroundings, because the cultural aspect of things is crucial. The environment will show you what is acceptable adversarial practice in the region and what to expect. Events are always part of a "basket of acceptable behaviors" linked to the values shared by the adversarial group. A group of bearded militants in the mountains of Algeria will not choose the same techniques as a South American guerrilla unit, or vegan activists in Germany. If you work in South America, google "security incidents in South America". If you work in the Middle East, do the same. Try to establish a scale of plausibility, although be conscious of how vague this can be. Your company may not be the real objective of the adversaries. These adversaries may want to discredit the government by showing its incapacity to protect foreigners on their soil. In that example, it is the composition of your workforce that matters. The underpinning assumption to this remark is that you should be aware of what is happening politically in the region where you have been deployed. You must know who's who in your environment. What alliances do exist between political groups in your surroundings, what is their relation with the government in place, how the government deals with irredentism and minorities, if these issues are relevant. You might not like it – you are a man of action, not an analyst – but it is crucial that you understand the world into which you and your employees are evolving. The danger is not far away. If there is danger, it will strike at close quarters and the analyses sent weekly from your headquarters will not help you face the crisis.

3.6.1 Becoming the Amateur Analyst

It will take time, you need to read books, devour newspapers, discuss cautiously with selected people, befriend specialists at local level, attend the OSAC meetings if such things exist where you have been deployed, exploit any opportunity ASIS has to offer and so on. Nothing that happens in your area of activity, incidents, politics, petty crime should escape your scrutiny. Does this mean that you must consider taking a degree in IR? Not necessarily, although you would probably not regret it. But what is absolutely necessary is that, at all times, you think in terms of threat from the global to the local and back. Your local threat obeys orders coming from a higher layer, except for minor misdeeds like vandalism, and theft, of course. If you protect a factory somewhere in the Sahel, sub-Saharan politics should have no secret for you. Follow what happens in the capital cities, check declarations, international conferences, read the local newspaper every morning, breath local, breath regional, breath global.

You do not need a degree to see how the situation is evolving in Mali, Niger, Nigeria. You just need to show some interest! Understand who's who around there. You will not be a wholesome security professional if you do not embrace the big picture. It is a bit painful at the beginning, but crucial to a suitable evaluation of the threat. Read the local newspapers between the lines. For 17 years, I lived in a country where journalists received awards and accolades from the government in black tie (or white thobe) events, that should say a lot of about their impartiality and objectiveness, and yet I was still able to understand regional and local politics with acute fairness by reading state-sponsored journalism. Believe it or not, you can still have fairly accurate idea of what happens in terms of political tensions by reading a totally biased and subordinate newspaper!

3.7 TERRORIST ATTACK CLAIMS: REALITY OR PROPAGANDA TOOL? THE LONE WOLF SYNDROME AND THE ENDORSEMENT OF INDIVIDUAL ACTS BY GLOBAL NETWORKS OF TERROR

A question that really challenges the understanding of the threat and its impact on our day-to-day activities is whether the attacks claimed by international terrorist organizations have been organized and monitored by them or whether they just use the acts of individuals murderers to make themselves look more important than they really are.

An interesting interview of Monica Duffy Toft,[4] a professor of international politics at Tufts university published in Conversation, analyzes the attitude of Daesh and the way it claims responsibility for terror attacks. It first establishes that Daesh claims responsibility in one of two ways: either through its own News Agency, called *Amaq* (this news agency reports through an encrypted app and is aimed at supporters, analysts and the media), or through its official information channel, the Nashir Media Foundation, considered as the direct voice of Daesh leadership. The purpose of these limited number of outlets claiming responsibility is to prevent rival organizations from falsely claiming responsibility on Daesh's behalf.

A claim of responsibility is usually the result of two things: either an attack deliberately planned and executed by members, soldiers, agents of the organization, something less easy now that international government agencies control and cooperation are in place, and those that they consider inspired by their propaganda.

According to Thomas Jocelyn[5] Long War journals, Deash calls members of the group *soldiers of the Caliphate,* a term they also use for Lone Wolves terrorists. According to Jocelyn, one can infer that when an attack has been planned by a terrorist organization (the Islamic state but also other groups or networks), the claim tends to mention specifics about the perpetrators and is usually released within the next 24 hours. When no personal details are provided about the perpetrator, there is a strong probability that the terror network had no knowledge of the planned attack. More surprising is the result of a research carried out by two terrorism experts Justin Conrad and Max Abrahams, asserting that only one in seven terror attacks are claimed by the terrorist group responsible. The authors remark that terrorist groups are mainly composed of two kinds of agents: One is rational leaders driven by strategic political objectives, the other, the operational foot soldiers, a mix of rational and irrational agents. The result of this is that, terror groups will claim responsibility only when they see a political benefit in the action, that is, when it serves their political purpose. When they understand that a terror act – organized by their network or not – might be detrimental to their objectives, they will not claim responsibility. This explains why some terrorist acts are never claimed by any terror organization (one might think about attacks in Kabul or in Pakistan tribal areas, where the victims are Muslims and so numerous that the return on investment would probably be detrimental to the cause.

The most important conclusion of Monica Toft's interview is the acknowledgment that groups representing hyper-violent operators do tend to act rationally and strategically. That means their actions and interests can be judged, patterned and predicted. In simple words, a solid analysis of the security environment means that our security practitioner should be able, provided they give sufficient thought to it, to contemplate the possible evolutions of the context and how it would be ripe for a terror attack or any other action against the protected target.

3.7.1 Emerging Threats, a New Type of Murderers

Do random knife attacks, vehicle ramming in innocent crowds, the blossoming of drones and so on show the decline of a globalized, organized threat against the West (Al-Qaeda/Daesh), or is it simply one of the cheapest but still effective tactics from an imaginative tool box?

Although the number of terrorist attacks seems to abate, one can only observe the change in the nature of these attacks. As I already mentioned in this book earlier, this is not really good news for the security practitioner, because the organized crimes, that could be foiled or heard about by government agencies and therefore that could have ended in a warning report by the security manager, are now probably a thing of the past.

The effectiveness of the anti-terror struggle shows the other side of the coin. I am thinking again about the word of warning of Grabo, that acts committed in very small committee, in the greatest secrecy by a very limited of number of persons, is almost impossible to foil. When I started my career as security director in a multinational company in the Gulf, at the beginning of the years 2000, we were in regular liaison with the local government agencies, which were well organized and managed very well to prevent attacks and uncover infiltrated network of extremists. Our information, as security director, was coming straight from the local or regional intelligence services that informed us as a matter of courtesy, and to make us sensitive to the existence of these networks in our work environment. The information was coming from the top, and this was quite reassuring. It seems that these days are now behind us and we are more lonesome than ever to observe and anticipate the threat developing in our immediate environment.

This, of course, does not alter the fact that even when information was cascading on us, we were still very attentive to what was happening in our organization. But the fact that many terrorist attacks are now the work of individuals – the famous lone wolves' pattern – makes our job more demanding. Since we need to observe and monitor the workforce, be aware of the possibility of having some of our guard force approached by external players, like members of their family, not a new phenomenon, but one that should be at the center of our reflection, since the cascading info from governments agencies might become less significant, without giving the feeling of spying or on employees or discriminating certain profiles over others. Not a comfortable situation, but we have to get used to it since I believe that it is the trend for the next few years ahead of us.

The question of the security practitioner, particularly if they operate in an industrial or corporate context, is why are these tactics privileged and what will be the impact on our security program?

3.8 WHY ARE THESE TACTICS CHOSEN?

Are these more individualistic tactics a consequence of the progress of the counter-terrorism agencies of the western world? I would like to think so. Security transcends borders, and I do believe that the civilizational and democratic values do mean something. A proof? The commitment of Britain to all the counter-terrorism agreements pre-Brexit that have been maintained. In spite of the sometimes acrimonious and ruthless negotiations that preceded their departure from the Union, Britain and their main security partners (France, Germany) never questioned their mutual commitment to the fight against terrorism.

3.9 THE EXAMPLE OF TERRORISM IN THE EUROPEAN UNION: FACTS AND FIGURES

Out of sheer curiosity, I had a look at the website of the European parliament to see what is the reality of terrorism in the European Union (EU). The following figures have been published on the European parliament website on 20 August 2021, and some of these are amazing and challenge the official communications by European leaders to their constituents and the perception of insecurity by the populations.

According to the 2021 Europol report on the Terrorism situation in the EU,[6] there were 57 terrorist attempts in the EU in 2020 (that includes successful, failed and foiled attempts), compared to 55 in 2019. Of those, 10 were jihadist terrorist attacks in Austria, France and Germany.

Figure 3.1 reflects the terrorist trends of the last seven years and confirms that there was a peak of attacks in 2017 and that it has been decreasing since.

Several facts do not match our intuitive feeling when it comes to terrorism. I guess we cannot really envisage that the EU would be distorting figures to satisfy political agendas, so let us consider these figures and let us try to analyze them.

Although they represent only a sixth of all attacks in the EU, jihadi terrorists were responsible for more than half of the deaths (12) and nearly all injuries (47). The total number of fatalities and injuries in the EU doubled from ten deaths and 27 injuries in 2019 to 21 deaths and 54 injuries in 2020. A total of 14 ethno-nationalist and separatist terrorist attacks took

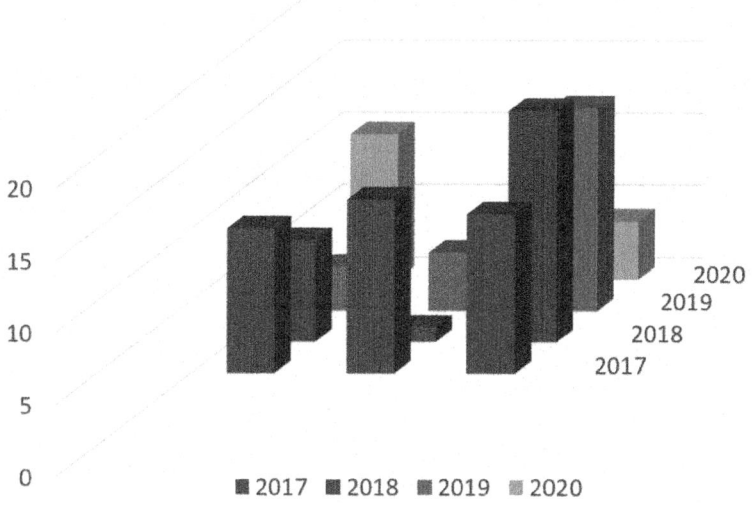

To make the reading of this information easier, I include the figures:

	2014	2015	2016	2017	2018	2019	2020
Arrests	395	687	718	705	511	436	254
Deaths	4	150	135	62	13	10	12
Attacks*	2	17	13	33	24	21	10

*Please note that the number of attacks include completed, foiled and failed attacks.

Figure 3.1   Religiously inspired terrorism in the EU

Source: Europol.

place in France and Spain, while 24 attacks were carried out by left-wing or anarchist terrorist organizations or individuals, all in Italy. In most cases, these attacks targeted private and public property such as financial institutions and government buildings.

In 2020, three EU countries – Germany, Belgium and France – experienced four terrorist attempts motivated by right-wing extremism. Only one of them, however, was completed.

3.10 FIGURES DIFFICULT TO CONFIRM

Second surprise: While I thought that our services had managed to foil a high number of terrorist plots, the figures announced by Europol do not seem to match the announcements of politicians in several European countries. For example, the French minister of interior at the time, Christophe Castaner, claimed that between 2013 and 2019, 59 terrorist attacks had been foiled by his services.[7] Of course, these figures do not seem to match the figures provided by Europol, hence my legitimate question. Are figures manipulated?

For Europol, Jihadist terrorism remains the greatest threat to the EU. In 2020, the number of completed jihadist terrorist attacks was more than double that of foiled plots (Figure 3.2).

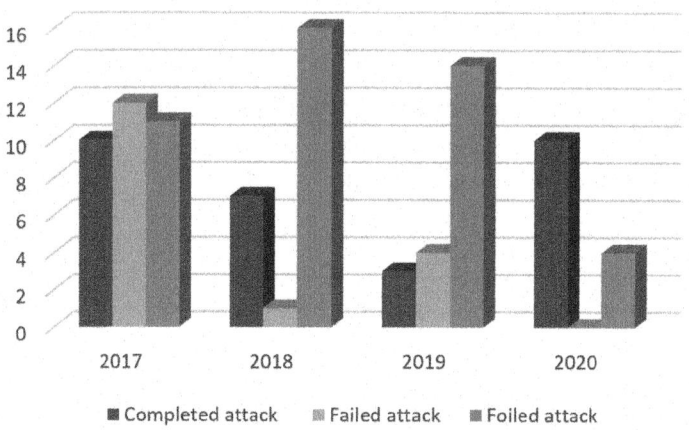

	2017	2018	2019	2020
Completed attack	10	7	3	10
Failed plot	12	1	4	0
Foiled plot	11	16	14	4
Total	33	24	21	14

Figure 3.2 Number of completed, failed and foiled jihadist terror attacks in the EU (2017–2020)

Source: Europol 2021.

3.11 CONFIRMATION OF THE LONE WOLF TREND

According to Europol,

> lone actors were behind all of the jihadist attacks, with four of the ten successful attacks carried out by EU citizens (what we call the bi-nationals). Some of the lone actors displayed a combination of extreme ideologies and mental health issues, with social isolation and increased stress as a result of the pandemic suspected to have played a role in some cases.
>
> *Europol*

This is an interesting remark. Indeed, the French government, and I guess of its European counterparts act the same, classifies most lone wolf attacks as non-terrorist attacks. Lone wolves end up being classified as suffering from psychiatric troubles and their acts are not considered as terrorist acts. A fresh example? Yesterday (11 May 2022), at the gate of a Catholic school in Marseille, a man – a French military doctor – coming to fetch his children, was stabbed ten times in the thorax and in the neck, by a Frenchman, Mohamed L. The attacker confided to the police that he had attacked "in the name of God" in order to fight "the devil". It seems to me that all the boxes of the lone wolf terrorist attacks are ticked? Wrong answer! For the police and the ministry, the terrorist motivation is not appropriate. Of course, I forgot to mention that the news bulletins forgot to indicate that the attack occurred in front of a Catholic school. Obviously, if you classify these kind of attacks as acts of madness committed by unbalanced people, the statistics have great chances to be distorted.

Old fashioned people like me find these manipulations unacceptable. Their authors showed no sign of madness when planning their attack, very often with the help of friends and family. This irresponsibility of the lone wolves' terrorists rather emphasizes the incapacity of the European justice system to face a political reality that does not match their ideology.

Anyway, this is not the topic of this book here, but I thought an American audience might be interested in learning about the difficulty for the liberal post-religious European system to deal with a well-organized enemy, which the European intelligentsia refuses to name. As the philosopher Albert Camus once wrote, ' "To name things wrongly is to add to the misfortune of the world". It seems that the European justice battles to understand that some of the terrorists are our enemies and should be considered as such. I thought that since 9/11, this principle was established.

125

Twenty years later, it is still far from being accepted by the European elites.

Anyway, what are the consequences for our security processionals? The fact that we fight an enemy and that we cannot justify measures to fight it and cannot organize awareness sessions to warn fellow employees in the organization.

I believe that this is the way things are evolving and this growing Woke culture will probably make this situation worse for us.

3.12 A SIGNIFICANT DROP IN TERRORIST ARRESTS

Another figure surprised me. The number of terrorists arrested in 2020 was lower than the number of arrests carried out in 2019. Here are the figures:

A total of 449 arrests on suspicion of terrorist offences were reported to Europol in 2020. This number was significantly lower than in 2019 (1,004). It is unclear whether this drop is due to reduced terrorist activity or is a result of diminished operational capacities of law enforcement due to the Covid-19 pandemic.

Europol

3.12.1 Increased Use of Simple Weaponry

The writers of the Europol report an interesting fact.

The lockdowns related to the pandemic and the closure of public spaces to mass gathering, such as shopping centers, churches and stadiums, seem to have led to a decrease in the use of explosives in terrorist attacks. In 2020, terrorists mainly resorted to stabbing, vehicle ramming and arson. Firearms were only used in the right-wing terrorist attack in Hanau, Germany, in February and the jihadist attack in Vienna in November.

Europol

This confirms my analysis of the situation but fails to explain underpinning assumptions regarding lone wolve attacks. Mainly that they come from the same portion of the population, that they are politically motivated under the guise of religion, and that the actors – the unbalanced perpetrators – almost never acted alone.

3.13 ONLINE RADICALIZATION: AN INCREASING THREAT

Another interesting part of this report concerns what is called the online radicalization, or how a disoriented youth is seduced by the Jihadist propaganda and how this propaganda contributes to the creation of individual modes of action.

> With the increased use of the internet during the pandemic, online communities played an important role in the dissemination of violent extremism. Following efforts by messaging apps, such as Telegram, to block terrorist groups, jihadist propaganda became more dispersed across multiple, often smaller online platforms, and right-wing extremists, particularly young people, increasingly used video games and gaming platforms to propagate their ideology.
>
> *Europol*

I will not even comment on the right-wing extremist dangers, which seems to be a fantasy shared by all and sundry in the leading circles of the EU.

A comparison of the figures of right-wing attacks measured against Jihadist attacks would have been interesting. As one can guess, it appears nowhere in this report. But this illusory equilibrium is incorporated in all assertions, trying to give the feeling that there is an equal danger coming from the right and from the left, from the Christian extremists and the Muslim extremists. The following is archetypal:

> Both jihadi and right-wing extremists tried to exploit Covid-19 for propaganda purposes, while left-wing and anarchist extremists incorporated criticism of government measures to combat the pandemic into their narratives.
>
> *Europol*

There are of course some truths in this comment, but the right-wing conspiracists that incorporated criticism of government measures did not lead to mass murder and individual assassinations. At best to some demonstrations of the Yellow Vest type.

This is a difference that Europol if it had not been a simple reflection of the EU dominant ideology of human rights and equality should have emphasized.

This leads me to the last item of this chapter, the endogenous threat.

3.14 THE ENDOGENOUS THREAT

We are not in the days of the Second World war where individuals of enemy nations could be parked in camp until the end of the war. Europe has turned its back to any action of this type, promoting human rights, open borders and a welcome of all immigration from developing countries, legal or illegal.

This generous attitude, diametrically opposed to the American attitude of Guantanamo, has of course consequences for the security practitioner. Legal and illegal immigrants are potential booty for organized Jihadist organizations on the European soil, and constitute an imminent danger for our society. Let me be clear, I am not saying that exogenous immigration is a constant threat. I am just saying that these uncontrolled immigration fluxes are a very practical way to infiltrate jihadists in our countries. There has been ample proof that several jihadists who participated in attacks in Europe had reached the countries via clandestine immigration networks.

That poses to our security practitioner a double problem. If you are tasked to evaluate the threat in a multinational company where a number of employees are issued from a certain sector of the population from where most attacks emanate, you cannot discriminate them overtly. And to be honest, it would be unfair to do so. Most of them have been happy to find a job and will show loyalty to the organization.

The problem is that you need to solve a problem that you cannot name.

If you are the director of security in a multinational company, particularly if you work in the Middle East, this problem will be acute and will be permanently at the back of your head. But in that case, you will find some support. While I was recruiting a guard force for a company installed in one of the Gulf sheikhdoms, I was asked not to recruit people from a specific nationality or origin, although I was very welcome to interview them. In that case, I received my orders from the top management and there was no ambiguity about where the danger could originate from. This was somehow comfortable, and in spite of that, we still had clandestine groups infiltrated in the workforce, who passed the recruitment interviews, and started recruiting potential accomplices and saboteurs, almost immediately after they joined the company. Fortunately, we managed to identify them successfully and the government agencies of the Sheikhdom did the rest. In that very case, I had the support of the management, and of the government agencies of two sheikhdoms, and that made the difference (we were in the immediate post-9/11 period). For those living under the diktats of human rights and equality, the situation will definitely be more difficult. Of course, all depends on your brief. And of the security environment. What I mean here is that threat is always target centric. It is the nature of your organization that will attract specific threat agents. This portion of the chapter might be totally irrelevant for you; but in some other circumstances, it can become your main problem and you must not bury your head in the sands.

3.15 THE FIFTH COLUMN: REALITY OR FANTASY? HOW EFFECTIVE CAN IT BE? HOW TO FIGHT IT?

The answer is simple: It can be a reality or it can be totally irrelevant to your situation.

The context, the environment rule. Depending on your situation, the location of your facility, the composition of the workforce, the geopolitical environment and the concerns of the shareholders, you might face a fifth column integrated in your workforce or you may not. The important question is once you think that you have employees who might want to harm the organization, in a stealth way, what should you do?

I think I have mentioned that security awareness is out of the equation. If you realize that a portion of the workforce might belong to a network that presents some danger for the company, it is not a good idea to advertise the problem. Talking to employees about the possibility of having potential adversaries within the workforce will not help. Security awareness should be used for basic security behaviors (photocopiers, shredding documents, doors closed after work, badges and vehicle identification stickers), not to point fingers at potential adversaries – who all are fellow employees – within the organization.

The conviction that there is an internal threat is of such importance that it should be reported only to the highest authority, in private. The response to such possibility must be a top-down approach and should involve the organization's management as well as government agencies. Discretion remains the most important part of it. And do not confide with other security personnel. Remember that a real secret is a secret that one repeats only to one person at a time, and that anxiety messages travel at the speed of light.

My experience of such situation is limited but real. If a possibility of internal attack is possible, you must act swiftly and in total secrecy. Make your case solid. As few people as possible must be informed and the response plan will soon pass into the hands of official services, who may decide to act while ignoring you entirely, an unpleasant situation, I have to say.

Anyway, my advice to you is to collect information, build your case and speak only to the boss, the real boss, and take it from here. Never sweep things under the rug, possible consequences are too dramatic, and you are a professional.

NOTES

1 On the evening of 14 July 2016, a 19-ton cargo truck was deliberately driven into crowds of people celebrating Bastille Day on the Promenade des Anglais in Nice, France, resulting in the deaths of 86 people and the injury of 458 others. The driver was Mohamed Lahouaiej-Bouhlel, a Tunisian living in France.
2 Seoul is located only 35 miles from the border between the two countries.
3 Dobbins R and Pettman BO (2002) *What Self-made Millionaires Really Think, Know and Do: A Straight-talking Guide to Business Success and Personal Riches*, Capstone.
4 Downloaded from https://theconversation.com/how-does-is-claim-respons ibility-for-a-terrorist-attack-78823 on 10 May 2022.
5 Retrieved from www.fdd.org/team/thomas-joscelyn/ on 10 May 2022.
6 www.europol.europa.eu/publications-events/main-reports/european-union-terrorism-situation-and-trend-report-2021-tesat
7 Retrieved from www.lemonde.fr/societe/article/2019/10/15/58-des-59-attentats-dejoues-depuis-six-ans-l-ont-ete-grace-au-renseignement-humain_6015520_3224.html on 10 May 2022.

4

The Securitization of Threats

I am going to consider the issue of the securitization of threats, a phenomenon that explains why some threats are given priority over others, and how this securitization issue may influence the perception of menace in your organization, from the CEO down to the employee. It is important that you, the security professional in charge, be aware of the political manipulations underpinning this securitization process in order to keep cool and not let yourself be influenced by a political process that may distract you from the real danger.

4.1 NOW A BIT OF THEORY…

What do I mean by placing the threat in context? When does a security threat become a securitized threat? You might think that threats, particularly security threats, are obvious, and speak for themselves, but it is not always so. Threats, or rather our perception of threats, are often the result of a political construction, called securitization. In my demonstration, I will use a concept of international relations called securitization that we owe to Barry Buzan, Ole Waever and the Copenhagen school of international security. I would like to establish a parallel with the issue of

DOI: 10.4324/9781003091080-5

securitization, in the field of international relations a term coined by Ole Waever in 1993 and often attributed to Barry Buzan, and which has now entered common usage.

What is securitization? To make it simple, securitization is an interpretation of a process where state actors transform certain subjects into matters of such importance that they morph into security issues (e.g., migrations, global warming, pandemics, etc.), granting them a kind of political priority over more classical conceptions of security (terrorist threats, criminals, saboteurs, vandals, threats normally dealt with by industrial security, police, army and specialized units).·

Buzan and the Copenhagen school of international relations observed that topics securitized may not be the most initially threatening (for a state), but that once one, or several of these threats, had been securitized, or being granted security status, they would often benefit from disproportionate means for treatment compared to other less glamorous perils. What this reflects is that the power of suggestion of a threat carries more power than its statistical value.

Waever and Buzan speak about states behaviors, but I think the same phenomenon exists in our industry and, amazingly, for very comparable reasons. To illustrate this theory, one can of course highlight the preponderant place reserved to terrorism in most of our risk assessment methods. In the country where I operated during most of my security career and where governments have issued very strict standards of security, it would be unthinkable not to mention terrorism as the principal threat against industrial assets, although the number of attacks on critical infrastructure is today negligible.

As part of my duties as a security consultant, I visited before the pandemics a facility that manufactures military equipment for the air force and the industry. The purpose of my meeting with the security team there was to lead what we call a Severity of Impact (SOI) workshop, in other words, a study of their assets and their criticality according to a set of established criteria. When this was done, I started a discussion about adversaries, attractiveness and dangers they thought they were facing. Like everyone else in the industry, they paid lip service to the terrorist threat, while, in reality, their main concern was the theft of equipment by contractors, and this at a very small scale anyway. Before the terrorism threat was granted the limelight, this facility had been operating for years in a relatively uninhabited suburb, without even a perimeter fence, and no feeling whatsoever of being a potential target. They were producing parts for the oil and gas equipment and military airplanes; they did not extract oil, gold or uranium! And yet, the budget they had at their disposal to protect their facility would be based on a risk assessment that puts the terrorist threat at the apex of the menaces.

To stay in line with our securitization theory, it is clear that the terrorist threat has reached securitization status and this is endorsed by all security departments for a single reason. It is almost the only way to secure funds to improve the security posture of a facility. Is this a bad thing? Not necessarily.

One can see that if the risk assessment said the main risk at your facility are work incidents and the second issue is the theft of tools, the C-suite of the company would refuse any improvement in the security posture of the plant.

It is generally said that, to be accepted, securitization should be accepted by the audience, irrespective of the reality – something anyway difficult to ascertain – of the threat. This audience can be quite varied in the security industry. I believe that there are, in fact, four actors to be considered.

4.2 THE FOUR MAJOR ACTORS

4.2.1 Policymakers

The securitization almost systematically needs to be supported by some sort of authority. The recent examples of issues like migration threatening Europe, and the coronavirus pandemic, illustrate that things happen when authorities decide things should happen. These authorities normally endorse an already existing situation, but their action is crucial in the process. Normally, authorities are not long in understanding how securitizing an issue will serve their political objectives. They are actually quite good at it and to be honest will securitize an issue only if they can find a benefit for them. In March 2020, while I was still working in one of the Gulf sheikhdoms, I was having my morning coffee in a coffee shop next to the office, I had a quick look at the local newspaper – as I do most mornings, particularly during the six nations Rugby tournament – and I could spot a few very obvious examples of how securitization serves political agenda (the public) as, and how it can be disseminated to an audience.

Here is the first snippet spotted on the newspaper:

Citizens of this Gulf Sunni monarchy could be punished for travelling to terror-exporting countries such as Iran under a new parliamentary proposal. I learned in this article that Iran do not stamp passports of pilgrims coming from Sunni countries. The article underlined the fact that entry to Iran without having the passport stamped was a clear threat to National Security... (dated 9th March 2020). It also stipulated that the new Iranian-exported terrorism through the spread to Covid-19 to the Sheikhdom had strongly damaged its economy.

Gulf News 9th March 2020

The second snippet reported that Saudi Arabia was now preventing entry and exit from the Qatif governorate to avert an outbreak of the coronavirus. 11 people from Qatif – Qatif being the eastern province capital of dissent in the kingdom, a place judged as very perilous for the regime, with aggressive Shia imams and population, had been diagnosed with the virus...

Gulf News 9th March 2020

But the best is still to come: Riyadh announced other precautionary measures, including suspending all educational and Koranic activities in Mosques in the country, because of the proximity of the faithful in a closed environment. To say the least, when governments take the lead in the securitization of a threat, it has immediately a normative effect.

Even on the domestic front, COVID-19 can play a role. I spotted a very small snippet mentioning that the local government had closed a few shisha coffee shops for fear of the virus. The government has had issues with illegal shisha coffee shops for a long time and has been trying to ban them from operating (meeting places for sedition?) on numerous occasions with little success. As soon as they close, they reopen nearby. These are, of course, small examples taken at random in one newspaper, on any day, in a very small country, but it shows how the securitization of threats – in our example the COVID-19 – can justify many things. And I am sure a study of the securitization of the COVID-19, migration, planet survival and gender equality would yield the very same results if we spent enough time studying the why and how. Nobody in the government seriously believes that closing shisha coffees will stop the virus from spreading, and the authorities have known for a very long time that Iranians authorities did not stamp Bahraini pilgrims' passports to avoid them administrative harassment on their return. As always, the question a security practitioner should ask himself when facing issues being securitized by authorities is simple. Why? And more importantly why now? And his or her job, is really to consider the question: if we take out the political agenda behind the securitization of a threat, what is left of its reality?

134

4.2.2 Bureaucratic Actors

The system that stems from the policymaker's decisions needs to be applied and controlled. When a topic is securitized, it needs to be supported by a set of administrative standards, directives or official procedures. Without this bureaucratic follow-up, securitization cannot be implemented and therefore cannot be financed. Finance is at the core of the process. Once a topic has been securitized (terrorism, climate change, drones, coronavirus, gender equality, etc.), it is crucial to give it an official appearance and structure (department, commission, authority, whatever), and this for a number of reasons: First, to confirm the imminence of the threat. If the government takes measures of that magnitude now, the problem has to be serious. Second, to reinforce a feeling of trust between the people and the decision makers. These people are looking after us and want to protect us against the threat. Proof? They create a commission that will study and fix the problem. Third, to cut short all further attempts of discussion about the legitimacy of the threat – the threat has now become an existential one for the government and the people, with rules, regulations agents and enforcers, and wanting to discuss it now would look tantamount to treason or sedition. Once a system has been put in place, it is almost impossible to dislodge. The commission and its servants may change tack, evolve according to situations, but it will stay active for a very long time with budgets, employees, cadres and agents – that all have a vested interest in the prolongation of the status quo. In other words, securitizing a topic, and transforming it into an existential threat, supporting it with bureaucratic structure and funds is the best way to bury it into a maze of unrelated procedures and prevent appropriate reactions to its evolution. The bureaucratic creation becomes then an autonomous entity the purpose of which becomes eventually to ensure its own survival, obtain bigger bigger funds and support the political agenda of the decision makers that presided to its creation. Threats are always securitized to satisfy a political agenda.

4.2.3 Technical Actors

Once standards, directives, guidance and others normative entities have been issued, people need to be designated to enforce them. Saying that one needs to be compliant is more complicated than it first seems. If a government issues specifications and regulations, it is necessary to have the people competent enough to ensure that designated targets become

135

compliant. It seems simple enough but it is not that so. For example, in some countries, governments have made mandatory the performance of a security risk assessment for all their industrial (and sometimes even non-industrial) sites. This is all very fine, but then three questions immediately come to mind: Which method are we going to use? Who is going to lead the evaluation? And who will validate the reports? Security consultants exist in many shapes and many colors. Some are rather technical people, others made their way up from man guarding, others are cash-in-transit professionals, others again are security analysts or executive protection professionals. Not to mention loss prevention practitioners (mainly in the retail service), investigators and K9 handlers. The list of professions in the field is endless, and because one has to feed one's family, any security person is ready to accept almost any security job. This means that securitization has strong, and I think positive impact on the capability of technical actors. Once an issue is securitized, technical actors (consultants, auditors, contractors, integrators and perhaps even manufacturers) need to respond to this demand. There will be a lead time, of course, but provided the decision makers and the bureaucratic actors stand firm, technical actors will respond.

4.2.4 The Public

By public, we mean the people who are on the receiving end of security. Employees, visitors, contractors will have to comply with the rules, adopt new behaviors, develop new routines. It is well known that people resist change. Their attitude will depend on a number of issues. The first one will be the trust. If the public feels that new security measures are reasonable, they will be more prone to accept them. Secondly, they – the public – must feel that a nonobservance of the rules will have consequences. If you create new rules and do not implement them, they will not be respected.

Different audiences can perform different functions by accepting a securitization.

There must be a general approval of this securitization. The atmosphere must be propitious to the adoption of new measures. For this, the media, the press, intranet and all the tools at the disposal of decision makers must be used to convince people and take them on board.

The recent coronavirus pandemic is a good example of this technique at work. Newspapers offer figures that are supposed to terrify the public, when figures, compared to other sources of deaths (like simple flu), are relatively mild. Yet decision makers have managed to create a world-wide trauma. This is the most extraordinary example of securitization of a topic, and it might be considered for a later study of securitization and its consequences! It is also a feast for conspiracy theorists who no longer know where to look to find ominous state wrongdoings.

4.3 CONDITIONS OF SUCCESS OF THE SECURITIZATION PROCESS

As said in the previous paragraphs, the securitization act, to be successful, must be accepted by the audience, regardless of the subject matter being a real threat.

4.3.1 The Eight Necessary Components of Securitization

4.3.1.1 A Motive
A threat, real or perceived, is not chosen out of the blue. For securitization to happen, there needs to be a reason, a motive or an excuse. It is quite accepted today that the attack on the Taliban and the military invasion of Afghanistan a few weeks after 9/11 had been planned long before the attack started. The United States had already decided to launch an operation in Afghanistan, and 9/11 was the morally impeccable pretext/excuse the administration needed. It was a bit more complicated to organize the attack against Saddam Hussein, but the quest for the weapons of mass destruction (WMD) was the perfect tool to ensure securitization. WMD suddenly became an existential threat not only for the United States but also for the whole free world, while before 9/11, it was just a threat for Saddam's own population. Securitizing the WMD issue made the attack against Iraq morally acceptable, and those who refused to join the coalition of the willing (therefore the unwilling) were branded as cowards and traitors to the cause. In that case, the project might have backfired, since Russia and France threatened to veto the decision. The United States, Britain and a few minor allies had to go on their own without the moral justification of the United Nations. But the frantic anti-French attitude – going to unheard levels of stupidity such as de-baptizing french fries (not really an issue for the French who consider the fries as a Belgian specialty) was the symptomatic result of securitization. Securitization brings any

137

issue onto an emotional register/level. When an issue has been success-fully securitized, that is when it has established a motive to justify an exis-tential threat; one suddenly feels liberated from any moral contingencies and feels entitled to do, suggest, impose almost anything!

4.3.1.2 A Securitizing Driver

The first, and to my experience, the most important agent in this process is the securitizing agent, which is the entity that creates the securitizing statement. It can be a government, a ministry, any entity with sufficient power to force compliance. The higher the authority, the lesser the resis-tance. Of course, this authority has a vested interest in securitizing a threat. When a ministry securitizes the terrorist threat, even when statis-tically it is negligible, it expects an increase in posture, a better position in the decision-making club, increased budgets for the leaders, increased power and reduced freedom for the people.

Obviously, there is a hidden agenda behind the securitization of an issue. Securitizing an issue is often a way to finance internal repres-sion, to tame an opposition (the securitization of the terrorist threat after 9/11 was masterfully played by some leaders to justify a violent cam-paign against their minorities and opposition parties). A domestic issue is often played, thanks to the securitization, to look as common sense response to attacks by irrational adversaries and as an act of protection of their population. Another political advantage of securitization, usu-ally played skillfully by the securitization motive construction, is that if a threat is successfully securitized, it tends to become an illegitimate subject for political and academic debate. Who would have dared to judge American actions in Afghanistan and in Iraq after the 9/11 attack? Who would criticize Saudi Arabia for protecting their populations from the scourge of violent extremism? Who would criticize a leader acting for the security of their population faced with the dangers of unrelenting violence?

There is therefore a risk of politicization of a threat to satisfy certain agendas that we, security consultants, practitioners and analysts need to be aware of. While we have to pay lip service to the general consensus, the security practitioner should be aware of these tactics if they want to understand the reality of the threat and do their job properly.

What is important is that the ability to securitize a given topic is highly related to the status of the securitization and whether there is a general acceptance, in a regional environment, that such issue could be regionally accepted as a security threat.

4.3.1.3 An Existential Threat, or a Threat That Can Be Credible as an Existential Threat

For us, in the security world, the worst possible threat as action is terrorism and therefore the worst possible threat agent is the terrorist. One cannot deny that the threat of terrorism after 9/11 was overwhelming and that the United States should not have continued to do security as if nothing had happened. But this event was not the first terrorist event of the period and will probably not be the last. But it was so audacious and so humiliating for the most military powerful country in the world that it could appear as a unique attack, which it was, obscuring all those attacks that announced it, and be naturally perceived by the American population, as an existential threat. This attack comprised all the elements of a blockbuster movie. Iconic targets attacked, live on TV watched by hundreds of millions of people, including myself, who could not believe their eyes. American heroes refused to cede to the threat and brought down a plane. The villains were Arabs and Muslims, often portrayed as villains in American films anyway. The nation, like after Pearl Harbor, was outraged, and like after Pearl Harbor, it unleashed a mountain of violence in the guise of retaliation. It was a drama and a trauma, of course, but it was equally the most extraordinary of pretexts to launch the project of remodeling the Middle East that had been in preparation for some time. The onslaught on Afghanistan and Iraq was triggered – but also justified – by 9/11. For the American people, it was an emotional appeal to revenge that guaranteed a total support for the Bush Jr. government, support it did not fail to use and sometimes abuse, with the mitigated results that we know.

I remember seeing on TV during the battle of Baghdad in 2003 an American soldier showing the inside of his helmet where a picture of the twin towers in flame had been inserted. To the question of the journalist, he said that he was in Baghdad to avenge 9/11 (meaning that he believed that Iraq was responsible for the attack, which it certainly was not. Saddam had no sympathy whatsoever for Saudis, for terrorists and even less for Saudi terrorists!). But emotionally Saddam was the culprit and had to be punished.

In other words, an overwhelming emotional element is crucial in the process of securitization (9/11, COVID-19).

4.3.1.4 An Event That Will Create the Occasion to Act

Securitization will only be made possible and accepted by the public if an event occurs, which creates a *sacred union* of the people behind the decision makers – in that case, the government, what some call the flag effect. This event will create blind support and will even demand retaliation, irrespective of the validity of the case. 9/11 is the perfect example. 9/11 allowed the Bush government to start two wars of aggression – that lost popularity with time but started with gusto and the total support of the American population. The Bush administration probably did not anticipate that 19 years after 9/11 they would still be present in Afghanistan, negotiating their withdrawal and power transition with the Taliban that they routed so easily two decades before! It is quite ironic that when people start a war, they always, always think that they will win it (although statistically there is only a 50% chance) and that they will do so quickly! The only short war I have seen in my life was the six-day war of 1967 between Israel and their Arab neighbors. A dangerous victory for Israel by the way, as the Yom Kippur war would strike with a vengeance only six years later…

Anyway, what is important is an action that creates an immediate urge for revenge, a visceral hatred against the perpetrators, an issue outstanding between parties. The trigger will not always work of course. The retaliation apparel must be ready and the decision makers ready to take a gamble. But all securitization process will start after a triggering event.

4.3.1.5 A Referent Element That Needs to Be Protected

Our country is often what comes first on the list. After 9/11, all security fell under the Homeland Security umbrella. The choice of Homeland as a word is of course significant since it carries a much stronger power than critical infrastructure. The department of homeland security (DHS) became an enormous authority with extraordinary budgets! When Margaret Thatcher in 1982 sent Britain's task force to the Falklands after the takeover of the tiny island by Argentinian commandos, it is more as a gesture of pride of a bygone empire than to save a few hundred British residents who had not been molested in any way by the Argentine soldiers. The referent can also be a lifestyle. As George Bush Jr. famously declared: *They hate our freedoms, our freedom of religion, our freedom of speech, our freedom to vote and assemble and disagree with each other.*

Amazingly, it will never be what is really at stake, the oil and gas extraction areas, the pipelines that crisscross the planet, the maritime trade routes, the freedom of navigation in certain areas of the world, that will be suggested as existential threats, while they often are. But if they are the material stuff supporting our lifestyle, they do not speak to our emotions. Nobody would accept to die for an oil rig or a pipeline. It needs to be something positive, linking to our status as human being, emotionally overwhelming: the planets, endangered species, the future of our children, global warming, things that do not smell of oil, diesel and dirty extractions. This is a problem for us, security practitioners, because we often deal with oil, gas and dirty extractions!

What matters is that we understand why we are in the crossline. If we understand why, we will have a better idea of who our adversaries really are. And if we know who they are, we can start the immensely important process of establishing their profile and start imagining which action they could carry out and devise some possible countermeasures.

4.3.1.6 An Audience

This audience is the target of the securitization of threats, the people who need to be persuaded that a particular issue has suddenly become an existential threat for the country, for the industry, for all of us. In our case, and when the decision makers are governments, the first audience are the decision makers in the major industrial groups. CEOs, presidents, chairmen of industrial groups and complexes are politicians cum businessmen. They are only interested in security when a situation materializes. They do not believe that terrorists are an existential menace to their industrial activity. Basic security is usually what they are ready to accept. By simple observation, they can see that the number of attacks on industrial sites is substantially inferior to attacks on administrations, military officers and civil servants, traditionally less protected – when protected at all – than industrial sites. The problem is that the government decision makers impose rules based on their appreciation of the menace toward themselves. They create standards that everybody, industries, administration and sometimes even the military, have to apply in order to protect effectively all and sundry.

Industry decision makers are always reluctant to commit to expensive physical security they believe is useless. The only place where I have seen an extraordinary enthusiasm for spending millions of dollars in security features is a company where most of the security department comprised American expatriates and this fervor lasted only until the last expatriates had been sent back home and the management transferred under local authority. After their departure, cheap and ineffective security resumed, minimum cost and business as usual. In a multinational organization, when the management is local, the attitude toward security is generally less generous and one needs a very good motive to convince CEOs and presidents of these groups that more security is needed!

4.3.1.7 Media with a Vested Interest

The adventure of the coronavirus made me add this element of securitization to my initial list of elements. This pandemic highlighted the importance, for the decision makers, to be able to count on a springboard that will create /support/ emphasize/ dramatize component number 2: the reality of an existential threat. The way media dramatized this pandemic will be taught, I hope, in schools of journalism for years to come.

On 20 March 2020, for example, articles on the coronavirus accounted for 90% of the articles published in the five or six press titles I read on my mobile phone every morning! The number of people infected, in emergency wards, dead and sometimes recovering in the world, appeared in big blocks of colors while the lack of civism from those who refused to apply the rules and mocked the idea of lockdown were designated as criminal behaviors.

The total support of the media, linked in part to it benefiting from the situation, is notable. But one can see very quickly how it impacts people and how important their role is in delivering rewards and moral punishments to those who do not abide by the rules. These media, usually leaning on the left side, at least in Europe, have decided to support policymakers in the pandemic crisis, realizing that their benefits (financial, image and political role) were in supporting it. With people locked down at home, online newspaper, TV programs and daily newspapers were given a makeover, to share the limelight with the other beneficiaries of the pandemic, the health care workers, who became the heroes of the day. Their deteriorating working conditions known for years in relative indifference were suddenly highlighted, their courage lauded, and they might have thought that they would be the winners of this when the virus recedes, something that remains to be seen.

It will be interesting to see, when the migration issue becomes eventually securitized, and it will because the survival of a civilization is at stake (the existential threat), if they will change their stand and support the decision makers. The calculation will probably be linked to whether or not they will benefit from this support. But one thing is for certain. If the media do not support the decision makers, the securitization will be much more difficult – if not simply impossible – to establish.

4.3.1.8 Capacity to Enforce the Securitization of a Threat

Before one can consider the securitization as a success, it is important to dispose of a system that forces decision-making audiences into compliance. If we talk about terrorism, it is not enough to suggest mitigation measures and issue directives or standards. Decision makers may pay lip service to the threat but will avoid paying for it at all cost! As we know, a subject successfully securitized will receive massive attention and huge financial resources when compared with non-securitized threats. Securitization as a course of action might work, with instances where budgets come from state contributions (UN, UNICEF, EU, etc.) but when real money is at stake, this is another story. Chairmen and presidents of private companies will be extremely reluctant to pay anything for a securitized issue unless there is a risk of serious retribution from governing bodies. If refusing or failing to comply with security regulations will meet with a substantial fine, a CEO replacement and or simply the closing of the firm, the chances to be listened to do increase. I have been able to compare this point when working in two different countries of the Gulf Cooperation Council (GCC). In country A, terrorism was officially a major threat, but no real security standards were created or enforced, and the government was keeping the security under their control, leaving the industry fend for themselves. In country B where shoot-outs between police and insurgents were almost a daily occurrence at that time, the government issued directives and standards that were rendered mandatory for all industries under the menace of immediate closure. The only difference between the two was that in one case the government was not threatened by their population, terrorism was a generic threat, not even confirmed by facts – there was not one terrorist attack during the four years I worked there – in the second case, there was a wave of discontent in part of the population and the sirens of Al-Qaeda spoke strongly to a part of a young and frustrated population. Securitizing the terrorist threat in the second country was the obvious way to keep in check all opponents and their sympathizers and, in the long term, to eradicate them, something the secret police and other services did pretty well and in a relatively short period of time. Therefore, securitization of the terrorist threat was used to satisfy a domestic political agenda. This government issued security directives made compulsory along with severe sanctions for noncompliance. These sanctions are what ensured the partial success of the exercise.

The COVID-19 pandemic has highlighted the fact that once a topic is securitized, it legitimizes extraordinary measures. We have observed: the closing of frontiers, the freezing of almost all commercial flights, the lockdown of entire population, the deployment of police forces to enforce these extraordinary measures, the restriction of the most basic liberties, the passive acceptance of extremely repressive measures, something a traditional democratic government would never have been able to impose in normal circumstances without triggering significant protests! This example highlights the power of securitization. What is interesting here is not that existential threats can coexist but that one can overcome the other brutally. The coronavirus has succeeded where saving the planet or maintaining Europe as a European cultured continent has failed.

Personally, I believe that the migration crisis from the third world toward the West will be the next securitized topic, because it ticks almost all boxes, and that this could lead to a general conflagration. It would be easy to securitize the issue of the migrants by saying that terrorists have infiltrated their ranks and present a major threat to our countries (it has already been said and proved, but nobody really saw the necessity of securitizing the topic probably by lack of urgency and/or other priorities).

But this is another story that takes us away from our job as security practitioners.

4.4 SECURITIZATION AND THE SECURITY PRACTITIONER

How is this securitization issue relevant to our job as security practitioner? Simply because we need to be aware of this phenomenon. We need to understand that what is presented as the quintessential threat to our industry at a specific time appears as such because some people, in higher circles, have decided that it would suit their overall agendas. It does not systematically mean that the assets we have been tasked to protect are under such threat. Being conscious of the phenomenon helps us take the measure of the relativity of the danger. But beware, do not mention it and never write it. Fighting the general consensus could get you to jobless-ness. Who would trust a security manager who says or writes: there is no threat, or even worse, this threat that we are told to fight is not what really menaces our industry! This is not what is expected of us.

As professionals, we breathe security threat on a constant basis. But we should be conscious that behind this consensus about threat, there is a thinking process at work that might harm our objectivity about the real threats we might be facing.

5

The Quest for a Method

5.1 INTRODUCING REFLEXIVE CULTURAL REALISM

I have already discussed the different techniques of prognostication that are available to the security analysts. The main conclusion of the analysis of these techniques is that all of them are expressed in a theoretical vacuum. As such a thing cannot exist, it simply means that all these techniques reflect the biases and prejudices of those who utilize them.

We have seen that there are ways and means to keep these biases under control, and during my inquiries with seasoned security analysts, I noticed that these professionals did not place much faith with theories of international security and that they privileged an understanding of the context to the theories that aim to explain the security environment. But I would like to share with you the result of many years of reflection about the topic of security analysis, of which threat analysis is, of course, the central point. I spent six and a half years working on a dissertation that measured how the support of theories of international relations could help analysts provide a better security analysis, anchored in the real, and rid of most biases. I understand that many of my readers are not IR[1] specialists, but I will try to explain how I organized my thought to make security analysis perhaps a bit more solid and provide a crash course in international relations, simplified to the extreme.

I started my reflection about security analysis and forecasting by applying the assumptions of a school of thought called Realism, which is rooted in a very long history of political thinkers, and historians, from Thucydides,[2]

Machiavelli,[3] and in modern times Morgenthau, Kissinger[4] and Brzezinski.[5] What do these realists believe in? They believe in very simple tenets. First, they have a pessimistic view of human nature, and because of this belief, they think that international relations can only be conflictual and that war is the natural ending to unsolvable situations. They place a very high value to state security and state survival. Some of their tenets have a crucial importance for threat analysis, particularly those that say that the purpose of nations – (that I translated in political entities) is to survive; the main currency of international politics is power; and political leaders are rational in their decision making. I cherry-picked some aspects of this theory that I thought could constitute some kind of basic principles of analyses.

Toward this end, I explored the relationship between existing forecasting techniques (summed up in Chapter 5) and selected tenets of some theories of IR. I evaluated then the extent to which their use has the potential to expand the analytical capabilities of private security analysts serving corporate customers. In considering the possibilities and limitations of IR approaches, I concluded that Realism alone could not provide a valid framework to improve security analysts' skills. I improved these tenets by adding some elements of social constructivism[6] and cultural analysis.[7] These three theoretical components constitute the backbone of an innovative approach to security threat analysis herein termed *Reflexive Cultural Realism* (RCR), a theory of security designed to explain politically driven security events in particular social and cultural contexts while allowing for forecasting based on an original way of building scenarios. This theory is applied through a specific *reading grid* (via a seven-step method) at all levels of political activity, from the global – the international – to the domestic – the immediate security environment. The background that took me to this method need not be discussed in detail, as this is not the purpose of this book. What I propose in this chapter is an approach that came as a logical conclusion after working on the topic in an academic way supported by three decades in the security industry. I believe that this method, by combining an innovative theoretical framework with a robust application process, is able to satisfy the demands of corporate customers by improving significantly the analytical and forecasting skills of the analysts serving them.

5.2 THE REFLEXIVE CULTURAL REALISM APPROACH: A SEVEN-STEP METHOD

The RCR is an original method that aims to provide a handrail that the analyst will follow from the moment they receive their task until they deliver their report. This method resembles others used in industrial security that practitioners are familiar with.[8] What makes this method unique is that each step is based on theory-orientated reflection instead of being based on facts or events. As a method, it is nothing more than a number of steps to be followed to keep the analysis process iterative, until its satisfactory conclusion.

The steps I propose to use to conduct the analysis are the following:

1. Analyze the request and reformulate the question (s) asked by the customer
2. Establish the limits of the questions and define customer's real expectations
3. Define forces, indicators, variables and any other data relevant to the problem posed
4. Develop one or several scenarios
5. Evaluate the chances of such scenarios occurring
6. Deliver the report
7. Archive the report for further use or reconsideration

Let us now examine each step of the method.

5.2.1 Step 1: Reformulate the Question Asked by the Customer

The head of a security consultancy[9] I interviewed during my research for a method remarked that the questions asked by the corporate customer were often very practical in nature. He reckoned that security analysts had to be able to provide answers to simple and straightforward questions such as: Do we need an escort? Do we need armored vehicles? Which hotels do you recommend? What are the risks in this region? Should we build a dam or launch any sort of project? It is concrete stuff!

The practicality of the question does not mean that the analyst should take the customer's request at face value and answer them without questioning their underlying assumptions and hidden biases.

As we have seen in a previous chapter, the customer's questions express concerns loaded with assumptions. These assumptions need to be identified, analyzed and readjusted when incorrect. It is essential that the analyst grasp the nature and the magnitude of the customers' fears. What triggered their concern about the perceived degradation of the security environment of their project? Which undisclosed apprehension motivated this practical question about the possibility of using armored vehicles?

147

Reformulating the question using the RCR approach means identifying the operating forces impacting the project and how and why the corporate customer perceives some of the threats posed by these forces as existential: concerns may have been triggered by alarmist reports from deployed consultants, warning of a deterioration of the security situation at ground level. Although they may not be properly equipped to act as analysts, security consultants have often developed an effective flair, and are particularly apt at reading social signs and their perceptions should be considered as important barometers by the analyst. For example, a question like 'Should we use armored vehicles for some of our employees?' suggests that the customer considers attacks against the personnel as a possibility. *Why* this question? And why this question *now*? This is what the analyst must expose. The underlying assumptions behind a simple and straightforward question must guide the analysts' reflection and help them reformulate the customer's question.

A power analysis should initiate the thinking process. Whatever the nature of the project, plant relocation, a joint venture, a factory construction, a cross-country pipeline or an industrial venture, it is an expression of some political power enforced on a geographically and often socially deprived area. Measuring the consequences of this power projection, as well as the disruptive impact this project may have on the local social fabric, seems an appropriate starting point for the analyst's reflection.

Then the level of resources used to secure this projection will assist the analyst to understand whether this project is welcomed or not in the area. The way the host country proposes to physically secure the project usually provides an indication about its local popularity and the importance the government attaches to it. As an example, any oil project in Algeria in the Hassi Messaoud area, the oil and gas production area in the east of the country, is the object of a massive Algerian military deployment (military camps surround each and every industrial compound) that says clearly that the government considers the contracts between SONATRACH[10] and any foreign partner as sacrosanct and the preserve of the Algiers central government. It clearly indicates that there will be a zero tolerance regarding threats. It also hints at the idea that the oil and gas joint ventures may not be perceived by the (local) population as benefiting them, leading to the idea that it could become, at some stage, a preferred target of terrorist groups roaming the Sahara desert. On the principle that the government will deploy forces they judge commensurate with the perceived threat to

148

their joint ventures, the resources dedicated to the project will also give a clue about the magnitude of the threat as seen from the hosts government perspective.

5.2.2 Step 2. Establish the Nature and Limits of the Questions as Well as the Expectations of the Customer

Once the concerns have been identified and the question reformulated to stimulate appropriate answers, the analyst can place their analysis in a broader context. The current trend in corporate security is to establish practical limits to the situation of insecurity, define the minimum level of security acceptable for their workforce, establish a threshold to their reasonable business involvement in a joint venture and so on. The limits usually take the form of practical limits (unacceptable incidents) beyond which the customer can reasonably decide to disengage and apply an exit strategy.

Whatever the problem at hand, it will be circumscribed within the limits clearly established in the report (traditionally, these are the risks incurred by their workforce, foreign and local, and must conform to the company's risk appetite).

5.2.2.1 Comprehend What the Corporate Customer Really Wants

Understanding the clients' concerns also means placing the project in its operating context. This context can be summed up in the security conditions of the operating environment. Security consultants are deployed in countries where the customers feel that their workforce is at risk. These are often countries of ethnic tension, political struggles and endemic violence. The workforce needs to be protected physically by security consultants, and the role of the analyst is to anticipate the possible evolution of the threats to measure the risk and suggest alternative outcomes to possible risk escalations (an evacuation plan is such a response). The field of application for both analysts and consultants is traditional areas of tension in the Middle East, South America and Asia.

Returning to the customer's expectations, the experience of seasoned analysts interviewed by the author reveal that they turn around very basic security issues. B., the head of the intelligence section of the consultancy, was adamant that the clients have already taken the decision when they contact the consultancy. What they are looking for is to ensure the security and safety of their expatriate personnel. Generally, the question is: *Can we*

stay or should we think about leaving the country? F-E C. confirmed this prag-
matist attitude in a conversation with the author:

> Actuality and the recent past push people to live in the *immediacy*.
> In the field of security, interlocutors are conscious that every-
> thing is volatile and try to see a clear way ahead, and now! And
> then, as analysts, we have another dimension, which consists in
> saying: there are heavy trends that you need to consider. We are in
> a functioning mode where the client wants an answer to an imme-
> diate concern. [11] [12]

Decision makers may also expect more than a straight 'yes-or-no'
answer to their immediate concerns, since, as Evans highlights: 'corporate decision makers want to understand the epistemology of risk'. G.V.,
a young and brilliant analyst for Russian affairs, sees this complementary
role of the analyst as central:

> Private security analysts are there to give to the decision maker
> elements that they will not read in the press. The traditional
> profile of analysts (diplomatic experience,[13] life in the target
> region, often mastering the language and equipped with an in-
> depth knowledge of the mentalities) makes them apt to grasp
> cultural issues often unknown by journalists. These analysts
> concentrate the open-source information, and thanks to local
> sources and a specific personal knowledge, often provide
> the decision maker with a different perspective than the one
> they may find in the media. We write papers about different
> clans, about the relationship between members of government
> in their President's inner circle, things that are not always
> known. These are items of information that add value to our
> reports.[14]

Defining the client's expectations may be disconcerting. When the
customer asks: 'Should we use armored vehicles?' there is more to it than
taking an educated guess and reply: 'Yes, I think you should'. Although
assertiveness is important in the way to convey the answer, serious
research is needed to justify the reply.

Customers want a robust answer to situations of perceived insecurity
and risk. At the same time, they want to understand the reasons behind
their choice, in order to justify their decision to their hierarchy. In an MNC,
command structures are complex and each decision maker reports to a
higher grade, and must be able to rationalize a decision.

5.2.2.2 Placing the Project in a Timeline

The purpose of placing the project in a timeline is to understand both the history of the project and its possible development. Events appear at specific times for reasons and the reasons that triggered these events and actions must be analyzed in terms of power variations in an often-overwhelming cultural context.

Yet looking at the situation from a theoretical standpoint will mean different things if the project is still greenfield,[15] if physical implementation has started, if personnel have been deployed and/or if threats are looming on the horizon.

A project is usually going through three phases: project, construction and maintenance, and operations. Each phase carries specific security concerns informed by different power issues. The construction phase, for example, is usually marred with theft of equipment, portable lights, vehicles, spare parts, powerful generators and expensive tools, which meet the demands of the local market and reinforce the criminal element. These threats, though, are not existential and rarely politically driven. Political threats (such as murders, abduction and kidnapping by terrorists, activists and regional insurgents) run at low intensity during this stage. Later, criminals and armed militant groups may join forces to combine political acts of sabotage with theft of items for resale. Their activities can expand to the abduction of expatriates, by criminals reselling their human cargo to terrorist groups for political and economic blackmail, through ransom.

Having these stages in mind is important for the analyst since each one has its own particular security issues at strategic, tactical and operational levels. In order to provide solid answers to pragmatic questions, the analyst will use the RCR approach to determine which forces are acting on the project (detrimental forces, social, political and criminal), and which stage-related threats can be culturally expected, based on past experience or analogical reasoning.

Depending on the time given, the corporate customer can expect a quick assessment or a full situation report. Interviews have revealed that, in the private security sector, customers can spend more time reading reports than their institutional counterparts. D.H. reminisces about his time at the British Ministry of Defense and how moving from the MoD to Jane's Publications presented him with more room for expression:

> In terms of word limits, in a previous life, I had to write 150 words assessments. In 150 words I had to write what happened and what

I thought. And it's pretty tough! So, in actual fact, when I came to Jane's, I had more words to play with. So, in a way, I was able to expand a little bit.[16]

B., another analyst who also honed his skills with the SGDN[17] and later transferred to the private security industry, remarked:

(In the private sector) we are lucky. Our readers can read one and a half page without (a) problem. We do not have the constraints and limitations of the MoD, for example. Some of our products can even be 4 to 5 pages long![18]

5.2.2.3 Placing the Project in a Cultural Environment

According to Evans, "current methods of terrorism risk assessment tend to focus on target vulnerability, terrorist resources and the consequences of a successful attack, but neglect the influence of terrorists' values and beliefs".[19]

The RCR approach is well equipped to address this shortcoming. The identification of potential adversaries to an industrial project (this can be politically motivated agents, violent non-state actors, but also petty criminals); understanding their motivations, and how the project may be perceived as a threat to their lifestyle, their values and beliefs; how it can, from their perspective, announce an unbearable modification in the societal fabric; the loss of power and prestige for their leadership; unwanted involvement of the central government in the area; and security consequences of this involvement for people and families, all are crucial elements of reflection.

The RCR can illuminate these threat layers, provided the analyst can collect the appropriate information. Often, in distant places, information can be fragmentary, distorted and almost impossible to collect. If the consultancy has security consultants deployed in the target region, their local knowledge should be used extensively since the value of the analysis will depend in a great part on the quality of the information they receive.

Understanding, for example, if local people can turn into violent non-state actors (VNSA) depends on an intimate knowledge of the social fabric, of the legitimacy and actual power of the local leadership as well as their capacity to transform this power into potentially harmful threats against the project. As Littlewood[20] highlights:

The ability of any VNSA to invest substantial resources, acquire or attain the necessary technical expertise, conduct such activity under pressure and in a relatively safe haven, and imbue within the organization a culture of learning relies upon multiple factors that cut across organizational structure and leadership, geography, time, availability of materials, the very culture of the actor and its constituents and the environment in which the VNSA operates.

This approach must guide the analyst who, without local information, may find their task unsettling and counterproductive.

5.2.2.4 How Will a Theory-Based Approach Improve on Existing Methods of Analysis?

For the corporate customer, the questions that matter are the *what* (what could happen?) and the *when* (when will they strike?). Yet these questions cannot be answered before the *who* and the *why* questions are properly addressed. And these questions can only be addressed when a theoretically informed approach that considers the issues of power and culture as primordial is developed. This is where the RCR approach will add value when compared to traditional risk assessment methodologies.

The question(s) asked by the customer and reformulated by the analyst should have revealed which threats are feared by the customer and the RCR approach should convincingly assert whether this fear is reasonable. How can this be achieved?

For many security agencies, the analysis starts with a collection of incidents that took place in the region for a determined period of time.[21] This exercise consists in compiling the security incidents of the last decade, and a study of how these incidents disrupted the activities of an industrial group, plant or network. It is based, essentially, on analogical reasoning. Many security analysts will consider past events as an acceptable way to predict future incidents. Often, the customer and local authorities, for lack of a better option, accept this 'reasoning by analogy' or sometimes even demand it.[22] The principle of extrapolation will suggest that similar attacks will occur in the future and security solutions are therefore devised to mitigate these 'expected' attacks.

From an RCR perspective, an extrapolation approach based on past occurrences should not form the basis for reflection. Previous incidents, if they constitute cultural indications, should not be given priority over a study of relevant political units, perceived interests and their potential means of action. A tactical study of previous incidents will certainly provide interesting information about preferred modi operandi and the level of violence to be expected, but this is not an objective of the analysis, rather a resultant. Posing the *who* question means identifying the adversary, assessing their motivations, measuring their capabilities and anticipating their potential for damage.

Past incidents happened because groups of interest, in a circumstantial situation of power, wanted to harm projects deemed incompatible with the group's status, interests, values and beliefs. In simple terms, posing the *who* question is determining which groups of interest operating in the project area would have a political interest to harm such a venture (and also which groups would support it!). Any compilation of past attacks therefore needs to be reviewed through a RCR reading grid, which is a theoretically informed vision to read the dynamics of power and forces in that specific environment as well as their current relevance.

Although some grudges are structural, others are circumstantial. The list of adversaries should be streamlined and only current threats should be investigated. These groups must be named! Currently, in many analyses I read, the adversary is labelled as 'the terrorist' or 'the criminal element'. This is not satisfactory since these groups, although culturally comparable, differ in their nature, their motivations, their capabilities, their conception of power and the way they are prepared to use this power to reach their objectives.

It is important that groups be named, and their values identified. If regional leaders and potential opponents share comparable political traits, they may promote different strategies to reach their political objectives and satisfy their followers. Desperate movements, for example, attract desperate people who may consider violence as their only means to alter the status quo or tilt the balance of power in their favor. Other groups will take the longer view and will follow a nonviolent path, looking for in-depth action and seeking alliances, whilst accepting a compromise. And others will play a double-language game, claiming a certain path and acting differently behind the scenes. All these political units belong to the same cultural groups, share comparable values and beliefs and yet use different strategies to reach their political objectives. The RCR is well fitted to understand the political perspective of these units and envision the plausible power strategies they would favor.

5.2.3 Step 3. Define Forces, Indicators, Variables and Data Relevant to the Question at Hand

Forces are influences and dynamics that drive events toward an outcome. They can be social, technological, economic or political (and often military). Forces can act at several levels, from the international to the domestic, and will be studied by the analyst in that order. Forces can be negative (threats) and positive (support). Forces can be centrifugal or convergent, but also sometimes centripetal. When the forces are mainly convergent, the task of the analyst is facilitated, since all elements point toward a single direction. As Clark remarked, "dominant forces and trends tend to be convergent phenomena that allow the creation of a few most 'likely outcome' scenarios, with indicators that can tell which is more likely" (2007, p. 184).[23]

When they are divergent, more reflection is needed. Integrating divergent information into the construction of the analysis is imperative. Divergent data regarding acting forces do not mean that the convergent model should be abandoned, and that dominant trends are no longer valid. But they may point toward new directions, an evolution of the context, suggesting that power may be shifting and that new strategies may be under construction.

Therefore, divergent data should not be discarded, but maintained at the periphery of the analyst's field of reflection, until confirmed or safely discarded.

5.2.3.1 From the 'Global Village' to the Village: Evaluating Forces at Different Levels

Analysts should start their reflection at the geographical periphery of the project and move toward its core. They should study the political and cultural significance of the project at international, regional and local levels.

Defining what the forces acting at international level are leads to some historical research in order to recreate the political environment that surrounded the original deal. This is the time where the project originated, where stakeholders, after an invitation from their respective governments met, where financial terms and conditions of the implementation were discussed and the contract between the parties signed.

Documented historical researches done through the RCR perspective will help understand which political and economic forces were at work then and how they shaped the success of the enterprise. The analyst should measure the politico-economic reasons behind the deal, and check whether these reasons are still perceived today as globally positive by the partners. Its political regional impact should be measured, and the possible security threats it can generate must be researched in the press and other open-source intelligence.

An agreement between a government and a western industrial power may generate some regional jealousy both with local leadership and within communities. This jealously may in time build into resentment, which can, in turn, feed a growing local animosity and make communities receptive to adversarial propaganda. Analysts must look for items of information that either confirm or invalidate such intuitive proposition. They will do so by using with rigor the RCR reading grid while collecting both convergent and divergent open-source information, asking questions such as: How can this project be perceived by the different political entities that compose the regional and domestic complexes? What are the traditional amities and enmities of each particular group? Will communities feel neglected, humiliated or betrayed by their central government? These emotional questions reflect cultural self-perceptions, and the wider the gap between the group's self-image and the perception of the way they are treated, the more fertile the ground for exploitation by adversaries.

When the project begins, the question of importance for the customer is: 'Are we going to face opposition locally and should we expect security troubles'?

Although reasons may be found at the global or regional level, the local level is the one where antagonistic relationship will crystalize, while it is also the level where information might be the most difficult to acquire. If this level has not been studied prior to the project decision, and my experience is that it is seldom the case, it must be researched by the analyst as soon as he joins the project. Understanding the forces acting at a domestic level is crucial.

Only theories that incorporate a constructivist-realist conception of power, and place it in a determinant cultural context, and the RCR is one such theory, can drive the analyst toward an understanding of how power, forces and threats will transform the reality. Interviewed analysts were not convinced that a rational evaluation of forces would provide a full understanding of the security risks facing the customer. As one of the analysts I interviewed aptly remarked, 'a Cartesian logic is not always applicable to regions where we operate'.[24] I concede that it may sometimes appear so, but there is always logic in a political move, even at a micro level and in culturally distant communities, and the task of the analyst is to grasp it.

Hobsbawm,[25] the great historian of the 20th century, highlights the importance of groups operating sometimes at a subnational level, preferably to more global stakeholders.

> For more than two centuries, until the 1970's, the rise of the modern state had been continuous, proceeding irrespective of ideology and political organization, be it liberal, social democrat, communist or fascist. This is no longer the case. The trend is reversing. We

have a rapidly globalizing world economy based on transnational private firms that are doing their best to live outside the range of state law and taxes, which severely limits the ability of even big governments to control their national economies. (...) Thanks to this development and the flooding of the globe with small but highly effective weaponry during the Cold War, armed force is no longer monopolized by states and their agents.[26]

Local groups of interests defined by a geographical logic, a legitimate leadership, a shared culture, a political project and possible access to weaponry to defend or promote their worldview have, with the end of the Cold War, broken the monopoly of violence previously enjoyed only by governments. In fragile political environments, where the customer usually operates, the legitimacy, the stability and security competence of the customer's partners should be examined.

The RCR approach allows defining and measuring forces in their cultural context and envisions their possible utilization. Through this reading grid, the analyst recreates a theoretically informed reality that can be acted upon.

5.2.3.2 Indicators
Indicators are the signposts that warn the analyst that some scenario is unfolding.

These indicators can be divided in three groups that reflect the three components of security risk:

1. adversary capability,
2. adversary intention, and
3. target vulnerability.

Although there is no consensus regarding the issue, it seems to me that the vulnerability of the target is an integral part of the security equation. Practitioners in corporate security already use this concept. The American Petroleum Institute (API 780) methodology, to name only this one, measures the Security Risk as a product of Threat × Attractiveness × Vulnerability. The corporate customer wants to know the relevance of their set up security position, and vulnerability is an important element of it.

For the private security analyst, the idea behind the compilation of indicators is that a coherent political unit, intent upon damaging a project, would undertake indispensable steps to be able to perform the detrimental action. Identifying these telltale events will confirm a trend about how a situation is evolving and provide valuable indications to the analyst.

The analyst should therefore establish: (1) what perceived advantage would induce local leaders to choose to harm the project over supporting it; (2) which form these actions could take, from the information collected; (3) create a list of indicators.

5.2.3.3 Variables and Relevant Data

Variables, like relevant data, are items whose modification (in number, value, expression, tone, character, etc.) will affect the unfolding of proposed scenarios. For example, the fact that the security force deployed to protect an oil and gas installation is reduced, without notice, in number or quality by the host country, is a variable that can be interpreted in different ways, all of which have an impact on the security of the project. This action may mean things as diverse as:

1. the host government is cash-strapped and must engage the facilities forces in other more important projects,
2. the security situation on site is improving and does not require anymore such levels of security protection,
3. the situation of the security forces in an irredentist area has become untenable,
4. or it may also be a sign from the government that their support for the project is waning.

This variable, the amount of protection dedicated to the customer's project or joint venture, must be examined through an RCR lens to understand what are the political/cultural reasons that triggered this action by the host government. Only then can the security consequences of the change in the variable be evaluated.

In summary, forces, indicators, variables and relevant data will be selected through a reflexive cultural realist perspective. The approach for each of these criteria will be normative in that each criterion will be observed as a social construct, in a particular cultural context.

5.2.4 Step 4. Establish from One to Three Scenarios

Establishing scenarios is the next logical step in the method. It allows imagining of what could be the impact and consequences of driving forces impacting the customer's project. Scenarios are about providing alternative futures to the customer to be acted upon.

From my interviews with security analysts, it appears that the provision of three scenarios, exploratory, normative and preferred outcomes, is a luxury they can rarely afford, because of time constraints. They usually have to settle for middle range scenario, lying between plausible and probable.

Many analysts do not feel it necessary to spend time on building scenarios. Yet when customers are expecting an in-depth report, it is a thorough approach to security forecasting. Analysts should feel comfortable with scenario building, and this skill needs to be routine, for all the advantages it brings to the comprehensive approach to a sensitive security situation. Their tasks are more about suggesting scenarios than about forecasting the future.

The principle behind the scenarios is simple. It is the plausible effects of the application of driving forces to a target situation along a defined timeline.

Specialists agree that the selection of relevant driving forces is the major tool for creating scenarios. Scenarios will result from the application of the selected driving forces on a target situation. But, as in physics or as in politics, the application of forces on a context will trigger reactions and the analyst will have to measure the driving forces against opposite or reaction forces that accompany all movement, such as inertia, contamination or synergy.

From the assessment of these forces, and depending on time constraints, the analyst will create one to three scenarios. Schwartz (1998), a *futurist* who performed political forecasting for Shell, suggests the following organization to create scenarios. He first recommends working with a team aware of the task at hand and that has come prepared to the first meeting. The purpose of the meeting is to answer the following questions:

1. What are the driving forces?
2. What do you feel is uncertain?
3. What is inevitable?
4. How about this or that scenario?

After the initial meeting, scenario planners are given 12 hours of reflection, and the meeting resumes the next day, usually with improved results. This is all very well, but a close reading of Schwartz's' book reveals several issues: to create a team dedicated to forecast in a transnational corporation such as Royal Dutch/Shell is far beyond the financial and organizational capabilities of any private security consultancy. Furthermore, the purpose of the Shell *futurist group* was to forecast an *unconditional* future, which is

159

different from the work of the private security analyst focusing on *contingent* forecast.

Could the Shell futurist group approach be retained as a possible guideline? How do the four questions approach measure when compared with the RCR approach?

Both methods begin with the necessity to study driving forces and their magnitude, and the threats they can pose to industrial projects. After that, they part company. The Shell model is constructed around judgment calls from the members of the panel. Even if forces have been properly assessed, there does not seem to be a proper technique to build up scenarios. The second and third question: *what is inevitable* and *what is certain* seem not to consider the enormous potential for biases. Researchers have highlighted the dangers of judgmental forecasts, notably remarking that they were strongly influenced by biases such as favoring a desired outcome (optimism bias), wishful thinking, lack of consistency and political manipulation.

The Shell model seems flawed in its conception, since it reflects essentially the cultural biases of their participants. Of course, all forecasting has an element of judgment. Forecasters use judgment in choosing models, in specifying parameters, in selecting historical data, in conducting uncertainty analyses and in interpreting results. Yet, in that approach, in the absence of real analysis, judgment calls seem to be accepted in place of reflection, making the results of these exercises highly unreliable.

The cultural aspect of the evaluation, central to the RCR approach and conspicuously absent from the Shell model, is a safeguard to counterbalance erroneous value judgment, caused by the apparent uniformity of the group of experts in terms of origin, cultural background and shared values that reflect the cultural and corporate climate of opinion.

This is where the RCR approach, with its emphasis on a constructivist approach about power and culture, would compensate these analytical shortcomings.

5.2.4.1 The Place of Power in Scenario Planning

The second issue of importance in scenario building is to understand the cultural nature of power in the target region. We need to assess if we are dealing with a *relative power* mentality, or with a *zero-sum game* mindset? Generally speaking, in areas of tensions, where the political legitimacy and cultural equilibrium are often fragile, there seems to be a zero-sum game mentality, historically constructed, religiously strengthened and culturally maintained, that says that if you lose an ounce of power to your enemy, they will use it to harm you. Time changes and mentalities evolve, but in areas of tension, they do so at an excruciatingly slow pace. The analyst must be aware of this determinant element of analysis.

5.2.4.2 Create an Indicators List

The RCR is well equipped to select indicators – that is, the elements that indicate the state or level of something – with a sociocultural perspective and attribute some preeminence to some indicators over others. People deployed on site, in our case the security manager in charge of the security of the workforce, should contribute to the preparation of the indicators list. Leaving their daily life in the target environment, they may have sound ideas about how some indicators will provide significant clues about the power struggles taking place among rivals and the impact of these struggles among communities. Grabo,[27] talking about strategic warning at international level reckons that

> in compiling indicators lists, analysts will draw on three major sources of knowledge: logic or long-time historical precedent; specific knowledge of the military doctrines or practices of the states concerned; and the lessons learned from the behaviour of the state during a recent war or international crisis.
>
> *2004, p. 26*

Grabo, in her statement, incorporates a constructivist-realist approach to the issue of power while incorporating cultural idiosyncrasies, giving a warning glimpse of the reflexive cultural realist theory I promote. She also warns us about the relative value of indicators lists, but supports their construction and maintenance. Her long experience with intelligence warning let her sadly admit that

> even if he (the analyst) helped prepare it (the indicators' list) in the first place, he will probably have very little need to consult it since he will know almost automatically that a given report does or does not fit some category on the indicator's list. Hopefully, he will from time to time consult his list, particularly if he begins to note a number of developments that could indicate an impending outbreak of conflict or some other crisis. If he does not expect too much, and remembers that at best he may hope to see only a fraction of the indicators on the list, he may find that the list is a useful guide to give him perspective on the present crisis.[28]

An indicators' list has therefore only a relative value and is time-contingent. Elements that compose this list are variable in essence. The indicators' list will have to be adapted, modified and revised on a regular basis, focusing on power and cultural issues.

5.2.5 Step 5. Evaluate the Chances of Each Scenario Occurring (Risk Intelligence)

The problem with scenario occurrence is mainly time constraint. The private security analyst/consultant will often be compelled to act fast, against their academic training and scientific instinct, and commit themselves to one report, one advice, trusting what is called their 'risk intelligence'. As interviewed analysts deplored, when faced with an immediate crisis, they lack time to establish several well researched scenarios and tend to suggest only what they see as the most plausible immediate development. British and French analysts I interviewed agreed that in such situations, their reports were assessed collegially, to make sure that they reflected the general feeling of the consultancy toward the event.

5.2.5.1 Encouraging and Developing Risk Intelligence

In his seminal book, *Risk Intelligence*, Evans[29] defines risk intelligence as 'the ability to estimate probabilities accurately'. His thought-provoking approach brings refreshing ideas to the issue of political and security analysis. Evans did not focus on the probability of occurrence of an event, but rather on the confidence the analyst puts into their analysis. For Evans, this trust in their own judgment should be delivered in figures rather than through words. His method for estimating this self-evaluation comprises the following steps:

> First you should gather all the information you can collect on the situation at hand. Be wide in your collection exercise, anything that, in one way or another, seems relevant to your assessment should be collected. Then, each piece of information collected should go through the grid of the question 'does this data make a statement more or less likely and how does it affect the probability that you are correct'? For Evans, 'the outcome of this process should be a hunch or feeling, the strength of which varies according to your degree of belief'. Finally, translate this feeling into a number that expresses that degree of certainty.[30]

This approach is unique because it does not focus on the probability of scenario occurrence but on the confidence analysts place in the scenario they propose, expressed in numerical (statistical) terms. This technique that will probably be met with fierce resistance by the security analyst community would solve, at least in part, several issues that plague the security forecasting business. First of all, it will clarify the issue of the interpretation of probabilities and denounce the illusion of communication. Verbal labels such as possible, probable and plausible, which are used regularly in security analysis reports, are subject to interpretation. Evans mentions a revealing example to illustrate that point.

> In one experiment, an intelligence analyst was asked to substitute numerical probability estimates for the verbal qualifiers in one of his own earlier articles. The first statement was: *'The cease-fire is holding but could be broken within a week'*. The analyst said he meant there was a 30 per cent chance the cease-fire would be broken within a week. Another analyst who had helped the analyst prepare the article said she thought there was about an 80 per cent chance the cease-fire would be broken. Yet, when working together on the report, both analysts had believed they were in agreement about what could happen.
>
> *Evans 2012, p. 117*

Although I have never put Evans' suggestion to the test, I intuitively feel that expressing opinions in figures would definitely improve and clarify analyses. As soon as analysts express confidence in a prediction as a probability, they commit to their analyses. They take responsibility. Such ground-breaking approach, when adopted, will change forever the way analysts approach the task. And it will make the RCR theory more pertinent, because the analyst would use the method to make their analysis more relevant and could express confidence in their reports.

5.2.6 Step 6. Deliver a Report

The form of the report and its contents are of utmost importance. The scope of the study will define the form and structure of the report. Some suggest that the scope of the study will determine the degree of prognostication. The wider the study, the more predictive, since the customers expect to be offered trends and perspective. But as the scope narrows down, the analyst should turn toward the descriptive mode. Narrowing the scope down means answering to a specific question. And the question demands practical answers rather than geopolitical considerations.

To this dimension, F-E C³¹ adds a practical requirement:

> The way reports are built is extremely important. This is a very strict exercise; the report must be coherent for the people in charge on site, the cadre in the headquarters in a tower in la Défense, and for the personal assistant who is preparing her boss' trip to the region. These three populations have usually no contact with each other and must, within the same report, find all the information they need. The analyst must therefore be very conscious of the form of the report. The more complicated the situation, the more accessible it must become, with a minimum of words, because we are constrained by the contingency of a very quick reading, two pages at most. The purpose is to be able to provide a report into which everybody should find the information they need.

The report explains, suggests, envisions a possible future, but does not pretend to provide solutions to the problem. Summarizing the general opinion of analysts interviewed, we can say that security analyses are not operational recommendations, a fact aggravated by their structural conciseness prevents theoretical explanations or justifications. This state of affairs will probably not change, but it does not mean that this invisible framework developed upstream should be neglected or ignored. An analyst should be, at any moment, able to substantiate their choices by using a robust theoretically informed approach in their analyses.

5.2.7 Step 7. Store the Analysis for Archive and Further Use

Once delivered and accepted by the customer, reports must be stored. Reasons for this are obvious: archiving the report offers the possibility to retrieve them when needed, and measure how accurate the analyses were. Reviewing old analyses would fight hindsight bias and definitely improve analytical skills.

There are other operational justifications to archiving reports. First, customers expect an analysis at M + 6 months, but experience shows that what analysts had often envisioned at M + 6 finally develops three or four years later. For the analyst, reviewing initial analyses and understanding why the time line differed may be very beneficial. Although most interviewed analysts admitted that monitoring old analyses and forecasts would benefit their analytical skills, all confessed that the immediacy and intensity of their work prevented them from looking backwards. It is a trend that needs to be reversed if analysts want to improve their risk intelligence. This could be extended to keeping track of all past analyses to understand where they were right, when assumptions were wrong and when and why theory selected data failed to deliver the proper picture.

NOTES

1   Acronym for International Relations.
2   The author of the Peloponnesian War (431–404 BC).
3   Machiavelli (1469–1527) wrote the Prince, a guide to political survival for the house of Florence (The Medici family).
4   Henry Kissinger was secretary of state under Richard Nixon and is one of the great names of political classical Realism.
5   Zbigniew Brzezinski was the secretary of state to Jimmy Carter and is also one of the great names of modern Realism.
6   Social constructivism is a theory according to which all human knowledge and development is the result of social interaction and language use, making it a shared, rather than an individual, experience. For constructivists, the most important aspect of international politics is social, not material, because social reality is not objective. For constructivists, the research should focus on ideas and beliefs that inform actors on the international scene. To sum up, reality is constituted by ideas, not material forces.
7   Cultural domain analysis is a set of methods for collecting and analyzing data about how people in cultural groups think about things and concepts that are related to one another. Cultural anthropology researchers glean insights from these data to gain a better understanding of different cultural worldviews.
8   American Petroleum Institute (2013); Biringer (2007), Vellani's Threat Analysis Group (2007), Somerson (2009) and Broder (2006), to name a few, compete with corporate security standards developed by MNCs to provide guidelines for corporate and industrial risk assessment specialists.
9   F-E C, Interview with the author, 25 June 2013.
10 SONATRACH: Société Nationale pour la Recherche, la Production, le Transport, la Transformation, et la Commercialisation des Hydrocarbures. The whole hydrocarbon industry in Algeria is managed by the government.
11 F-E C wrap up interview, 25 June 2013.
12 Dylan Evans, 2004: 107.
13 During my interviews with analysts, I have noted that a number of these young analysts are often sons or daughters of diplomats.
14 G.V., interview: 25 June 2013.
15 A greenfield project is a project still in its planning phase.

16 D.H., Interview with the author, 19 Mai 2011, London.
17 Renamed in 2009 Le Secrétariat General de la Défense et de la Sécurité Nationale.
18 B., interview with the author, 25 June 2013.
19 *Ibid.*
20 Littlewood (2016).
21 A decade, for example, in API 780 methodology, a mandatory methodology for many industries in the Gulf Co-operation Council (GCC) countries.
22 Several industrial organizations in the GCC will accept only past incidents as a source of forecast.
23 Clark (2007).
24 Discussion with B. 25 June 2013.
25 Eric John Ernest Hobsbawm (1917–2012), a self-confessed "unrepentant communist", was professor emeritus of economic and social history of the University of London at Birkbeck. He wrote many acclaimed historical works, including a trilogy on the nineteenth century: *The Age of Revolution*, *The Age of Capital* and *The Age of Empire*, and was the author of *The Age of Extremes: The Short 20th Century 1914-1991* and his recent autobiography, *Interesting Times: A Twentieth-Century Life.*
26 Hobsbawm (2008).
27 Grabo (2004).
28 Grabo (2004, p. 29).
29 Evans, D. (2012) *Risk Intelligence: How to Live with Uncertainty.*
30 *Ibid.*
31 F-EC, discussion with the author, 25 June 2013.

6

Anticipating the Threat
Introduction to Forecasting
Principles and Techniques

6.1 WHAT WE REALLY ARE SUPPOSED TO BRING TO THE TABLE

We are an aide to decision. For the people who pay us, our value resides in our ability to anticipate an attack. What the decision makers want to understand is whether they constitute a possible target, and what will be the costs to protect the productive assets (people, property and information) from such attacks.

What they need, I have noticed, is a clear and simple explanation, convincing arguments and an estimation of the costs. The last point is always a problem, since many of us, security practitioners, are not really aware of the exact costs of the equipment. Because our job is mainly projection and analysis, we tend to think that if something needs to be protected, the cost is irrelevant. But one should understand that it cannot be the position of the CEO or general manager. If I had to resume a career in security today, I would probably get much more interested in costs than I have been in the past. This might be the real convergence. The fact that since we are an aide to decision-making, we should be able to provide a full range of services,

DOI: 10.4324/9781003091080-7

from the risk analysis – the analysis, to the risk treatment – the financially estimated solution.

In a time where attacks on industrial sites are less common than they were a few years ago, the issue of cost will become more central to the survival of our business *raison d'être*.

To make it simple, the more generic we are, the less credibility we have. If we can't talk figures, we are at a disadvantage. Having simple figures is an enormous advantage for a practitioner and might make a lot of difference with your customer. In my former company, for example, we could provide the gross price of all the basic stuff a facility needs: the price of the kilometer of fence, raw; the price of the kilometer of the same fence equipped with CCTV cameras, microwave system, fiberoptic on the fence; the price of the main gate with basic equipment, and with crash and raise arm barriers, CCTV, bollards, etc. Having simple figures that the decision maker could play with immediately always had a positive effect on the conversation – meaning we were the consultancy that won the contract.

6.2 LIMITS OF OUR ANALYZES

Of course, it is a complex exercise because our narrative regarding the risk is limited by the boundaries of acceptability our customer has established without letting us know. There are things we can say, and others we can contemplate and keep for ourselves. The culture is what establishes the limits and we must be very aware of them.

Our job is an exercise in balance, in equilibrium, and consists in providing a list of credible and acceptable threats, so that they can sound acceptable to the highest echelon of decision-making – providing solutions that are equally acceptable for our customer, and in trying to associate it with a timeline. I will not insist on the last point, since a timeline is hardly ever respected, in security as in any building project. But it must be there, because to obtain the required budget, the decision maker will have to justify to the shareholders, how long it will take to reduce the risk – meaning to implement the recommendations of the risk treatment – to an acceptable level of responsibility. CEOs like their shareholders are very eager to get the burden of responsibility diverted.

Threats are the dominant element of the risk evaluation. Characterizing the facility, the HQ or the plant is an exercise in listing items, characterizing the assets that compose the target to protect. Measuring their criticality is also an easy task when competent and knowledgeable people perform the assessment. The other stages of the security risk assessment (SRA), vulnerability, risk measurement and risk treatment, all develop from the correct assessment of the threats. Get the threat wrong and the value of your risk assessment is zero.

Let us have a look at existing methods to anticipate, forecast, prognosticate the consequences of undesired situations, and see if these methods could improve the way we organize our reports.

6.2.1 Analysis and Forecast

Several years ago, as part of a personal research for my PhD, I had the opportunity and the privilege to interview security analysts in Dubai, the UK and France. I conducted semi-structured interviews with some brilliant and dedicated analysts who really impressed me by their knowledge and their maturity. Among a set of prepared questions, two of them aimed to evaluate how analysts perceived the relationship between analysis (the what-has-just-happened) and prediction (what-will-probably-come-next). As a reply to my first question "Should every analysis be predictive?" one of the analysts, an experienced specialist of East Asia, declared that an analysis was of "no interest for the decision maker if the risk at one month, three months or six months was not taken into account and clearly defined". Another senior analyst argued that the wider the object of the study, the more predictive it should be, and should the object be restricted in scope, the more the analyst should adopt a descriptive attitude: "Readers, he said, do not always appreciate us providing great strategic reflections. They want to know what happened and what might happen next".

To the question: "What is the purpose of a good analysis?" I received this very thoughtful answer that the type of analysis (and therefore its purpose) was determined by the event itself. "Normally an immediate analysis of an event will be written within two hours, its purpose being to inform the security manager on site and help his thinking before he meets the local decision makers. A second analysis usually follows, three or four pages long, which is a comment on the event. Analysts can return to the event after a few days". Our first analyst remarked that when an event is analyzed, a political and security forecast couldn't go very far without becoming pure speculation.

During these interviews, contradictory views were sometimes expressed. For some, the relationship between analysis and forecast was not clear: "I have not really given any thought about it" one analyst admitted. Another bluntly rejected the idea: "Analysis and forecast are two different things and while analysis adds value, forecasting is pure speculation". Yet, when I asked whether the purpose of a good analysis was: (1) to forecast, (2) to suggest trends or (3) to provide tools for thought to decision makers, all interviewees concurred that all three objectives were somehow equally important.

One analyst suggested that their task as analyst was more to announce and propose scenarios than to predict the future. Another one I had previously interviewed in Dubai had provided a relatively comparable answer. She told me that if by predictive I meant to identify and analyze trends and try to understand how, in a certain context, they may set to become long-term threats; in other words, if we were evaluating a current situation, identifying the forces at work and trying to forecast possible outcomes, then it could be a yes. She admitted that she was always a bit uncomfortable with the term of predicting. As a matter of fact, the word prediction has charlatanic connotations while the word forecast is perfectly acceptable. So, when you can, use the latter and avoid the former.

An analyst I met in London, editor of two top intelligence journals at the time of the interview, confided:

> I think the meaning of analysis needs to be predictive. I come from a MoD[1] background where this is a necessity. Intelligence analysis and even all analysis have to be something that can be acted upon and there are therefore a series of steps to follow on. Our publication (tries) to be predictive because we are trying indirectly to influence policymakers.

These various comments, all stemming from knowledgeable professionals with experience in both government and private intelligence circles told me unambiguously that the relationship between analysis and prediction was far from being established in the profession. Although all agreed that a security analysis plays a great part in highlighting trends, there was a reluctance to accept that the purpose of a security analysis was to predict. The duality of their answers that the future is unpredictable but that analyses should uncover trends suggests that there is a consensus at least on the fact that some parts of the future, or rather some futures (scenarios?) should be studied.

6.2.2 Forecasting Principles and Concepts

This senior editor of an intelligence journal emphasized the fact that, as part of the commissioning process, contributors to the publications placed under his responsibility were made aware that their articles *needed* to be predictive. He confided:

> To prevent the 'so what?' commentary from the customer, we impress on our contributors that they must answer the questions: what does this all mean? Why is this important going forward? Why is this important in six months' time? We do not prescribe how far contributors should predict, but we say: please, tell us what is going to happen and why this is going to happen.

Forecasting is a multidimensional exercise. It can be approached from different perspectives and undertaken at different levels. One always forecasts for a purpose. Security analysts do it to respond to specific demands, to satisfy the purposes of particular agendas. The director of the Department of Strategic Analysis at a major continental security private organization, summarized these objectives as an *accompaniment of clients in their international negotiations* (good repute studies, due diligence, decisional network cartography), and *a physical assistance in the implementation of projects in often degraded and volatile environments*. He added that an early warning tool was offered to corporate customers that measure transversal threats such as terrorism and organized crime, a standard practice in corporate security. He agreed that all these tasks have an element of forecast in their approach.

In this book, pragmatic in nature, I privilege the discussion about challenges facing private consultant/ analysts serving multinational corporations operating in unstable and degraded environments and deploying expatriate personnel while assuming responsibility for a local workforce.

My purpose is to improve the analytical capability of international security consultants and analysts, by providing them with advice, support, guidance and method. I intend to evaluate existing techniques that have either been tested in an academic context or applied in the field. I aim to help improve corporate security forecasting and advocate a theoretical discussion about principles, methods and techniques.

6.3 EXTRAPOLATION, PROJECTION AND FORECAST

Any concept must be expressed within limits to be workable. For us, security practitioners, this principle is equally valid. Whether we are assigned in an office in Washington, London, Paris or Milan to provide an in-depth analysis of a recent worrying situation, or whether we are deployed as a security consultant looking after an expatriate workforce in a far-off and not so pleasant place, we have to provide reports about what is currently happening on the basis of the information available, which can be what the local newspaper writes – more often about what it keeps silent about – what we see, what we hear and what we are told. To be more precise, all these sources create in us an image of the unfolding situation and it would be more correct to say that we report a *perception* of what is happening rather than what is really happening. This report, in spite of its shortcomings, forms the bedrock from which analysts in offices in western capital city will estimate the possible evolution of the situation. This projection is, of course, of crucial importance for the decision makers who need to know, mainly, if they should stay, go under cover, adopt a low profile or evacuate / exfiltrate / extricate their personnel. What is the real value of an analysis based on impressions and tainted with fear and anxiety, or sometime the lack of it? Gill and Phythian tell us that "broadly speaking, analysts are deployed to produce two main types of analysis: tactical (short term or limited in area) and strategic (long term or more extensive in area)". These analyses may not be our main source of concern, but we may find an interest in understanding them better. The road from security consultant to security analyst is sometimes surprisingly short and I believe that all consultants should have an idea of what is being produced in their headquarters.

To put it simply, the analysts' task is (1) to describe and evaluate a situation on the basis of what they know, see, hear and are being told; (2) analyze these elements to make them intelligible to decision makers, and (3) suggest possible / probable developments of the situation in order to provide valuable information to justify business decisions (we stay, we downgrade, we go). Seen from this perspective the importance of the third task cannot be overlooked. This is what really matters to the customers.

Clark (2007) defines three different approaches to predictions: extrapolation, projection and forecast. Although these three words are often used interchangeably, they actually mean very different things and I suggest that we, security practitioners, become familiar with these three concepts.

- Extrapolation

Extrapolation is probably the method most commonly used by journalists and analysts faced with an unexpected situation. Jouvenel (2010) underlined that "prediction, whatever the method employed, is based mainly on the extrapolation of trends observed in the past. It postulates that everything will change in the same fashion, to the same rhythm, and in the same direction".

Extrapolation, confirms Clark, is "the most conservative method of prediction. In its simplest form, extrapolation extends a simple curve on a graph based on historical performance". It is also the technique most commonly used by analysts because of the time constraints imposed upon them: the analyst will resort to extrapolation because it is the easiest thing to do, the quickest and the most susceptible to being granted immediate acceptance. And to be honest, extrapolation is often accurate in the short term because inertia, this natural resistance of forces, may maintain the illusion that things will remain the same forever. Inertia, in physics as in human organizations, makes status quo the normal unfolding of things. Consultants and analysts facing an unexpected and sudden situation will favor extrapolation, if only to buy time. Remember that a first report will normally be produced within two hours of the incident.

- Projection

Projection is an extrapolation to which a pinch of uncertainty is added. A projection accepts that forces created a situation, but considers the possibility of these same forces exerting themselves differently in the future. Of course, this suggests that a projection needs a bit of time to get produced. One needs to study the political reasons behind the incident, the convergence of events that led to its occurrence, and whether the convergence of interest was a one-off or whether other incidents could occur again. In places of great instability, the game of alliances at regional level, always susceptible to change, will modify the balance of forces, and this alteration will/might/could impact on the *course of events*. But changes in alliances may take some time and maybe difficult to assess in the immediate aftermath of an attack. Projection should be therefore more reliable than extrapolation, but is more uncertain in its implementation since it requires information that may not be available to the analyst or the field consultant. For Clark, "projection predicts a range of likely futures based on the assumption that the forces that have operated in the past will change, whereas extrapolation assumes that they will not".

Clark also remarks that even the best-prepared projections seem very conservative when compared to the reality years later. New political, economic, social, technological or military developments create results that were not foreseen by experts in a field. But this type of general forecast is of no real concern to us, security people. We are not interested about the way the world will change, but how changes might affect a security situation. There might be disruptive events that impact a security situation in practical terms. The way drones, who have been in existence for quite some time, are now used as threats could be considered as this type of disruptive technology, not because it is new, reconnaissance drones were used for decades, but because it is now used in a manner that impact security.

To take these disruptive events into account, from an analytical standpoint, one needs to move to the highest level of prognostication: the forecast.

- Forecast

One might think that to forecast is to tell what the future will be. A weather forecast tells you what the weather will look like tomorrow, and the day after and the day after, often until the end of the week. Although they may sometimes be wrong, the weather forecast *never* provide weather alternatives. They are assertive and quite often, correct in their predictions! This is what a forecast is supposed to be. Alas, this is not really an objective anyone can reach when it comes to the unfolding of human affairs. Man is the limit, not the sky, although the sky was sometimes used by soothsayers to predict the course of human actions. Be that as it may, soothsayers are not in great numbers anymore in our modern world and even they were prone to spectacular errors and mistake. Our modern thinkers have reduced the field of forecasting to something more rational and less mystical. Forecasting is therefore about defining a target question focusing on a unique and precise situation, and answering this precise question in a logical, informed and authoritative way. Clarks (2007) considers that the major objective of forecasting is to define *alternative futures* of the target question. He posits that "the alternative futures are usually scenarios. The development of alternative futures is essential for effective strategic decision-making. Since there is no single predictable future, customers need to formulate strategy in the context of alternative future states of the target".

This is very much in line with what we endeavor to achieve: provide a faithful interpretation of what just happened (the undesired security event), suggest the most probable evolutions to those situations (scenarios) and deliver good advice to decision makers who pay for our expertise. More cannot be expected from us.

6.4 FORECASTING APPLIED TO INTERNATIONAL SECURITY

6.4.1 About Scenarios

In this section, I want to discuss the nature and purpose of scenarios as well as how they can contribute to improve the decision-making process. Scenarios are things that security practitioner are quite familiar with. The API 780 or the ISPS[2] suggest a number of scenarios that can/should be used to evaluate our vulnerabilities and recommend mitigations measures. But scenarios have limits. One cannot use too complex scenarios because they make the whole risk evaluation process – beginning by the vulnerability study – far too complicated. If we want the threat to be realistic, we also need to make our work readable. This is a very difficult balance to reach.

Anyway, security practitioners are quite comfortable with scenarios. However, our choice of scenarios should be limited, reasonable, believable and adapted to the situation we are dealing with. There are constants in threats. Linear assets, like pipelines or trains, have a limited number of threats. Although we deal with these threats intuitively, we need to be conscious of the limitations of our target. Our targets show intrinsic limitations that can narrow the threat a bit. Linear assets – trains, pipelines do not lend themselves well to hijacking. Ships can be boarded and rerouted. People as target need to be observed for some time to discern patterns, etc. Ports, commercial and industrials are also subject to recurring threats. It is important that we consider only credible threats, link these threats to what happened in the past while adding a flavor of what could happen in the future. Our evaluation of the threat must be a mix of possibilities, past events and exploration. Coming back again to the appearance of the drone as a means of attack, it is very clear that no current threat evaluations could be submitted to a customer without having considered drones as a means of attack.

But listing threats according to past events and projections might not suffice. Forecasting international security – and/or in our case forecasting the threats against assets deployed abroad should rely on theoretical and methodological principles. Armstrong was the first academic to establish principles as a basis to build forecasts. He wrote: "Principles should be supported by empirical evidence" (Armstrong 1985: 2001). By that, he meant that some sort of order should preside at any attempt to forecast a security situation. I think that, in our work, some issues should become routine.

First of all, the customer's request needs to be analyzed. Do not assume that you know what the customer wants, or fear. The question you receive may well pull you away from what you think is important or relevant, but the fact remains that the one who defines what is important or relevant is the customer. In other words, clean your slate before reading the task assigned to you. You might receive your task directly from the customer, or from your direct supervisor. Your supervisor has already edited the request according to his understanding (and preconceptions) to make it workable and in line with what your organization normally provides. Having the task pre-edited for you is an issue since you might start working on biased premises and "miss the point". Your task number one therefore, is to try to get the exact request/question/problem provided by the customer. A second point is that you must, at all costs, fight the temptation that consists in twisting the question in a certain way because you have elements of answers at the ready. Like in any job, security professionals try to make their life easier, and, when possible, use previous analyses, tables, assessments that they have already produced in comparable circumstances and that they can adapt with minimum efforts. In many consultancies, being professional means working fast. The consequence is that the cut and paste philosophy is very much part of our daily life. Now, if Peter's principle is to be believed,[3] and I am a believer, your supervisor may have missed the point with the question, and, eager to produce a document (and an invoice), failed to grasp the causes underpinning the anxiety of the customer. Therefore, if you can diplomatically get the exact question of the client, it will give you the right basis to start thinking. Forecasting should not be about producing a document, but about thinking. Why this question? What feeling does it reflect? The question asked is of course the result of a business concern. Therefore, a business approach must be adopted and only an answer to this business concern is of any value to the decision maker. Reasons can be multiple: it may be a lack of trust in a business partner, in the host authorities, in the locally employed workers, a lack of confidence in the business model, a worry about the impact of recent events on the worker's attitude, a fear of a sudden escalation of violence in the region where their expatriates are deployed, it can be many things and a conjunction of things. All sort of factors had created a feeling of anxiety mixed with one of urgency in the higher echelons of the organization. Yet, the reasons behind the request are often not mentioned. Questions are often of the short, lapidary type; most of the time it can be resumed in *what* questions? "Following what just happened, what should we do?" They are the convergence of a number of worries, some conscious, some unconscious and our job is to untangle them. Understanding the reasons behind the customer's request will help the analyst provide appropriate answers through relevant scenarios.

Security forecasting in an international context, or in a business venture carried abroad, must be performed with three crucial elements: (1) a target question; (2) a purpose and (3) an audience: this is called the *contingent forecast*.

Armstrong who was a precursor in the idea of forecasting, still remains an inescapable reference. His 'principles' are, all at the same time, advice, guidelines, prescriptions, condition-action statements and rules. Through his demarche, Armstrong intended to firmly establish forecasting in the realm of natural or empirical science. He insisted on the fact that these principles have a purpose. This purpose is simple: *forecasting aims to provide decision-makers with tools or at least aides for decision.* Armstrong suggested that the forecasting process should comprise the six following stages[4]:

6.5 INCONSISTENCY AND BIAS

When one thinks about analysis, the first word that comes to mind is bias. For serious analysts, controlling consistency and getting rid of biases are imperative requirements. Biases are numerous, varied and often imperceptible. All analysts I have spoken with, through many years of interaction, are conscious that bias is detrimental to analysis objectivity and accuracy and therefore to any attempt to forecast. Yet, all interviewees were convinced that their own biases were negligible, peer-controlled and almost insignificant in terms of intellectual rigor.

This bias issue is all the more difficult to control when it is not acknowledged by individuals and when both the analyst and the customer share identical worldviews. Being the product of identical societal constructions, this is, of course, as far as we are concerned, almost always the case.

Although forecasting is based on principles, processes guide it. A process is defined as a number of stages unfolding in a rigorous and logical manner from the definition of the problem to the delivery of the solution. The four-step standard methodological process recommended by Harvey[5] is:

1. Choice of forecast method;
2. application of forecast method;
3. combination of forecasts;
4. evaluation of forecasts.

The downside of forecast is that it complicates and often renders unnecessarily cumbersome a threat evaluation. Customers are often expecting assertive statements, or narratives, on which they can base decisions, rather than scenarios implying different levels of consequences and probabilities, transforming a simple exercise into a complex demonstration, and an unexploitable "gas factory". Furthermore, the fact that the prognosticator cannot be rigorously assertive in his evaluation becomes a handicap.

Before we embark on exploration of scenario techniques it is important to clarify a few points.

Envisioning trends is a conceptual effort. Successful attacks may trigger copycat attacks, or they may not. Understanding the evolution is most of the time an exercise made with some hindsight. And hindsight is not what your customer is interested in. This is what really makes the difference. A journalist can launch ideas about undesired security events trends (drones, stabbing techniques, beheadings, etc.). Everything is permitted to him because he is paid to write stories, no matter how realistic the stories are. Writing a book about whether the United States and China are on military collision course can sell copies because it is thrilling idea. Nobody will rebuke the journalist if their prediction never materializes. The purpose was to write an exciting story and the public got their thrill. Their position is comfortable, because they write to entertain. Their assessment must be pleasant to read, must have a dramatic or emotional impact, display heroes, villains and secret meetings. The reality can be adjusted to fit the objective. Your situation is far less comfortable. You are paid to define how the security threat might evolve in the future in order to give decision makers tools to make decisions and enforce security policies and budget for reasonable mitigation measures. You are at a disadvantage here, because your customer probably reads everything he can find on the situation in the news and follows news channels *live* in his office. Journalists have the authority granted by the importance of their channel, their prestige is magnified by interviews of specialists (very often other journalists having a very shallow understanding of the situation, but they speak with authority, in an ominous atmosphere, helped with map that most of the time also display color on the screen. Your customer is not a security specialist, he is a businessman. He is not really convinced that the anchor speaking with authority about the situation in the country where your customer has deployed a facility with hundreds of local and expatriate workers, probably already in a panic mode, is less competent than you are. You have to convince him that you are. But you start with a handicap because you are on your own, you do not benefit from a good cartographer, your voice is not that of a professional media anchor, and you speak with less clarity than a seasoned journalist. Unless you have reached the absolute security mastery in that you manage to say very little but tick all the other boxes that will impress the client.

Be that as it may, never forget that you are at a disadvantage from the onset. You have this dual challenge of being honest, that is to try to really understand how the security landscape might evolve, while being assertive enough to be credible and vague enough not to be seen as a war-monger! It is always a difficult equilibrium to reach.

6.6 DISRUPTIVE EVENTS AND DISRUPTIVE TECHNOLOGIES

Forecasting is based on the idea that some disruptive events can quickly change the path of events. Disruptive events are events that were not envisioned at the time of the threat evaluation and that will change the threat spectrum significantly. These events can be many things. They can be political, diplomatic, economic, social (ethic, tribal) in nature. For example, the evanescence of the Afghan army, handsomely trained and paid for years by the United States when confronted to the ragtag Taliban militia, is definitely a disruptive event. It was not anticipated by anyone – perhaps except by those military staff who trained these soldiers and lived among them – those who are never believed in high circles. If you work as a security manager in Afghanistan, in Pakistan or in Central Asia, this event has already had – an impact on the security of the facilities and the people placed under your protection.

These disruptive events change the flow of politics, disrupt existing alliances, help creating new ones that are not always clear to the security manager on site. Yet, they are crucial. These disruptive events should be the starting point of our reflection.

179

Often, disruptive technologies are the techniques that might be used as a possible consequence of disruptive political events. But not always. They can be modern technologies but they can also be abandoned techniques that reflect the trend of the day. Disruptive events might wake up wrath in areas that were peaceful for some time, and new MOs may replace the old tactics. Disruptive events may have resulted when a few skilled adversaries would join the adversary you have already portrayed bringing with them skills acquired in other theatres of operations. And this is something that will rarely be brought to your attention unless you managed to build a network of local support within the security work-force and perhaps local policemen. I managed to achieve this in one of my jobs and the result was absolutely fantastic!

We should also consider disruptive techniques that is types of attacks that are not the flavor of the day at the time of the evaluation but that could appear and trigger copycat attacks. Disruptive events can be political (attack, terrorism, change of regime, coup, etc.), economic (introduction of new industrial players in the region, that do not satisfy the inhabitants, and their tribal leaders), social events (a change of support by a new government for a new ethnicity or tribe that threatens the life of a previously advantaged group), the list is endless, but if you work for a big consultancy, their analysts are usually quite good at describing all these potential disruptive events that are not predictable but consist in serious possibilities, and you must not hesitate to contact them. Disruptive technologies complicate the matter! So many things can happen that we have not foreseen. Military (and civilian) observers on Bastille Day 2019 military parade when French inventor (and army reservist) Franky Zapata flew above the crowds carrying a rifle in a demonstration of the potential military applications of his Flyboard invention.

The French army is considering using this incredible invention for military purposes. The "soldier" of the craft, a kind of *Flying Frenchman*, however, wasn't French military: According to France24, the pilot was a former watercraft racer turned inventor, operating his gas turbine-powered "Flyboard Air," a hoverboard-style vehicle that his company Zapata Racing claims can allow flight up to an altitude of 10,000 feet with a top speed of 93 mph.

It's unclear what, if any, formal relationship exists between Zapata Racing and the French Armed Forces, but Zapata has long expressed a desire to further develop the platform for potential military applications. And, of course, we do not know what the military capabilities of this "disruptive "technology can be. Would it sustain a submachine gun recoil?

What are the limits of the invention? How loaded could the flying man carry and still fly safely and reach the objective. Could an attacker carry explosives, or bombs to be dropped on a target? It is still too early to know what paths are opened by this device, but the security professional should follow these technologies and the interest should be proportionate to the possible threat it could mean to the specifics of the facility you are tasked to protect!

This new technology, even it can be only imagined as being used by individuals or small units of highly trained specialists, opens an incredible potential of new threats for the world of industrial security. The demonstration of Zapata's flight,[6] when he successfully crosses the Channel solo, propels us into a new technological era. Although such equipment is probably costly and its pilots will undergo some serious training, there is no reason why it would not end under the feet of determined adversaries. An Hoverboard, neatly hidden in a pick-up or any vehicle could be used by one or two adversaries for an attack on a refinery, a nuclear facility, or any other high-security installation. A quick flight and a determined attack would be regarded by its author as an incredible success and a magnificent gain in terms of image or reputation. The hoverboard is one of several new techniques that are being improved nowadays. Another French inventor is busy working on a flying motorbike[7] that is advancing satisfactorily. There are not only French projects and I guess most technologically advanced armed forces are working on similar or comparable projects. Once the technique is acquired, it will not take long before it is obtained by malevolent people that will want to use them against our facilities.

For example, the apparition and use of drones in terror attacks by the end of the 2010 decade (and counter-terrorism almost immediate response) in Saudi Arabia – drastically altered the threat spectrum. When the first attacks by drone were registered, my Saudi clients requested immediate responses about the way to defeat drones' attacks or drone surveillance! They thought immediately that the Houthis enemies, under Iranian guidance, would use this new means and threaten their industrial cities and facilities. Security managers – particularly the very techno savvy Saudi ones – react nowadays at the rhythm of social medias. A good video of a surveillance drone flying over an industrial facility on the web quickly turns viral and triggers and immediate demand in the world of industrial security, a demand that requires an immediate response!

Some other times, very old modes of attacks suggested a long time ago in the heydays of Al-Qaeda in the Arabian Peninsula, are resuscitated and become, for short period of time, an ingenious and effective modus operandi. For example, using a lorry as a ram (Nice and Germany) had been suggested by one the thinkers of Al-Qaeda as early as 2000.

These disruptive techniques coming on top of disruptive events, make forecasting an incredibly complicated exercise so much so that the practitioner must remain modest at all time and aim at simplicity. Although modesty and simplicity may not be the business-like solution.

Several reasons to that. To start with, disruptive events and disruptive techniques have a life of their own and are not exclusive of each other. They can happen at different times, impact the security landscape differently, and are not subject to arithmetical compatibility. One disruptive event and a disruptive technique are events that you cannot combine for prediction purposes. You cannot intertwine them, put them in a table and end up providing a probability of attack. Simply said: you do not add them or multiply them or whatever equation you have in mind.

6.7 SO, HOW DO YOU START?

Is this a reason to stop reflecting and stick to extrapolation and projection techniques? If time is against you, I suggest that you keep to these two techniques. Same recommendation if your customer is a difficult person. He will probably challenge any prediction he distastes. In that case, stick to simple techniques. They are relatively safe and you cannot lose much credibility. If you have more time, or if your customer insists on a qualitative threat analysis – in other words more than two pages of work, you should go for the forecast. But a word of warning. Be assertive with your forecast. Although you know that the chances of your forecast materializing are infinitesimal, you must be assertive in your report. Because the most important element that you must maintain with your customer is your credibility. Avoid the *may*, the *might*, the *could* and the *possibly*. Always remember Dylan Evans sentence: 'who would trust a man who says I'm not sure?'

My suggestion is that you should analyze disruptive events first. What kind of disruptive events could occur? What unexpected thing could modify the security landscape. If you have been deployed for quite some time, you have some ideas. For example, when I was working in a gulf sheikhdom, media reported regularly and in a very flattery way the sojourns the prime minister was doing in Europe to get his cancer treated. In the traditional media culture of the region, each return home was hailed by titles like "we congratulate our sheikh for successfully passing his medical tests" and other journalistic pearls. These trips were becoming so frequent that it had become impossible to hide them and the government decided to make them public, highlighting the courage, the bravery and the extraordinary resilience of the prime minister. Such an event qualifies as disruptive not only because it hampers the work of the most prominent minister in the country but also it probably announces the probability of a more disruptive event that might follow the death of the man. A security manager is not an international security analyst, or a political scientist and he often finds himself in a lonely situation when he tries to apprehend the situation. As I always say, ask for support, meet fellow practitioners, join ASIS or the OSAC chapter, and trust in yourself. Your bet could be as good as the bet of the best experts. Try to envision the worst possible situation but keep optimistic. My experience is that every time a strong man dies, his death is not followed by upheaval. I lived through a few of these situations, and most of the time, the tough leader had organized his succession and things remained the way they were. Of course, this is my experience and you may have had another one. But violent death can lead to chaos, while long term illness leaves time to rulers to organize their succession. And brutal death is difficult to predict, by definition. To make things simple, observe, inform yourself, discuss and plan. Your job, once a disruptive event is in the making, is to follow the press, every day, and transform the propaganda into more or less reliable information. Who are the ailing leader's main competitors? Do they take action while the man's health is waning? Do they organize demonstrations? How does the population seem to react? What does the head of state do, or announces? Where does he travel? What kind of meetings are held in the country? Can you notice a change in the newspaper op-ed? How do your local colleagues react to the event? All these possibilities must be explored. Will the role be taken by another leader more open to negotiating with the opposition? Will this modify international, national and regional alliances? Who in the country would benefit from this death and what kind of actions could they start if they are bold?

I know what you will tell me: this is not my job, this is what analysts do in my HQ in London, Madrid, Houston or Canberra. True, and you can ask them to draft notes for you, but do not forget that you are the man in the field. You see, with your own eyes, you observe, you feel, they don't. But take their advice seriously as they are often brilliant academics as well as good analysts. I was working recently on a security project in Pakistan and the analysis of the city that was provided to me by analysts observing the situation from Paris was absolutely remarkable. I had travelled to

Pakistan a few years back, and it reflected exactly the existing tensions that I remembered could be found in the country. So, on the one hand, hone your skills and become passionate about the politics of the place where you work, and, on the other hand, get all the help you can!

The reason behind trying to imagine plausible scenarios that would follow a disruptive event (the death of the king, or the prime minister or the regional warlord) is a political exercise, but you can perfectly rationalize it since it is not overly complicated. A list of possible disruptive events should allow you to list the groups that could react to the disruptive event (be it political, economic, tribal, social, religious, etc.). These groups, already in existence and normally regularly assessed and measured by your HQ analysts should then be measured against the traditional threat criteria discussed in a previous chapter.

A disruptive event would be any event – coup, attack, kidnapping and abduction, murder, destruction, etc. that alters the existing balance of political power in the area where you operate. This event – because it is political in nature, will often trigger reactions from some of the groups, associations, tribal or ethnical entities, groups of influence, criminal gangs, or any entity with at least a power of nuisance. These reactions can be political-covert – change in alliances, modification of behavior toward your facility or management, influence on the local employees that will modify the security posture, etc. These covert alterations, may not be self-evident and it might take time before you realize that something has changed in the atmosphere. Hence the importance of recruiting some local security personnel and to establish with them a relation of trust. Although they might be reluctant to report a change for a number of reasons (fear, loyalty, family reasons) in the atmosphere, a changing behavior should always alert you. Those who worked abroad for some time, know what I mean.

My experience taught me that a good reading of people (in the sense of population) and an intuitive reaction to a change in behavior is one of our most important qualities as security professionals.

The second option would be a politically overt reaction. (This should stem quite logically from the nature and size of the disruptive event itself). It can go from a refusal to carry on working for the organization, riots, demonstration, workplace violence between employees, events that will be reported to you and that need a response – or perhaps no response – from yourself. These incidents are rarely spontaneous and result from a strategy. The idea is always to establish a *rapport de force* that will limit your capacity to solve the problem and consequently weaken the image of the security department by way of consequence. If security looks weak or lost, then more assertive events can take place, events that needs to be prevented or controlled. It goes from these incidents the same way as it goes in politics. The underpinning strategy is to embarrass the management and to show that security is the adversary of the local workforce and therefore cannot be trusted.

6.8 HOW TO LINK DISRUPTIVE EVENTS TO DISRUPTIVE TECHNIQUES?

Disruptive events, depending on their nature, will concern only specific adversaries. A change in political regime, a contract signed with a tribal leader, a change of alliance between local warlords and a change at the helm of your organization will only trigger reactions from specific groups that have a vested interest in the change. Your analysis of the situation must therefore be political. If you just landed the job and are not really aware of the repartition of people in the workforce, and how the repartition advantages one specific group for a specific reason, to the detriment of another group, have a chat with the HR manager. I have found these people to be very useful allies, provided you do not tread on their toes trying to propose your services for background checks and preemployment screening! You need to understand who composes the workforce, why some got the job (merit, influence, nepotism, business or political deals), what the deal was, and what the disruptive event considered will or might change. How many representatives of each group are there? Who might react violently to the disruptive event? Would this disruptive event trigger some workplace violence within the company's workforce? HR people, in this evaluation, are your allies. They usually have recruited the employees themselves in recruitment campaigns, and know the files of most of them. Was there a deal with anybody to recruit some specific tribe/ethnicity/party political members, unionists, or even gang members (Yes, it is possible)? Regarding the consequences of this disruptive event, who wins? Who loses? What is the power of nuisance of the losers? What is the top management attitude regarding the possible outcomes? How do they want you to operate? These are urgent and always complicated actions to be treated with caution, discretion and diplomatic skills, but they are part of your job.

185

When you have a clearer picture of the elements that could evolve into a threat, begin a traditional threat analysis (nature and types, number and means, etc.) for each of the group you have identified.

In the following section, the nature and purpose of scenarios will be discussed, as well as how they can contribute to improve decision-making. The nature and complexity of forecasting suggests that only multidisciplinary analysts can succeed at it. Be reassured, even top-analysts fail. Who, among this myriad of think-tank analysts, envisioned the collapse of the Soviet Union? No matter how self-assured and famous they are, nobody has an all-encompassing knowledge sufficiently credible to make judgment calls integrating variables as diverse as geography, international politics, new technologies, cultural beliefs, societal determinism, local political or tribal balance of power and use them effectively and rationally to create plausible scenarios. A versatile analyst is a requirement to provide a decent forecast provided this person is conscious of their limits. You can do the job.

6.9 THE ISSUE OF BIAS IN FORECASTING

For analysts, controlling consistency and getting rid of biases are well-known impediments. Biases are numerous and often imperceptible. I discussed with many analysts and all of them were very conscious that bias was detrimental to forecast objectivity and accuracy, but all were convinced that their biases were minor, peer-controlled and almost negligible in terms of intellectual rigor and analytical outcome.

This bias issue is all the more difficult to control when it is not acknowledged by individuals and when both the analyst and the customer share identical worldviews. Being the product of identical societal constructions, this is, of course, often the case.

6.10 USE DIFFERENT METHODS

From Harvey's earliest recommendations, one infers that different forecast methods or techniques are available to the analyst and that some may be more appropriate than others to answer specific questions. One also assumes that there may be different ways of applying a method, that several methods can be combined and that outcomes need to be measured against the reliability of the methods and techniques employed. Some techniques will be more adapted to qualitative demands while others will integrate statistics and provide quantitative data to answer or illustrate qualitative assertions. Often, analyses and forecasts will include both qualitative and quantitative data. Nevertheless, whether they are the epicenter of an argument or simply support each other, qualitative and quantitative data will have eventually to be transformed into a judgment call and interpreted. From the choice of the forecast method to the evaluation of forecasts, judgment calls will eventually determine the outcome, and analysts will have to make choices, ineluctably tainted with biases and prejudices, although principles and processes intend to alleviate those. By multiplying the safeguards, forecasting theoreticians want to provide impeccable methodologies that will minimize interference, inconsistency and biases. Harvey[8] remarks that "forecasts can be sub-optimal in two ways: inconsistency and bias". People intent on improving their forecasts should minimize these components of forecast error. Inconsistency is a random or unsystematic deviation from the optimal forecast, whereas bias is a systematic one.

Seasoned analysts are very much aware of these dangers, as this anonymous article extracted from the yearbook of an authoritative security organization underlines: *Delivery of correct forecasts requires multiple layers of audit, both internal and external, to discipline both the individual's judgment and avoid 'group think', information from human source's conflicts of interest, political preference degree of risk aversion, competence and access.*

Audit is indeed a feature all security analysts approve of and are familiar with. All analysts I interviewed concurred that their work, was systematically audited, collegially assessed and sometimes peer revised before publication or delivery. However, if auditing seems to be the norm, one should understand that it is only one of the guidelines that practitioners should use to improve their forecasting capabilities both in terms of accuracy, impartiality and relevance. Harvey established a list of seven principles aimed to improve judgment in forecasting and avoid suboptimal performance at different stages of the forecasting process. They are:

1. The value of checklists
2. The importance of establishing agreed criteria for selecting forecast methods
3. The retention and use of forecast records to obtain feedback
4. The use of graphical rather than tabular data displays
5. The advantages of fitting lines through graphical displays when making forecasts

6. The advisability of using multiple methods to assess uncertainly in forecasts, and
7. The need to ensure that people assessing the chances of a plan's success are different from those who develop and implement it. (Harvey 2001: 59)

The purpose of these principles is to make forecast less prone to flaw, bias and partiality. They are not principles[9] as generally assumed, but rather guidelines in the form of stages of an implementation method, or even a template, that analysts should follow to ensure that phases are dealt with in the correct sequence and that none is neglected or forgotten. By following these recommendations, the forecast can only benefit from a recognized and accepted methodology and gain in credibility.

As I mentioned earlier, one forecasts for a purpose, which often means to provide material for decision-making. The forecast should be contingent – or to use Clarke terminology *target-centric*. It should also be bespoken to the personality and the expectations of the customer.

This section has shown that a lot of thinking has been dedicated to methods and techniques. It seems though that much less research has been dedicated to the way to "feed" these sequences. There is a crucial need to theorize the way analysts should populate each step of the methods, both in terms of questions asked and in terms of responses provided. Without a solid framework to support the analyst in their quest for a workable description of reality, and therefore of the reality of threats, any method will reflect the biases of a group of similarly educated people, sharing comparable prejudices toward misunderstood cultural idiosyncrasies and inclined to respond in a similar way – because of shared cultural codes – to misinterpreted or misunderstood political situations.

Having spent a great part of my working life practicing security in what we now call emerging countries, I know by experience that in such regions, where most of the International Joint Ventures in this early century operate, *power* remains the main currency at local level. Political groups, even sometimes very small ones, are constantly fighting for more of it, resulting in persistent rivalry, politically motivated violence reflecting unstable, (or sometimes very stable) balances of power. In such places, the relative legitimacy of governments and the existence of actionable forces determine the real level of security the host country is likely to provide and what the Multinational Corporations (MNC) management can reasonably expect.

If brute power is the currency in such regional politics, it is the capability of host nations to protect the MNC's assets that provide the paramount condition of international business projects: that is *security*. To understand the security equation, the security analyst is well advised to apply a strong realist approach to the situation at hand. For those who are not familiar with the concept of political realism, I will let Keohane (1986) highlight its simple tenets:

> Even as long ago as the time of Thucydides, political realism contained three key assumptions: (1) states are the key units of action, (2) they seek power, either as an end in itself or as a means to other ends (3) they behave in ways that are, by and large, rational, and therefore comprehensible to outsiders in rational terms.

When I studied theories of international relations, I thought that I had discovered the recipe that would allow me to identify and evaluate any threat with certainty and authority. But my experience contradicted the first tenet. I agreed that nation-states were the key units of action in international politics, but in the world of security, there were usually many other contenders to power, who often were the main causes of threat (as in threat-as-agent) in many projects I had worked on, and therefore could not be ignored. That these smaller entities also sought power and acted in a rational way, provided you understand their cultural codes, made perfectly sense to me. If nations are the *major* stakeholders, and will remain so for some time, they are not without adversaries and competitors. Most of the post-Cold war conflicts are the consequence of political entities suffocating under the imperial blanket suddenly freed from it and fighting to gain autonomy, independence and recognition. They all fight to become nation-states that will in turn defend their newly acquired interests in the free-for-all international polity. This seems quite a logical development and is to be expected from most social groups. But these groups vying for power have an uncanny attraction to foreign (exogenous) projects on their soil and the excellent ratio of ease of attack / financial benefits / international coverage that makes expatriate workforce an almost irresistible magnet (and target)!

All political entity has in its DNA the desire to increase their power, their freedom of action and – at least initially or in principle – the well-being of their own people. These principles apply even to the lowest form of human collectivity, the ethnic group, the tribe, even the clan, (one is tempted to say the gang) provided such entities share a historically embedded common culture, similar political interests and aspirations and are ready to fight for them. The recent example of the rise and fall of the Islamic state (ISIS or Daesh) shows that an entity without a land can acquire one quite rapidly and behave, for a while at least, like a sovereign state. The plight of the Kurds, a political entity of close to 40 million[10] people spread on 4 nation-states unwilling to release their grip on an ethnically coherent human group is also a painful example of this principle. Therefore, we will keep the realist principles as a sound basis for observing and analyzing a threat, but will replace tenet No.1 by saying that any group with common interests, a dedicated leadership, political ambitions, a capacity to sustain itself economically and a willingness to fight, can qualify as a unit of action. After all, the struggles for power of Greek cities of Antiquity and Italian cities of the Renaissance are often cited as fine illustrations of realist behavior and these cities did not qualify as nation-states in a Westphalian sense.

6.11 THE LIMITS OF FORECASTING

Forecasting security events is not about foretelling the future but about suggesting possible or rather plausible outcomes, favorable or unfavorable. The most practical tool to do this is to use informed scenarios.

The core argument of this chapter is that prognosticating generic events, what Schrodt labelled the *unconditional forecast*,[11] is not only impossible, but unproductive since a forecast request is a demand created by a customer for a purpose. Corporate customers have to take decisions to protect their shareholders' investments and human assets deployed abroad. They are accountable for the security and safety of their people and must have the best possible picture of the possible threats in order to make appropriate business prudent decisions. As Morlidge (2011a) postulates:

> every forecast is created for the purpose of making a decision. Without a purpose, forecasting is an idle pursuit not worthy of our efforts, and without clarity about the future about the nature of the decision to be made, a forecast is unlikely to fulfil its purpose, whatever it is.

A security forecast, thus, is performed for an audience, a sponsor, a customer, or anybody with a power of decision. The purpose of a forecast is not to predict the future but rather to provide guidance. There is a misconception shared up to the highest level of decision-making that makes the words forecast and prediction synonyms. As Morlidge (2011a) underlines:

> Forecast providers and customers of the process can have conflicted views of what a forecast represents. There is sometimes a mistaken belief that forecasts paint an immutable picture of futures. In reality, forecasts are intended to prompt interventions, some of which may change the course of events, thereby invalidating the predictions.

6.12 PREDICTION, CONTEXT AND PURPOSE

The relationship between prediction, context and purpose is central to our understanding of the limits of forecasting. Both contents and formulation of the forecast will depend heavily on the context from which such a request originates. In the world of intelligence, international politics or corporate security, the question asked by the customer, the context in which the question is being asked, the nature of the problem, the constraints of time, a multiplicity of pressure factors, the potential consequences of action not only define the limits of the forecast, but give it a unique orientation.

A security forecast is always milieu-related and must be expressed within constraints imposed by a definite context in order to satisfy the corporate decision maker specific needs. Furthermore, as Neustadt & May (1986) aptly remarked that

> even with situations and concerns clearly defined, one set of questions need to be answered before debate turns to options for action: What is the objective? What is action supposed to accomplish? What conditions do we want to bring in place of the one existing now? Knowing how the concerns emerge, how the situation evolves, how the constraints multiply, can help.

By understanding the events, as well as the context from which the question stemmed, the analyst can answer questions and alleviate concerns purposefully and with relevance. If the *why* and the *how* are acknowledged with confidence, if the limits of the questions are properly established, the forecast has more chance of fulfilling its purpose. To this effect, I will develop Clark's[12] concept of the target-centric approach and then examine methods of forecasting that have been tested, mainly in an academic research context.

6.13 THE TARGET CENTRIC APPROACH

The first task of practitioners dealing with a security analysis is to define the limit of their work to the target question itself in order to avoid the danger of unconditional prediction. Stick to the question. Understand the question, clarify the target or targets, and define the threats to understand the vulnerabilities.

A target-centric approach is a focused approach. The target cannot be generic. On the contrary, it should be defined with precision. A question such as *What do we do at our headquarters in Islamabad?* For example, is not acceptable. What do we do should be expressed in practical terms: Do we stay? Do we evacuate? Do we reinforce security? Do we leave a skeleton staff? Our headquarters in Islamabad, must be clearly defined and the contours of the questions clear for all. Are we talking buildings only or do we include the expatriate and local workforce working in the building? If the purpose is to protect first the people and then the building, this must appear quickly in the definition of the target. It then becomes necessary to increase the scope of the question accordingly. The bus station opposite the main entrance needs to be included in the study, the compounds where employees reside, the restaurant where many of them enjoy lunch, the route they use every day to come to the office, the different parking areas they use on a daily basis, all these items, that we could sum-up as the environment of the employees, need now to be included in the target, before or at least along the building proper. One can suddenly see that the scope of work has increased and that contrary to what one initially could think, a target centric approach may require more work than a generic prognostication about an unwanted situation. A target centric approach generates pertinent and practical recommendations and a serious set of security procedures.

When the environment characterization is firmly established and the areas of protection clearly defined, one must turn toward a study of the threat. What are the most plausible threats that the target could face? Threat-as-agent and threat-as-action. A precise description/definition of these malevolent forces and how they might threaten our target should come next. Defining the threat-as-agent as terrorist, as many risk assessment methods recommend, for example, is not a pass. If you envision the terrorist threat as being crucial, and you are perfectly entitled to do so, then you need to be more specific. Terrorists? What kind? Linked to which movement or ideology? Stemming from where and with which kind of background? Which tactics do these people normally use and which level of sophistication or violence should we expect? What could be their motives? Why would they want to attack the target (s)? With which resources? Do they have the capabilities? Which tactics could they select to strike?

Target and threat, in the target-centric approach, are inextricably linked and their combination must guide your thinking.

A target centric approach has several advantages: It tends to reduce bias and overconfidence by approaching a situation through a practical lens. It generally avoids generic verbiage about the danger of the terrorist threat, or the criminal networks that threaten the corporation – these statements are a pure waste of time and of no interest to the customer. The narrower the study, the less room there is for small talk, and therefore for bias and prejudice. Both are normally significantly reduced and easier to control.

A target centric-approach mixes the needs for theoretical and practical items of information. Both the regional analyst, in their Washington or London office, and the security consultant deployed abroad, can look for and collect relevant items of information to work toward the resolution of target-questions and replace these collected items into a theoretically informed framework that will contribute to rationalize a normally emotional situation. There again, target and threat need to be analyzed from both a theoretical and a down-to-earth perspective (always the *why* and the *how*).

Last, the target-centric approach is a flexible concept that "lends itself readily to techniques, such as Delphi, for avoiding negative group dynamics".

The Delphi technique mentioned by Clark[13] is part of specific forecasting techniques I am now going to describe and evaluate. Almost all of these techniques are the product of post-World War II US think tanks and were tested and developed, mainly in academic and institutional environments.

6.14 THE PSA TOOLBOX: PRINCIPLES, METHODS AND TECHNIQUES

Private security analysts have at their disposal an array of predictive (or prognostication) techniques that they can use to approach or refine their evaluation of the threat. These techniques are not new, and as Clark (2007) writes, "They have evolved over the past five centuries, as mathematics and science have evolved. They frequently reappear with new names, even though their underlying principles are centuries old". The choice of these techniques depends mainly on the situation at hand, the time constraints and the resources available. Armstrong (2001) tells us, for example, that "role-playing appears more recommended when dealing with conflict while a simple extrapolation exercise can be sufficient when short-range results are sought".

Yet, the result of my interviews with seasoned professional analysts revealed that none of these techniques, apart of course for judgmental methods – meaning the absence of any structured method, were used in consultancies. Analysts were ignorant of most of the components of these techniques and sometimes not even aware of their existence. I was told that no analyst was ever trained in forecasting, at least in the private sector, and this surprising statement was confirmed by analysts I spoke with. Be that it may, even when these techniques were acknowledged, they were dismissed out of hand for reasons such as lack of time and customer's pressure for immediate comments, that made these techniques discon-nected from the realities of life. Yet, these techniques exist and should be at least known and understood before discarding them. The question we must ask ourselves is: Can these techniques improve the quality and rele-vance of our analyses and to which extent?

I have selected in this chapter, five classic techniques available to forecast/ prognosticate security situations. Most have their origin in economic context, but not all. They have been used by pundits and discussed and tested by academics often on a student population and in think tanks. There is an ample body of literature to discuss the pros and cons of each of these techniques and how and when to use them. None, however, provides a comprehensive solution. This is why Armstrong recommended that "when selection is difficult, combine forecast from different methods".

6.15 TECHNIQUE 1: JUDGMENTAL METHODS

Forecasts produced through judgmental methods are elaborated by sub-ject matter experts (analysts or deployed security consultants) based on their knowledge, experience, skills and intuition. They are the simplest and most common prediction technique. Judgmental techniques fit the natural intellectual inclination of most analysts who like to produce their work in isolation. Analysts using judgmental methods, which are basically an intuitive approach, can often reach notoriety in some circles because of their credentials, attitude and media exposure. Their success is not always linked to the accuracy of their prediction, but rather to the assertiveness of their character and a solid political or media network. Yet, as Evans (2012)[14] remarks, "they do not always strike it right because they often overestimate the extent of their knowledge, they will make more mistakes in judgment than people with greater risk intelligence, but they will also project more charisma and authority".

Since onlookers often mistake confidence for competence, these analysts tend to be overconfident and very disdainful of existing techniques, which they reject because, when it comes to analysis, they do not believe that safety lies in numbers. The analyst's duty is to acquire more knowledge, more expertise, and project more competence. For the devotees of the judgmental method, knowledge, experience and literary style are everything, forecasting techniques an encumbrance; these experts see the quality of their analyses taking the shape of a regular hyperbole, fed by their accumulated knowledge, experience and professional exposure. The result is a strong forecast, expressed assertively, which has the best chance to convince the decision maker.

Judgmental forecasts are therefore prone to psychologically documented shortcomings. For Stewart, "all judgement forecast, will be affected by inherent unreliability, or inconsistency in the judgment process. Psychologists have studied this problem extensively, but forecasters rarely address it".

Researchers and theorists have described two types of unreliability that can reduce the accuracy of judgmental forecast:

1. the unreliability of information acquisition,

For Stewart, "judgements are less reliable when the task is more complex, when the environment is uncertain, when the acquisition of information relies on perception, pattern recognition, or memory; and when people use intuition instead of analysis."

Judgment-based forecasts are bound to reflect the natural inconsistencies and shortcomings of human nature, such as an accumulation of various biases and flawed assumptions. Judgment calls can only be generated on the basis of the information collected, and analysts cannot grasp the whole picture of variables and indicators necessary to fully understand a situation. This also applies to analysts working in groups.

The problem of information acquisition has been well summarized in the *known and unknown unknowns,* attributed to Donald Rumsfeld, but which clearly predates his famous declaration.[15] There are indeed known and unknown *unknowns* that will not be made available to the analysts in general and there is not much one can do, except try to know more, read more, think more, individually and collectively.

2. the unreliability of information processing.

The second shortcoming has been identified as a weakness in data processing. Harvey identified six possible explanations for the lack of reliability of judgment:

1. A failure of cognitive control.
2. An overloading working memory.
3. A recursive weight estimation during learning.
4. Learning correlations rather than learning functions.
5. Reproducing noise.
6. Deterministic rule switching.

Harvey (2001) has proposed six principles to facilitate improved judgment in forecasting. He recommends:

1. *The use of checklists of categories of information relevant to the forecasting task*

Variables should not be used only on the basis of recent history, as is often the case, but should also take into account recent or expected changes in variables. The analyst should use a checklist of variables that past experience has shown to be relevant to the forecast and complete it with new ones, case related. Harvey remarks that people are frequently influenced by information that is not relevant to their tasks; checklists can serve to remind people of factors relevant to their forecast only and to warn them against being influenced by other categories of information. The proposed basis to compile the checklists is defined as the 'accumulated wisdom within an organization'.

2. *The establishment of explicit and agreed criteria for adopting a forecast method*

Security analysts need to decide which techniques they will use for the specific forecast. Although the forecast will remain judgmental in nature, the choice of a method may ensure procedural consistency, with the added advantage of keeping some biases in check.

196

3. *Keep records of forecasts and use them appropriately to obtain feedback*

Harvey, like several others, insists on the issue of feedback. Feedback can improve judgment and help control hindsight bias. *Hindsight bias is the most important factor of continuous and repeated inaccuracy.* The hindsight bias causes forecasters to overestimate the quality of their initial forecast, and is a well-known memory distortion. Can anything be done to reduce hindsight bias? Simply warning people about its dangers seems to have almost no effect. Evans joins Fischoff in suggesting that the best remedy is "to record predictions as one makes them and review the notes regularly".

4. *Study data in graphical rather than tabular form when making judgment forecast*

Although this recommendation stems from sales-related forecasts, it is an interesting suggestion. It may not always be suitable to security issues, since variables and indicators in security that can be presented in a graphic form are rare. Yet, when possible, analysts should endeavor to use graphs, charts and pies to express quantities, in order to support their discourse while being aware of the possibility of falling into the *quantitative fallacy*'s trap. Security analysts might think they will gain credibility by involving in their report figures, numbers, statistics and the like. Information appearing in tables, graphs or numbers is surrounded by an aura of authority difficult to surpass. Nobody would deny that serious information should appear in tables, graphs or numbers, whenever possible. Schwartz (1998), though, objects that "important questions about the future are usually too complex or imprecise for the conventional languages of business and science and that the language of stories and myths are often preferred to the language of mathematics".

Hackett Fischer (1970) refers to the systematic use of figures as the *quantitative fallacy* concept which consists in the idea that

> the facts which count best count most. It is a criterion of significance, which assumes that facts are important in proportion to their susceptibility to quantification. Many ideational and emotional problems which lie at the heart of problems cannot be understood in quantitative terms.

This issue is not recent. Historians who promoted cliometrics in the mid-1960s were determined to bring a scientific approach to history. Forced to focus on what could be measured, cliometricians failed to integrate variables such as opinions, ideas, myths, propaganda and cultural

197

beliefs, dwarfing the field of historical research. There is no possible denial that figures and graphs have their use. But their purpose should be to illustrate a statement, not to drive the discourse. Schrodt warned us about the abusive use of figures and the danger of data mining which he defines as "taking a very large number of variables, cramming them into a generic model, crunching the numbers and then accepting the results irrespective of whether they make any theoretical sense". Using figures for the sake of figures is tempting because it is easy, it looks impressive; and it actually works in applications where one is interested only in unconditional forecast 'to the exclusion of explanatory or manipulation of the underlying variables.'

But it also leads to what Hackett-Fischer (1970) labelled the *fallacy of statistical impressionism,* which occurs whenever a historian (in our case a security analyst) "casts an imprecise, impressionistic interpretation into exact numbers".

What all this tells us is that some situations lend themselves to the use of numbers and graphs while others simply do not and that circumspection, as well as common sense, must be applied to ensure an appropriate use of figures, if at all, in a security or threat analysis.

5. *Use more than one way of judging the degree of uncertainty in forecasts*

Armstrong has also recommended using multiple methods to reduce bias and inconsistency in forecasts. And those who gave some thought about judgmental forecast have to my knowledge supported this suggestion.

6. *Have different people write and validate the forecast*

Finally, Harvey recommends that the person responsible for developing and implementing a plan of action should not be the person who also estimates its probability of success.

The report written by one analyst should be evaluated by one or more peers before it could be considered as definitive and ready to dispatch.

In spite of its apparent lack of method, judgmental forecasting should not be discarded offhandedly since, as Armstrong himself admits, in many situations, experts can make excellent forecasts. Experts' opinions, however, are traditionally marred with biases and shortcomings. For Armstrong,

> much is known about the cause of these limitations and there are solutions to reduce their detrimental effects. Some solutions are simple and inexpensive, such as "there is safety in numbers" and "structure the collection and analysis of experts' opinions.

I am of the opinion that Harvey's principles should be used as guidelines to limit and control the inevitable biases of judgmental forecasts. Analysts use judgment in choosing models or methods, in specifying parameters, in selecting historical data, in conducting uncertainty analyses and in interpreting results. Judgmental forecasts remain the favored and more reliable source of international security forecasting, in spite of its acknowledged deficiencies.

6.16 TECHNIQUE 2: THE DELPHI TECHNIQUE

The Delphi technique is the least unfamiliar of the techniques used in forecasting, contingent or unconditional, and was known, at least by name, by most analysts I interviewed. It is a method for obtaining independent forecast from a panel of experts over two or more rounds, with summaries of the anonymous results provided to the participants after each round. Designed by individuals at the RAND[16] Corporation in the 1950s, this technique has been widely used for supporting judgmental forecasting and decision-making in a variety of domains.
The Delphi process is

1. *Anonymous* and controlled by what some call a judge, and which authority must be acknowledged by the group
2. *iterative* since the conclusions of the first rounds are communicated to each panelist for deeper reflection
3. *reasonable* in its outcomes since the forecast is fostered from the anonymous estimate of experts on the final round

When is the use of Delphi technique appropriate? Rowe and Wright suggest that the process should be used "to elicit and combine expert opinion when expert judgement is necessary because the use of statistical methods is inappropriate, when information is scarce – and one must then rely on opinion". Moreover, they suggest that Delphi may also be appropriate "when disagreements between individuals are likely to be severe or politically unpalatable". They posit that studies have shown that collections of individuals make more accurate judgments and forecast in Delphi groups than in unstructured groups, but that does not mean that Delphi will prognosticate right. The reality is less conclusive. According to the famous GIGO[17] theory, the Delphi technique is as good as what it is made of, to begin with the panelists. In my experience, it is uncommon that panelists possess an equivalent level of expertise and experience. The consequence of this unbalance often is that the most experienced panelists will be very reluctant to change their opinion between rounds, because they consider that their seniority gives them a better assessment of the situation than that of their younger colleagues. Young analysts, on the other hand, will be influenced by old hands, and the fact that panelist's opinion tend to converge over rounds may simply be the result of experience obstinacy on one side, and youthful lack of self-confidence on the other. In Delphi, the forecast is generally accepted when opinions converge, but I fear that they tend to converge toward the most senior analysts preferred outcome and most forceful ego.

The second issue is the one surrounding the *nature* of the questions. As we have already emphasized, *bias* infiltrates questions. The phrasing in questioning is important and emotional words or phrases have an impact. Therefore, if one wants to minimize a bias response, one should frame questions in a balanced manner, use clear and succinct definitions and avoid emotive terms, avoid incorporating irrelevant information into questions and give estimates of uncertainty as frequencies rather than probabilities or odds.

There is empirical evidence that the untrained mind is not equipped to reason about uncertainty using subjective probabilities, but is able to reason successfully about uncertainties using frequencies. When historical frequencies are not obvious, perhaps because the event to be forecast is really unique, then the only way to assess the likelihood of the event is to use a subjective probability produced by judgmental heuristics.[18] These cognitive shortcuts can lead to overconfidence. Evans warns us that

> these heuristics can also push the analyst toward availability heuristic (based on the principle that anything easily retrieved from memory is usually perceived as more probable than the absent past event), wishful thinking (another form of optimism bias), confirmation bias (the tendency to pay more attention to information that confirms what we already believe and to ignore contradictory data), and mind-reading illusion (the tendency to think that we are better at reading other people than we really are), all items of a polymorph overconfidence bias.

Finally, the Delphi technique, from a cultural standpoint, cannot avoid reflecting the biases and prejudices of the judge and panelists in the selection and formulation of questions. In spite of its collaborative method, it tends to aggregate prejudices and produce a short-sighted response to any issue. Claiming fairness, it reduces contestation and creates monolithic answers. All this should make us seriously think about the value of the Delphi technique. Some critics of the RAND Delphi technique trials argued that the Delphi technique was sloppily executed; that questionnaires tended to be poorly worded and ambiguous and that the analyses of responses were often superficial. Explanations for the poor conduct of early studies could be that its apparent simplicity encouraged people without the requisite skills to use it, or that early Delphi researchers had poor background in the social science and hence lacked acquaintance with appropriate methodologies.

Grabo, basing her judgment on 40 years of experience in an American intelligence context, warns: "it is obvious that the technique should be applied with care". Should it be dismissed without any further ado? Maybe not. In spite of inconsistent application of the techniques, research has shown that Delphi-like groups provide better forecasts than other judgmental approaches. To achieve optimal results, researchers suggest the use of experts with appropriate domain knowledge, the use of heterogeneous experts, and the use of between 5 and 20 experts. For Delphi feedback, provide the mean or median estimate of the panel plus the rationales from all panelists for their estimates, then continue Delphi polling until the responses show stability. Generally, three structured rounds are enough. Obtain the final forecast by weighing all the experts' estimates equally and aggregating them. In phrasing questions, use clear and succinct definitions and avoid emotive terms; frame questions in a balanced manner; avoid incorporating irrelevant information into questions; when possible, give estimates of uncertainly as frequencies rather than probabilities or odds and finally use coherence checks when eliciting estimates of probabilities.

Needless to say, these conditions are never met in the corporate world of security. With consultancies, time constraints would prevent these recommendations from being implemented. In corporate security analysis, time is of the essence. Nevertheless, the above recommendations can be considered as generic guidelines to be used or at least approached whenever possible.

Delphi could be practicable if a pool of comparably skilled and experienced analysts were working on the same "patch", with a reasonable time allowance to reach results. But this is not often the case. And the bias fight would be almost impossible to win anyway.

6.17 TECHNIQUE 3: ROLE-PLAYING

I must confess that, although I know many security analysts, I have never met a single one of them who participated in a role-playing exercise in their professional life. Yet, a substantial amount of literature on the topic exists. Academics in various fields have studied at length the pros and cons of role-playing, and led numerous experiences on the relative accuracies of different prediction techniques. I shall succinctly sum up these findings, with the caveat that the context in which they were obtained was more academic than professional. Many of the "experienced" security analysts I know would be extremely reluctant to lend themselves to a role-playing act, which they would consider as histrionic and undignified. Armstrong defined Role-playing is as "a way of predicting the decisions by people engaged in conflicts". Role-playing is considered the preferred method for predicting decisions in situations in which parties interact. It is especially useful when there are conflicts between them, involving large changes, and where little information exists about similar events in the past.

Studies have shown than role-playing was better at providing accuracy than other techniques. They also revealed that, besides providing more accurate forecasts, role-playing could enhance the understanding of a situation. Role-playing can provide participants with information about how they feel about other's actions and how others react to their actions. Researchers reported that Germany used it in 1929 to plan their war strategy. It was also suggested that decision makers could use role-playing to test new strategies. And last, role-players can identify outcomes that experts did not consider. Role-playing has rather good press with the academic and forecasting community.

I am rather less favorably inclined toward this technique for several reasons: First, because it is based entirely on an emotional evaluation of a situation – and I think I made it clear that emotions differ enormously from one culture to another – and second because little research has been done regarding the validity of procedures when conducting role-playing sessions. According to Armstrong, we do not know whether it is best to ask role players to act as you would act in this situation or to act as you think the person you represent would act. Finally, there is a major unknown in the evaluation of the threat. If the actors are acting, who writes the scenarios? Who defines the cast? And who outlines the assumptions? It seems that, as it is conceived, role-playing focuses and relies on a kind of emotional dynamic, where emotive reactions to conflicts situation seem to have precedence over reflection. And, as for the Delphi technique, it integrates as part of "the rules of engagement" the assumptions, biases and cultural prejudices of the participants. It may therefore be an interesting exercise in social psychology, when conflicts between culturally comparable adversaries take place in the corporate world (e.g., struggles between management and trade unions in a European or American context) but do not seem fit to help analysts working on establishing the validity of threats in far-off and culturally distinctive places.

In summary, in spite of the good score realized by role-playing in comparative prediction techniques, I would not recommend the technique also because case studies and results were measured and obtained in academic (or think tank) environments and because role-playing lacks theoretical underpinnings, ignores complex determinisms, cultural differences, historical background and cultural relativity of decision-making. Even if role-playing has, to date, been more accurate than alternate procedures, in particular when compared with experts' opinions, more research is needed to test the reliability and validity of the findings.

6.18 TECHNIQUE 4: GAME THEORY

Game theory is the study of mathematical models of strategic interactions among rational agents. It has applications in all fields of social science, and has been considered by many as a relevant technique in the security. In Bueno de Mesquita' words, "Game theory is a fancy label for a pretty simple idea: that people do what they believe is in their best interest!". Game theory sits on the opposite side of role playing on the decision-making axis. While role-playing appeals to the emotional side of decision-making, game theory postulates that the decision maker will always act according to a cost-benefit analysis of a situation. In game theory, winning is everything and passes by a rational only approach. But what really is game theory? It has been described as

> a formal, mathematical method of studying decision-making in situations of conflict. It expresses its ideas in terms of how things should be, given certain assumptions; one of these is that decision makers will act rationally. Being mathematical, these ideas have been expressed in quantitative, numerate forms (known as pay-offs).

Yet, there is more to game theory than this definition, and there are different variants. The two best-known expressions of the game theory are the minimax principle, and the non-zero-sum variable (also known as mixed-motive game). The minimax principle is a rule that says that players will seek to maximize their gains or to minimize their losses, in a zero-sum situation, a simplistic vision of pure conflict. The non-zero-sum variable considers outcomes where players can win and lose, and where cooperation can emerge as alternative to pure conflict. Born from the Cold War, one may wonder whether the theory was not trailing behind the reality of the two superpowers Great Game, oscillating according to the different stages of the relationship, from detente to containment, from domino effect theory to rapprochement again, adapting and justifying with hindsight the options made by the protagonists on the Cold War timeline.

Game theory was heavily criticized in the 1960s for its lack of relevance to the real world. It was argued that in the field of mixed-motive game (another name for non-zero-sum game), no unambiguous definition of rationality was given and that the playing out of the mixed motives game involved consideration of factors such as trust, which are not encountered in the zero-sum game. In a comprehensive review of the use of experimental games to test game theory hypotheses, researchers concluded that game theory is not descriptive and will not predict human behavior, especially in games with imperfect information about the pay-off matrices. In short, game theory was discarded on the basis of its intellectual aloofness and lack of social empathy. As Barkin (2002) pointed out,

> in a perfect game-theory world, we could model the strategic interactions generated by a given foreign policy decision, and deduce what our adversary's best option is. But in our imperfect world, there is always the possibility that our adversary will think of a better option in response than we had thought.

Academics have also criticized it over its lack of predictive validity. Three academics[19] reviewed all game theory articles published in the leading US OR/MS journals and found that, on average, less than one article per year addressed a real-world application. Armstrong[20] stated firmly: "I have reviewed the literature on the effectiveness of game theory for predictions and have been unable to find any evidence to directly support the belief that game theory would aid predictive ability".

Green's researches in conflict forecasting, based on six different types of conflicts, revealed that game theory experts, on average, did not perform better than chance in forecasting decisions made during real-life conflicts.

One may wonder what is therefore the predictive value of game theory in spite of the enormous efforts devoted to research over six decades.

Has game theory therefore become another artefact of the Cold War intellectual paraphernalia? In a world where power was equated with the military arsenal of two superpowers, it may have demonstrated valid aptitudes for forecasting, although it was never confirmed. In a multipolar world where forces are so plentiful, indistinguishable and asymmetrical, it appears as obsolete. In security, it appears even less valid to discuss threats.

6.19 CONCLUSION

This discussion shows the interest that pundits and academics showed in forecasting techniques particularly during the rivalry of the two super powers. A lot of reflection and model-building led to sophisticated techniques, tried and tested in academic context, but never applied in the security corporate world. These methods, were in fashion when the world was bipolar, simple, and where MAD[21] ensured that long careers in academia could be based on the status quo. The world has changed, and the state of anarchy, violence and risk is today far less structured and potentially much more unstable than during the Cold War period. Whether these principles fit the threats that security practitioners are facing in today's world remains to be seen and is essentially a matter of opinion. I believe that terrorist groups are political entities led by leaders who pursue political goals and therefore act rationally and consequently are subject to the same laws and rules of analysis.

Security analysts confine themselves to judgmental methods, out of dignity, perhaps, but mainly out of practicality, time constraints and customer's expectations. It does not mean this "intuitive" and very personal work has no value. If it remains controlled and peer-reviewed most biases should be kept in check. Should we consider these techniques as enhancing the skills of private security analysts and should we deplore that they are not more used in private consultancies? I can raise three objections against them. First, they suffer from a disease of obsolescence. Born in the specific context of the Cold War, measuring similar items in comparable cultural environments (the West), they assumed identical rules, values and behaviors. This must have been, at the time and in these circumstances, an acceptable reasoning principle, but the world has changed, the zones of friction have geographically drifted to culturally different areas, where western values are not shared by many actors, and where rules of play are not shared anymore, resulting in the irrelevance of these techniques. Second, they tend to privilege emotions over reasoning/rationality. Of course, emotions are crucial to any situation. But emotions are not standardized and peoples react differently to situations. Leaders use emotions to support their policies, take their constituency where they want them to be. The logic used in their application is tainted with cultural and cognitive biases, leading to wishful thinking and other unacceptable preferences. All of them carry aboard the cultural biases of their participants. These biases are not acknowledged as such, and are therefore never challenged or questioned. The last drawback of these techniques is that they are expressed in a theoretical vacuum. They are based on the idea that collectable items are supposed to speak for themselves. They do not. They cannot. They will not. They are interpretations and as such they are not impartial. A theoretically informed approach is necessary to make situations intelligible, and this approach must encompass the perspective of *all* stakeholders, to allow the corporate customer to make informed decisions.

These techniques can be useful when dealing with situations of cultural equivalence, when analysts and the target population are culturally comparable, but in culturally different environments, in regions of deployment where the customer has no physical power, where the workforce is vulnerable even when officially placed under the protection of a host, they cannot provide analysts and consultants with a meaningful advantage in analysis capability. Therefore, they provide information of little significance for the decision maker.

NOTES

1 The British Ministry of Defense
2 International Ship and Port Facility Security.
3 The **Peter principle** is a concept in management developed by Laurence J. Peter in 1969, which observes that people in a hierarchy tend to rise to "a level of respective incompetence": employees are promoted based on their success in previous jobs until they reach a level at which they are no longer competent, as skills in one job do not necessarily translate to another.
4 Exhibit 3 Stages of forecasting in Armstrong 2001, page 8.
5 *Ibid.*
6 Accessible on YouTube: www.youtube.com/watch?v=v8d6oGPRri8 or www.youtube.com/watch?v=SG4dt-gLrdo

7   www.youtube.com/watch?v=yrPekQ0iExs
8   *Ibid.*
9   A principle is a fundamental truth or law as the basis of reasoning or action (The Concise Oxford dictionary 9th ed.).
10 Estimations of the Kurd population oscillate between the figures of 30 and 45 million spread over four countries: Syria, Turkey, Iraq and Iran.
11 An unconditional forecast says what a situation will be at a certain date. It is not a reasonable exercise.

    It does not take into account the disruptive events that will modify the projection, neither the possible modifications of forces applying on the situation.
12 *Ibid.*
13 *Ibid.*
14 *Ibid.*
15 "There are known knowns; there are things we know that we know. There are known unknowns; that is to say, there are things that we now know we don't know. But there are also unknown unknowns – there are things we do not know we don't know".

    Declaration by Donald Rumsfeld on 12 February 2002, before the invasion of Iraq.
16 The RAND (Research and Development) corporation is an American non-profit global policy think tank created in 1948 by Douglas Aircraft Company to offer research and analysis to the United States Armed Forces. It is financed by the US government and private endowment, corporations, universities and private individuals. It is probably the most famous think tank on the planet.
17 Garbage In, Garbage Out. Simply meaning that if one bases the analytical process on wrong, biased or unreliable data, one cannot expect to get correct answers, but only reach more biased and irrelevant conclusions.
18 A heuristic is a mental shortcut that allows people to solve problems and make judgments quickly and efficiently. These rule-of-thumb strategies shorten decision-making time and allow people to function without constantly stopping to think about their next course of action.
19 Riesman, Kumar and Motwani (2001).
20 Cited in Green (2002: 324).
21 Mutual assured destruction (MAD) is a doctrine of military strategy and national security policy in which a full-scale use of nuclear weapons by an attacker on a nuclear-armed defender with second-strike capabilities would cause the complete annihilation of both the attacker and the defender.

And now...

We have come to the end of this book, in which I have tried to combine some theories of security studies with other theories of international politics along with several decades of personal security experience in volatile and unstable environments, in order to provide an aide for security practitioners and suggest theoretical approaches for threat evaluation and anticipation.

My goal was to equip the security practitioner with some tools that would complement and enhance their professional skills and field experience.

Without wishing to transform a security practitioner into a political analyst, I wanted to get these two characters get closer to each other.

Obviously, my first job in the Middle East after a 15-year sojourn in Africa had been a cultural shock and triggered my interest in political sciences and international politics. I realized then that I would not be able to do my job effectively if I tried to do it in a vacuum. Security certifications were of course a must and obtaining them was not negotiable. But an engagement with the environment is also a necessity. Once deployed, you become engulfed in a cultural and security environment, which may not always be hostile, but that definitely needs comprehending.

This work on threats remains to me the most interesting part of any risk assessment. If an asset characterization is quite straightforward, the threat assessment is the first conceptual portion of the risk assessment. Threats exist, or so we think, but often cannot be proven. For some decision makers, they result in useless expenses. The security practitioner, when he or she presents what he/she believes to be a valid threat evaluation to the decision makers, walks on a tightrope, and risks one's credibility, having to appear reasonable with the people who can allow the budget to provide an appropriate protection to the facility.

To provide the right mitigation measures, one must get the threat assessment right. Or at least be convinced that the threat evaluation is correct.

I do not know if I have reached my goal. What I can hope is that some of the ideas developed in this book found an echo among some members of the security community I have been so proud to be a member for all these years.

REFERENCES

American Petroleum Institute (2013). *Security Risk Assessment Methodology For The Petroleum And Petrochemicals Industries*. ANSI/API780. Washington DC: API.

Armstrong, J. Scott. ed. (2001). *Principles of Forecasting: A Handbook for Researchers and Practitioners*. Boston: Kluwer.

ASIS International. (2015). Risk Assessment Standard. ANSI/ASIS/RIMS RA.1-2015. Alexandria, VA: ASIS.

Barkin, J. S. (2008). 'Realism, Prediction, and Foreign Policy', Paper prepared for the annual meeting of the *International Studies Association*, San Francisco, 28 March 2008.

Barkin, J. S. (2010). *Realist Constructivism: Rethinking International Relations Theory*. Cambridge: Cambridge University Press.

Biringer, B. E. (2007). *Security Risk Assessment and Management: A Professional Practice Guide for Protecting Buildings and Infrastructure*. John Wiley.

Biringer, B. E., Matalucci, R. V. and O'Connor, S. L. (2007) *Security Risk Management And Management: A Professional Practical Guide For Protecting Buildings And Infrastructures*. Hoboken: John Wiley and Sons.

Broder, J. F. (2006). *Risk Analysis And The Security Survey* (3rd ed.). Burlington, MA: Butterworth-Heinemann.

Clark, R. M. (2007). Intelligence Analysis: A Target Centric Approach. Washington, DC: CQ Press.

Dobbins, R. and Pettman, B.O. (2006). *What Self-Made Millionaires Really Think Know And Do: A Straight Talking Guide To Business Success And Personal Riches*. Chichester, UK: Capstone.

Europol. Europol.europa.eu/media-press/newsroom/news/Europol-report-latest-situational-analysis-terrorism-in-eu.

Evans, D. (2012). Risk Intelligence: How to Live with Uncertainty. New York: Free Press.

Fondapol (2019). www.fondapol.org/en/study/islamist-terrorist-attacks-in-the-world-1979-2019.

Garcia, M. L. (2006). *Design and Evaluation of Physical Protection Systems*. Oxford, UK: Butterworth-Heinemann.

Gelles, M. G. (2016). *Insider Threat: Prevention, Detection, Mitigation and Deterrence*. Oxford, UK: Butterworth-Heinemann.

Grabo, C. M. (2004). *Anticipating Surprise: Analysis for Strategic Warning*. Lanham, MD: University Press of America.

Green, K. C. (2002a). 'Embroiled in a conflict: whom do you call?' *International Journal of Forecasting*, 18, pp. 389–395.

Green, K. C. (2002b). 'Forecasting decisions in conflict situations: A comparison of game theory, role-playing and unaided judgment'. *International Journal of Forecasting*, 18 (2002), pp. 321–344.

Green, K. C. (2005). 'Game theory, simulated interaction, and unaided judgement for forecasting decisions in conflicts: Further evidence. *International Journal of Forecasting*, 21, pp. 463–472.

Green, K. C. and Armstrong, J. S. (2007a). 'Structured analogies for forecasting'. *International Journal of Forecasting*, 23, pp. 365–376.

Green, K. C. and Armstrong, J. S. (2007b). 'The value of expertise for forecasting decisions in conflicts'. *Interfaces*, 37, pp. 287–299.

Green, K. C., Armstrong, J. S., and Graefe, A. (2007). 'Methods to Elicit Forecasts from Groups: Delphi and Prediction Markets Compared'. Foresight, 8, pp. 17–20.

Green, K. C. and Armstrong, J. S. (2011). 'Role thinking: Standing in other people's shoes to forecast decisions in conflicts'. *International Journal of Forecasting*, 27, pp. 69–80.

Hackett Fischer, D. (1970). *Historian Fallacies: Toward a Logic of Historical Thought*. New York: Harper Perennial.

Harvey, N. (1995). 'Why are judgements less consistent in less predictable situations?' *Organizational Behavior and Human Decision Process*, 63, pp. 247–63.

Harvey, N. (2001). 'Improving judgment forecasts', in J. S. Armstrong (ed.), *Principles of Forecasting*. Norwell, MA: Kluwer Academic.

Hobsbawm, E. (2008). *Globalisation, Democracy and Terrorism*. London: Abacus.

International Monetary Fund (2020). www.imf.org/external/pubs/ft/ar/2020/eng/.

Jouvenel, H. de. 'Pour une prospective géopolitique', *Revue internationale et stratégique*, 4/2010 (No. 80), p. 40. Available at: www.cairn.info/revue-internationale-et-strategique-2010-4-page-41.htm (Accessed: 5 January 2015).

Keohane, R. O. (ed.). (1986). *NeoRealism and Its Critics*. New York: Columbia University Press.

Kepel, G. (2021). *Le prophète et la pandémie*. Paris: Gallimard.

McNicholas, M (2016). 2nd ed., *Maritime Security an Introduction*. Oxford, UK: Butterworth-Heinemann.

Morlidge, S. (2011a). 'The Forecasting Process: Guiding Principles'. *Foresight*, 22, Summer 2011, pp. 5–11.

Morlidge, S. (2011b). 'Guiding Principles: Reply to commentaries'. *Foresight*, 22, Summer 2011, pp. 44–45.

Neustadt, R. E. and May, E. R. (1986). *Thinking in Time: The Uses of History for Decision Makers*. New York: Free Press.

Price, J. C. and Forrest, J. S. (2009). *Practical Aviation Security: Predicting and Preventing Future Threats*. Butterworth-Heinemann.

Rand. (2015). www.rand.org/blog/2015/07/the-1970s-and-the-birth-of-contemporary-terrorism.html. Retrieved on 3 June 2021.

212

Reisman, A., Kumar, A. and Motwani, J. G. (2001). 'A meta review of game theory publications in the flagship US based OR/MS journals', *Management Decision*, 39 (2), pp. 147–155. https://doi.org/10.1108/EUM0000000005420

Schrodt, P. A. (2002). Forecast and Contingencies: From Methodology to Policy. Paper Presented to the American Political Science Association Meetings, Boston 19 August-1 September . Available at: http://polmeth.wustl.edu/media/Paper/schro02.pdf

Schwartz, P. (1998). *The Art of the Long View: Planning for the Future in an Uncertain World*. John Wiley.

Somerson, I. S. (2009). *The Art And Science Of Security Risk Assessment*. Alexandria: ASIS International.

Stewart, T. R. (1987). 'The Delphi Technique and judgmental forecasting', in J. S. Armstrong (ed.), *Principles of Forecasting*. Norwell, MA: Kluwer Academic.

Stewart, T. R. (2001). 'Improving reliability of judgmental forecasts', in Armstrong, J. S. (ed.), *Principles of Forecasting*. Boston, MA: Kluwer Academic.

Vellani, K. H. (2007). *Strategic Security Management: A Risk Assessment Guide for Decision Makers*. Oxford, UK: Butterworth-Heinemann.

Wikipedia contributors. (2022, September 9). Lone wolf attack. In *Wikipedia, The Free Encyclopedia*. Retrieved 06:42, 19 September, 2022, from https://en.wikipedia.org/w/index.php?title=Lone_wolf_attack&oldid=1109422856.

INDEX